T0159513

MARY ROBERTS RINEHART RETURNING FROM THE WAR ZONE
AND CAPTAIN FINCH ON S. S. "ARABIC."

KINGS, QUEENS, AND PAWNS

*An American Woman
at the Front*

MARY ROBERTS RINEHART

Introduction by Rick Rinehart

TAYLOR TRADE PUBLISHING
Lanham • Boulder • New York • London

Published by Taylor Trade Publishing
An imprint of The Rowman & Littlefield Publishing Group, Inc.
4501 Forbes Boulevard, Suite 200, Lanham, Maryland 20706
www.rowman.com

Unit A, Whitacre Mews, 26-34 Stannary Street, London SE11 4AB

Distributed by NATIONAL BOOK NETWORK

British Library Cataloguing in Publication Information Available

Library of Congress Cataloging-in-Publication Data Available

ISBN 978-1-63076-095-3 (pbk. : alk. paper)
Library of Congress Control Number: 15024921

∞™ The paper used in this publication meets the minimum requirements
of American National Standard for Information Sciences—Permanence of
Paper for Printed Library Materials, ANSI/NISO Z39.48-1992.

Printed in the United States of America

INTRODUCTION

THE first American journalist permitted to visit the front in the early months of World War I was not a battle-tested Ernie Pyle or Hemingway-esque larger-than-life character, but rather a diminutive yet fearless woman who had made her way to the war zone through a combination of charm and subterfuge.

In 1915 Mary Roberts Rinehart was arguably the most popular woman in America, and inarguably one of the country's most successful authors of romances, mysteries, and plays, in addition to regularly contributing stories and essays to such popular magazines as the *Saturday Evening Post* and *McClure's*. After first cracking the top-ten best-seller list with *The Man in the Lower Ten* in 1909, she rang up three more best-selling books before her departure for Europe and the Great War. And more was to follow: her prolific output and enduring popularity did not wind down until 1953, with the publication of her last book, *The Swimming Pool and Other Stories*. However, her success in writing was merely a medium through which she could satisfy her lifelong temptation toward adventure, often taking her places and putting her in situations hitherto known only to men. Such was the implausibility of much of her life—especially for a woman of the early twentieth century—that one biographer quoted a line from Shakespeare's *Twelfth Night* to describe it: "If this were play'd upon a stage now, I could condemn it as an improbable fiction."

* * * * * *

Mary Ella Roberts was born in Allegheny, Pennsylvania (now a part of Pittsburgh), in 1876, in what has traditionally been referred to as "genteel poverty." "All week the house was busy enough, although there was no money," she wrote of her early childhood in a family cluster that consisted of her grandmother, Aunt Sade, and Uncle John, as well as her own parents. "There never was any money in those days." Her father Tom was a dreamer, ostensibly the proprietor of a sewing machine shop, but in his heart an inventor whose several patents were "paid for in agony . . . later lapsing without result to him." Maybe in spite of himself, the business nevertheless prospered—albeit briefly. He moved his family to their own home in 1880; two years later he was managing the Domestic Sewing Machine Company in Pittsburgh. However, by 1887 he had lost his franchise as well as his job. The small family picked up and moved to a less expensive, more austere neighborhood; Tom took to the road to sell everything from wallpaper to insurance policies.

Mary graduated from high school at the height of the Panic of 1893, fully expecting to pursue a career in medicine. However, the Panic changed all that: "Now when I spoke of going to college there was a curious silence," she later recalled. "My music lessons ceased. One day I came home to find that my belongings had been shifted to my sister's room on the second floor, and that two strange men had rented the room on the third." At about this time she submitted three short stories to the local newspaper in an effort to improve the household finances. All three were accepted for the disappointing sum of $1 each, after which she declared that her career as a woman of letters was over. Prophetically, however, her Uncle John remarked that there was enough plot in one of the stories to make a book.

Medicine still intrigued her, so she lied about her age and talked her way into Pittsburgh Training School for Nurses at Homeopathic Hospital in August 1893, a place where surgeons who had learned their trade during the Civil War still insisted that maggots could be used to cleanse a dirty wound. Her first assignment was to remove from the operating room a bucket containing a human foot. Though this incident certainly shocked her, it did not make her physically ill. She reckoned at that moment that she was cut out for not only nursing but also the greater dramas in life. In her autobiography, *My Story*, she wrote:

> And the emergency ward had drama. One morning I came on duty to find the battered body of a man who had been beaten to death with an iron pipe. One cold evening that fall just before going off duty, I turned down the bed for a burly policeman, crying as though his heart would break, while he placed on it the body of a small newsboy, burned and dying from the fire he had built to keep himself warm. A woman was brought in slashed in thirty places by a jealous rival with a knife; a pretty woman. She recovered.

Indeed, her acceptance of the horror of life at such a tender age well prepared her for the dreadful conditions on the Belgian Front years later. While her mysteries and romances may have been breezy and circumspect, her work as a journalist was at times direct and unrelenting. As she herself affirmed, "Why all the evasion, the fear of acknowledging what we know exists, goes on? A big emergency hospital deals with life itself. It cannot evade."

In her early days at the hospital she also became acquainted with the "rather severe" Dr. Stanley Marshall Rinehart, whose legendary scowl frightened away just about every nurse except the steely Mary Roberts. Dr. Rinehart, a very young (twenty-five years old in 1894) surgeon, and thus probably not of the maggots-as-antiseptic school, was known not only for his skill with the knife but also for his perfectionism and fierce temper. However, Mary saw another side to him that clearly attracted him to her, because it was something that she so lacked as a weary and overworked nurse:

> I was in the children's ward, and he had some cases there. More than that, he loved children. He would walk in, apparently very severe, looking through his pince-nez at the children, and they would rush to him and surround him. He was very gentle with them, and he would play with them. It seemed very strange to me, that playing. Neither then nor later had I that gift of being a child with children. . . . Later on when my own children were born I was to look back with much heart searching at the neat tidy machine which had fed and bathed and nursed those little wrecks of humanity. I had missed something there. But I was always tired.

Their acquaintance grew into a friendship, and then into a romance. Ever the risk-taker, Mary flouted hospital policy by agreeing to an engagement with a fellow staff member. Very soon thereafter the hospital's chief engineer stumbled upon a tryst, and word spread like an epidemic. Confronted with the facts by the hospital board, Dr. Rinehart responded to their accusations by yelling at them and telling them that it was none of their business. With the meek request that Mary not flaunt her engagement by wearing a ring, the board simply "went away."

It was to be a two-year engagement, interrupted by a personal tragedy that Mary seemed to react to with disturbing detachment, even nearly forty years after the incident—which she recalled, almost as an anecdote, in *My Story*. Long despondent over his own failures as well as those precipitated by the nation's continued economic depression, Tom Roberts shot himself through the heart and died while on a business trip to Buffalo on November 14, 1895. Away from the hospital and caring for a woman left alone with her illegitimate daughter to die of cancer, Mary received a telegram bearing the news. "It stunned me," she simply said of her response. The balance of the detail imparted in *My Story* is merely clinical:

> Early the next morning I bought a paper to see if there was any explanation. There was indeed. It was blazoned on the front page. He had gone to a hotel in Buffalo and killed himself. Shot himself.
> I had not even known he owned a revolver.

Indeed, prior to recounting the circumstances surrounding her father's suicide, she had shown more compassion in defending the cancerous mother and her love child against the people who had ostracized them both:

> She had had a child, and had had the courage to ac-
> knowledge it, so she was dying alone. Ever since that
> time, I have felt the cruelty and bitterness of our atti-
> tude toward the unmarried mother and her child. How
> stupid we are, that two wrongs can ever make a right.

Although later in life her politics could only be described as conservative, she showed a tendency—illustrated by these two events—to elevate the disen-
franchised who accepted life as it was and met it head
on over those who, notwithstanding the opportunities
available to them, were confounded by it. In short, she
did not abide weakness, most especially in herself.
Unlike her father, she made no excuses.

Mary Ella Roberts became Mary Roberts Rinehart
on April 21, 1896, and, after intervals of illness and
residual exhaustion brought on from her two years of
work at the hospital, found my grandfather forming in
her belly in December of that year. While none of her
three pregnancies was easy, all were ultimately successful, yielding first Stanley Marshall Rinehart Jr. in
1897, then Alan Gillespie Rinehart in 1900, and finally
Frederick Roberts Rinehart (Ted) two years later. By
all accounts, both those of her own hand and those
of her biographers, marital life and motherhood did
not constitute the crowning achievements of her life.
"Once again, however, the world was a small place,"
she told readers in *My Story*, "smaller than ever." She
further complained that she didn't dine out for ten
years (because of Dr. Rinehart's late office hours) or
sleep the night through for seven (because the boys
apparently kept no particular hours).

There were moments of true crisis, however, that
fully engaged her attention as wife, mother, and (work-

ing with her husband) medical practitioner. When Ted became gravely ill at six months and "solemn processions" of medical men would only shake their heads and go away, Dr. and Mrs. Rinehart would stare them down and will their child to live. He did. A year later, after he had swallowed enough carbolic acid to sicken a grown man, Ted again was given up for lost. In the family mythology (at least as my father tells it), Ted was in fact presumed dead at one point following this incident and laid to rest (if temporarily). His sudden gurgling and crying told his parents he was not quite ready to be taken. Uncle Ted lived on to become a favorite of my father's (thus our common name, Frederick) and, except for a bout with alcoholism, enjoyed a long, loving, and exuberant life.

In 1904 the Rineharts were riding high with a house full of children and servants, a busy medical practice, and a stock portfolio worth $12,000. In her spare minutes Mary would dash off a few lines of verse and shop them around to popular magazines such as *Munsey's* and the *Pittsburgh Sunday Gazette*, where she published for the first time under the name of Mary Roberts Rinehart. On a visit to New York to try to sell a collection of her poems, she and Dr. Rinehart decided to pay a visit to the stock exchange for a first-hand look at how their money was growing. Instead, they witnessed a panic of the first order and came home knowing that their entire savings had been wiped out. Not only that, but they were $12,000 in debt as well. ("We might as well have owed twelve million," she wrote.) And even though Dr. Rinehart received a salary as city physician (and presumably a small stipend for representing the state board of health in the county), patient fees for an office visit were only $2, with perhaps an additional dollar for an office prescription. The practice of medicine was not then the lucrative profession that it has become today, and though Stan Rinehart earned more than most, every dime went to support the household—even after, "save one strong girl," all the servants were dismissed.

But this was not a precipitous ledge with a view to a deeper despair; it was the foot of the arc of a life that would make Mary Roberts Rinehart a household name in just a few years' time. Mary Roberts Rinehart was no Tom Roberts: faced with adversity, she declared that she "had found a way to help" the family after a short story was accepted by *Munsey's* for the sum of $34. And they wanted more:

> I began to work now, to write fast and furiously, to listen with a sinking heart to the postman, to glance at the mail in a maid's hands and know at an incredible distance the envelope containing a returned manuscript. Now and then one was accepted. The checks at first were small, from ten to thirty dollars, but money was not important. I was learning a new profession, and being paid while I learned.

By the middle of 1906 she had sold forty-six stories and made $1,842.50.

Notwithstanding the presence of a muse in her life, she did not succumb to the sort of creative self-indulgence that has isolated so many artists from their families, and ultimately broken them. She was fiercely devoted to her family and claimed in her autobiography that she would never work when the boys were in the house: "the slam of the front door" and "the shout of 'Mother' was the signal to stop." Except for slipping away for an hour or so under pressure of a deadline, she early on established a routine that did not allow her work to interfere with family life.

Still, possibly because she was exploring uncharted terrain for a woman of the early twentieth century, she did a bit of hair-splitting when it came to defending exactly what it was she was doing in those hours alone in the house. While freely referring to writing as her "profession," she refused to admit that it was a "career." Years later, when her reputation as a writer was well established, she wrote, "I did not want a career. The word has never been used in the family and never will be. I 'work' when and where I can, but there is no real career, and never has been." Webster's simple definition of career is "course of life"; for profession, it is "a calling or occupation." By these narrow terms she differentiated her craft from that of writers who would sacrifice everything for the greater interests of their art.

In retrospect, she was true to her ethos—at least as far as writing goes. Inadvertently, however, she did make a career out of something else, and that was building and promoting the American institution that she herself became. The emotional sacrifices made by her family for the greater good of the institution were, at times, equal to those of any relative who has lived in the penumbra of a personality who belongs to the public as much as she belongs to her husband and children.

The cornerstone for this particular institution was laid toward the end of the first decade of the new century, when, at the urging of her Uncle John, she submitted a book-length manuscript to a publisher. (Not knowing one publisher from another, she picked one by the "simple method of taking a story by Anna Katherine Green from the book case" and noting the name. The fortunate imprint was Bobbs Merrill in Indianapolis.) Though intended as a satire of the mystery genre, *The Circular Staircase* was taken seriously by the critics, who stressed the "relief of humor in a crime story." "I kept to myself," Mary later recalled, "the deadly secret that the book had been written as a semi-satire."

The Circular Staircase, which had sold 1.25 million copies, was followed a year later by *The Man in the Lower Ten*, which was the #4 best-seller in 1909, and *The Window at the White Cat* and *When a Man Marries* as the #8 and #10 best-sellers in 1910. The pattern continued pretty much unabated for the next twenty-five years, with subsequent top-ten best-selling novels in 1915, 1918, 1919, 1921, 1922, 1923, 1927, 1930, and 1936. Indeed, when book club and paperback editions are taken into account, Mary Roberts Rinehart was in all likelihood by 1950 the all-time best-selling fiction author in the United States since the birth of the Republic.*

* * * * * * *

Notwithstanding her rising literary success, by 1915 Mary Roberts Rinehart wanted something more: to witness history first-hand, and perhaps even become part of it. When war broke out in 1914, all she could

---

*An article in the January 19, 1946, issue of *Publisher's Weekly* cited a list developed by Irving Harlow Hart of the Iowa State Teachers College ranking the top one hundred authors of best sellers in fiction from 1895 to 1944. Mary Roberts Rinehart led the list, followed by Winston Churchill. John Steinbeck ranked fifty-fourth, and Ernest Hemingway ninety-sixth.

think about was leaving her young family behind and getting to Europe to report on the fighting—all contrary to her own ethos of always putting the family first. Initially resistant, Stan Sr. ultimately agreed that Mary should go, hoping that, like most journalists, the closest she would get to the war would be London. Little did he know that her subterfuge as a representative of the American Red Cross would get her across the English Channel and beyond, and she had already made arrangements with the *Saturday Evening Post* to fully fund the trip in return for a book's worth of dispatches of her experiences. George H. Doran quickly published them as *Kings, Queens, and Pawns* later that year.

Hailed as "the best of the war books" by newspaper magnate Lord Beaverbrook, *Kings, Queens, and Pawns* gave Americans their first glimpse into the grim reality of what was happening on the other side of the Atlantic. (It also dispelled rumors of German atrocities against Belgian women and children that had been reported in American newspapers.) Since Mary Rinehart's stated purpose in visiting the front was to report on conditions at the hundreds of temporary hospitals across Belgium in France, she spared no detail in describing what she saw:

> Every sort of building is being used for these isolated hospitals—garages, town halls, private dwellings schools. At first they had no chloroform, no instruments. There are cases on record where automobile tools were used in emergency, kitchen knives, saws, anything. In one case, last Spring, two hundred convalescents, leaving one of these hospitals on a cold day in March, were called back, on the arrival of a

hundred freshly wounded men, that every superfluous bandage on their wounds might be removed, to
be used again.

Furthermore, she wrote, "much that we regard as
fundamental in hospital practice is ignored." Infection
and fever spread throughout the wards, and in one
particular hospital a single thermometer was available
for sixty typhoid and scarlet fever patients.

Unsurprisingly for someone whose views on the war
were evolving, such graphic descriptions were directed
toward her audience at home in a chapter titled "How
Americans Can Help." But it was not just about urging
donations of medical supplies:* Mary Roberts Rinehart
also became an early and vocal advocate of American
entry into the war on the side of the English, French,
and Belgians, both to bring a quick end to hostilities
and to deal with the humanitarian crisis they had created and that she had witnessed first-hand. Moreover,
she had a sympathetic spirit in her Canada-born publisher George H. Doran, whose ties to England went
beyond swearing allegiance to the Crown; in London
on that fateful August day in 1914 when England
joined the war, he was called upon by the Ministry
of Information to do some "publicity" work in the
United States.** He eagerly agreed, and became the
Ministry's conduit for what could only be described

---

*In a perfect example of being careful what you wish for, upon her
return to the United States Mary Roberts Rinehart was put in charge
of coordinating relief for war-torn Europe, described as "an avalanche
of money and supplies."
**The Torontonian had moved to New York to reestablish his publish-
ing business in 1909.

as pro-English propaganda. *Kings, Queens, and Pawns,* though overtly not propagandist, certainly sent the right message.

But it was not a popular one at the time. America was still largely isolationist in 1915, and even the sinking of the *Lusitania* by a German submarine that May was not in itself persuasive. Many Americans were either pro-German or at best neutral, some dismissing as lies the accusation that the Germans were using poison gas. But as the situation in Europe continued to stalemate, sentiment in America started to shift and was solidly in the camp of joining the war effort when Germany resumed unrestricted submarine warfare in January 1917—in a sense inviting the United States into the war. Upon learning of Germany's ill-considered offer to help Mexico reclaim Texas, Arizona, and New Mexico in exchange for joining Germany in the fight against the United States, Congress voted to declare war on Germany on April 6, 1917.

Patriotic fervor had by now reached a fever pitch, prompting the editors at the *Saturday Evening Post* to ask their most esteemed female writer to pen a piece about sacrifice, particularly of the familial kind: in short, they wanted Mary to write about how mothers should allow, if not encourage, their sons to join up and go to war. At first appalled by the idea, she later relented, especially because only recently she and her husband had given Stan Jr. permission to join the army. (Ultimately all four Rinehart men enlisted, including Stan Sr., commissioned as a major in the Army Medical Corps.) After twelve straight, grueling hours, during which she wept continuously, she produced "The Altar of Freedom," perhaps one of her most influential essays* and one that spoke directly and, in her by now familiar voice, personally to mothers.

* * * * * *

For Mary Roberts Rinehart, there were to be some rewards from her two months reporting from the front; indeed, it might be said that the experience informed much of the rest of her life. Now recognized as a serious journalist, she was asked to cover the 1916 Democratic, Republican, and Progressive presidential conventions by the Philadelphia Public Ledger Syndicate, during which she met and befriended the "Bull Moose" party candidate Theodore Roosevelt. On a trip to Glacier National Park in 1915 she was introduced to a group of Blackfoot Indians, who were so impressed with this woman who had been to the Great War that they inducted her on the spot into the tribe, bestowing on her the name "Pitamakin," or "Running Eagle."** And following the cessation of hostilities in 1918, George Doran offered Stan Jr. a position in his company, which Mary helped secure with the acquisition of a substantial share of Doran stock—all a prelude to her underwriting the firm of Farrar and Rinehart (later Rinehart and Company before merging

---

*A piece she wrote for the *Saturday Evening Post* in 1947 was arguably her most widely read and was certainly ground-breaking for its time. "I Had Cancer" detailed her personal ordeal with breast cancer and encouraged women to self-examine, a hitherto forbidden topic of discussion.
**The Blackfeet were in fact in desperate straits, as the government had failed miserably to transform a tribe of hunters into farmers on barely arable land. Upon her return to Washington, Rinehart went directly to Interior Secretary Lane and demanded relief for the tribe, "pouring out her rage." Lane acted immediately.

with Holt and Winston) ten years later, for which she is seldom given credit.

"It will take a hundred years to paint this war on one canvas," Mary Roberts Rinehart writes in the early pages of this chronicle, reprinted here just as it appeared in 1915. Here, then, exactly a century later, is *Kings, Queens, and Pawns*, brushstrokes on that great canvas.

Rick Rinehart
Essex, Connecticut
July 2015

CONTENTS

CONTENTS

KINGS, QUEENS AND PAWNS

KINGS, QUEENS AND PAWNS

FOR KING AND COUNTRY

MARCH in England is spring. Early in the month masses of snowdrops lined the paths in Hyde Park. The grass was green, the roads hard and dry under the eager feet of Kitchener's great army. For months they had been drilling, struggling with the intricacies of a new career, working and waiting. And now it was spring, and soon they would be off. Some had already gone.

"Lucky beggars!" said the ones who remained, and counted the days.

And waiting, they drilled. Everywhere there were squads: Scots in plaid kilts with khaki tunics; less picturesque but equally imposing regiments in the field uniform, with officers hardly distinguishable from their men. Everywhere the same grim but cheerful determination to get over and help the boys across the Channel to assist in holding that more than four hundred miles of battle line against the invading hosts of Germany.

Here in Hyde Park that spring day was all the panoply of war: bands playing, the steady tramp of numberless feet, the muffled clatter of accoutrements, the homage of the waiting crowd. And they deserved homage, those fine, upstanding men, many of them hardly more than boys, marching along with a fine, full swing. There is something magnificent, a contagion of enthusiasm, in the sight of a great volunteer army. The North and the South knew the thrill during our own great war. Conscription may form a great and admirable machine, but it differs from the trained army of volunteers as a body differs from a soul. But it costs a country heavy in griefs, does a volunteer army; for the flower of the country goes. That, too, America knows, and England is learning.

They marched by gaily. The drums beat. The passers-by stopped. Here and there an open carriage or an automobile drew up, and pale men, some of them still in bandages, sat and watched. In their eyes was the same flaming eagerness, the same impatience to get back, to be loosed against the old lion's foes.

For King and Country!

All through England, all through France, all through that tragic corner of Belgium which remains to her, are similar armies, drilling and waiting, equally young, equally eager, equally resolute. And the thing they were going to I knew. I had seen it in that mysterious region which had swallowed up those who had gone before; in the trenches, in the operating rooms of field hospitals, at outposts between the confronting armies where the sentries walked hand in hand with death. I had seen it in its dirt and horror and sordidness, this thing they were going to.

War is not two great armies meeting in a clash and frenzy of battle. It is much more than that. War is a boy carried on a stretcher, looking up at God's blue sky with bewildered eyes that are soon to close; war is a woman carrying a child that has been wounded by a shell; war is spirited horses tied in burning buildings and waiting for death; war is the flower of a race, torn, battered, hungry, bleeding, up to its knees in icy water; war is an old woman burning a candle before the Mater Dolorosa for the son she has given. For King and Country!

CHAPTER I

TAKING A CHANCE

I STARTED for the Continent on a bright day
early in January. I was searched by a woman
from Scotland Yard before being allowed on the platform. The pockets of my fur coat were examined;
my one piece of baggage, a suitcase, was inspected; my
letters of introduction were opened and read.

"Now, Mrs. Rinehart," she said, straightening,
"just why are you going?"

I told her exactly half of why I was going. I had
a shrewd idea that the question in itself meant nothing.
But it gave her a good chance to look at me. She was
a very clever woman.

And so, having been discovered to be carrying
neither weapons nor seditious documents, and having
an open and honest eye, I was allowed to go through
the straight and narrow way that led to possible destruction. Once or twice, later on, I blamed that
woman for letting me through. I blamed myself for
telling only half of my reasons for going. Had I
told her all she would have detained me safely in
England, where automobiles sometimes go less than
eighty miles an hour, and where a sharp bang means
a door slamming in the wind and not a shell exploding,
where hostile aëroplanes overhead with bombs and unpleasant little steel darts, were not always between

one's eyes and heaven. She let me through, and I went out on the platform.

The leaving of the one-o'clock train from Victoria Station, London, is an event and a tragedy. Wounded who have recovered are going back; soldiers who have been having their week at home are returning to that mysterious region across the Channel, the front.

Not the least of the British achievements had been to transport, during the deadlock of the first winter of the war, almost the entire army, in relays, back to England for a week's rest. It had been done without the loss of a man, across a channel swarming with hostile submarines. They came in thousands, covered with mud, weary, eager, their eyes searching the waiting crowd for some beloved face. And those who waited and watched as the cars emptied sometimes wept with joy, and sometimes turned and went away alone.

Their week over, rested, tidy, eyes still eager but now turned toward France, the station platform beside the one-o'clock train was filled with soldiers going back. There were few to see them off; there were not many tears. Nothing is more typical of the courage and patriotism of the British women than that platform beside the one-o'clock train at Victoria. The crowd was shut out by ropes and Scotland Yard men stood guard. And out on the platform, saying little, because words are so feeble, pacing back and forth slowly, went these silent couples. They did not even touch hands. One felt that all the unselfish stoicism and restraint would crumble under the familiar touch.

The platform filled. Sir Purtab Singh, an Indian prince, with his suite, was going back to the English lines. I had been a neighbour of his at Claridge's Hotel in London. I caught his eye. It was filled with

cold suspicion. It said quite plainly that I could put
nothing over on him. But whether he suspected me of
being a newspaper writer or a spy I do not know.

Somehow, considering that the train was carrying
a suspicious and turbaned Indian prince, any number
of impatient officers and soldiers, and an American
woman who was carefully avoiding the war office and
trying to look like a buyer crossing the Channel for
hats, the whistle for starting sounded rather inadequate. It was not martial. It was thin, effeminate, absurd. And so we were off, moving slowly past that line
on the platform, where no one smiled; where grief and
tragedy, in that one revealing moment, were written
deep. I shall never forget the faces of the women as
the train crept by.

And now the train was well under way. The car
was very quiet. The memory of those faces on the
platform was too fresh. There was a brown and weary
officer across from me. He sat very still, looking
straight ahead. Long after the train had left London, and was moving smoothly through the English
fields, so green even in winter, he still sat in the same
attitude.

I drew a long breath, and ordered luncheon. I was
off to the war. I might be turned back at Folkstone.
There was more than a chance that I might not get
beyond Calais, which was under military law. But at
least I had made a start.

This is a narrative of personal experience. It makes
no pretensions, except to truth. It is pure reporting,
a series of pictures, many of them disconnected, but
all authentic. It will take a hundred years to paint
this war on one canvas. A thousand observers, ten
thousand, must record what they have seen. To the

reports of trained men must be added a bit here and there from these untrained observers, who without military knowledge, ignorant of the real meaning of much that they saw, have been able to grasp only a part of the human significance of the great tragedy of Europe.

I was such an observer.

My errand was primarily humane, to visit the hospitals at or near the front, and to be able to form an opinion of what supplies were needed, of conditions generally. Rumour in America had it that the medical and surgical situation was chaotic. Bands of earnest and well-intentioned people were working quite in the dark as to the conditions they hoped to relieve. And over the hospital situation, as over the military, brooded the impenetrable silence that has been decreed by the Allies since the beginning of the war. I had met everywhere in America tales from both the German and the Allies' lines that had astounded me. It seemed incredible that such conditions could exist in an age of surgical enlightenment; that, even in an unexpected and unprepared-for war, modern organisation and efficiency should have utterly failed.

On the steamer crossing the Atlantic, with the ship speeding on her swift and rather precarious journey, windows and ports carefully closed and darkened, one heard the same hideous stories: of tetanus in uncounted cases, of fearful infections, of no bandages—worst of all, of no anæsthetics.

I was a member of the American Red Cross Association, but I knew that the great work of the American Red Cross was in sending supplies. The comparatively few nurses they had sent to the western field of war were not at the front or near it. The British, French, Belgian and Dutch nursing associations were in charge of the field hospitals, so far as I could discover.

To see these hospitals, to judge and report conditions, then, was a part of my errand. Only a part, of course; for I had another purpose. I knew nothing of strategy or tactics, of military movements and their significance. I was not interested in them particularly. But I meant to get, if it was possible, a picture of this new warfare that would show it for the horror that it is; a picture that would give pause to that certain percentage of the American people that is always so eager to force a conservative government into conflict with other nations.

There were other things to learn. What was France doing? The great sister republic had put a magnificent army into the field. Between France and the United States were many bonds, much reciprocal good feeling. The Statue of Liberty, as I went down the bay, bespoke the kindly feeling between the two republics. I remembered Lafayette. Battle-scarred France, where liberty has fought so hard for life—what was France doing? Not saying much, certainly. Fighting, surely, as the French have always fought. For certainly England, with her gallant but at that time meagre army, was not fighting alone the great war.

But there were three nations fighting the allied cause in the west. What had become of the heroic Belgian Army? Was it resting on its laurels? Having done its part, was it holding an honorary position in the great line-up? Was it a fragment or an army, an entity or a memory?

The newspapers were full of details that meant nothing: names of strange villages, movements backward and forward as the long battle line bent and straightened again. But what was really happening beyond the barriers that guarded the front so jealously? How did the men live under these new and strange conditions? What did they think? Or fear? Or hope?

Great lorries and transports went out from the French coast towns and disappeared beyond the horizon; motor ambulances and hospital trains came in with the grim harvest. Men came and, like those who had gone before, they too went out and did not come back. "Somewhere in France," the papers said. Such letters as they wrote came from "somewhere in France." What was happening then, over there, beyond the horizon, "somewhere in France"?

And now that I have been beyond the dead line many of these questions have answered themselves. France is saying nothing, and fighting magnificently. Belgium, with two-thirds of her army gone, has still fifty thousand men, and is preparing two hundred thousand more.

Instead of merely an honorary position, she is holding tenaciously, against repeated onslaughts and under horrible conditions, the flooded district between Nieuport and Dixmude. England, although holding only thirty-two miles of front, beginning immediately south of Ypres, is holding that line against some of the most furious fighting of the war, and is developing, at the same time, an enormous fighting machine for the spring movement.*

The British soldier is well equipped, well fed, com-

* This is written of conditions in the early spring of 1915. Although the relative positions of the three armies are the same, the British are holding a considerably longer frontage.

fortably transported. When it is remembered that
England is also assisting to equip all the allied armies,
it will be seen that she is doing much more than holding the high seas.

To see the wounded, then; to follow the lines of hospital trains to that mysterious region, the front; to
see the men in the trenches and in their billets; to
observe their *morale*, the conditions under which they
lived—and died. It was too late to think of the cause
of the war or of the justice or injustice of that cause.
It will never be too late for its humanities and inhu-
manities, its braveries and its occasional flinchings, its
tragedies and its absurdities.

It was through the assistance of the Belgian Red
Cross that I got out of England and across the Channel. I visited the Anglo-Belgian Committee at its
quarters in the Savoy Hotel, London, and told them
of my twofold errand. They saw at once the point I
made. America was sending large amounts of money
and vast quantities of supplies to the Belgians on both
sides of the line. What was being done in interned
Belgium was well known. But those hospital supplies
and other things shipped to Northern France were
swallowed up in the great silence. The war would not
be ended in a day or a month.

"Let me see conditions as they really are," I said.
"It is no use telling me about them. Let me see them.
Then I can tell the American people what they have
already done in the war zone, and what they may be
asked to do."

Through a piece of good luck Doctor Depage, the
president, had come across the Channel to a conference, and was present. A huge man, in the uniform
of a colonel of the Belgian Army, with a great mili-

tary cape, he seemed to fill and dominate the little room.

They conferred together in rapid French.

"Where do you wish to go?" I was asked.

"Everywhere."

"Hospitals are not always cheerful to visit."

"I am a graduate of a hospital training-school. Also a member of the American Red Cross."

They conferred again.

"Madame will not always be comfortable—over there."

"I don't want to be comfortable," I said bravely.

Another conference. The idea was a new one; it took some mental readjustment. But their cause was just, and mingled with their desire to let America know what they were doing was a justifiable pride. They knew what I was to find out—that one of the finest hospitals in the world, as to organisation, equipment and results, was situated almost under the guns of devastated Nieuport, so close that the roar of artillery is always in one's ears.

I had expected delays, a possible refusal. Everyone had encountered delays of one sort and another. Instead, I found a most courteous and agreeable permission given. I was rather dazed. And when, a day or so later, through other channels, I found myself in possession of letters to the Baron de Broqueville, Premier and Minister of War for Belgium, and to General Melis, Inspector General of the Belgian Army Medical Corps, I realised that, once in Belgian territory, my troubles would probably be at an end.

For getting out of England I put my faith in a card given me by the Belgian Red Cross. There are only four such cards in existence, and mine was number four.

From Calais to La Panne! If I could get to Calais I could get to the front, for La Panne is only four miles from Nieuport, where the confronting lines of trenches begin. But Calais was under military law. Would I be allowed to land?

Such writers as reached there were allowed twenty-four hours, and were then shipped back across the Channel or to some innocuous destination south. Yet this little card, if all went well, meant the privilege of going fifty miles northeast to the actual front. True, it gave no chance for deviation. A mile, a hundred feet off the straight and tree-lined road north to La Panne, and I should be arrested. But the time to think about that would come later on.

As a matter of fact, I have never been arrested. Except in the hospitals, I was always practically where I had no business to be. I had a room in the Hôtel des Arcades, in Dunkirk, for weeks, where, just round the corner, the police had closed a house for a month as a punishment because a room had been rented to a correspondent. The correspondent had been sentenced to five years' imprisonment, but had been released after five weeks. I was frankly a writer. I was almost aggressively a writer. I wrote down carefully and openly everything I saw. I made, but of course under proper auspices and with the necessary permits, excursions to the trenches from Nieuport to the La Bassée region and Béthune, along Belgian, French and English lines, always openly, always with a notebook. And nothing happened!

As my notebook became filled with data I grew more and more anxious, while the authorities grew more

calm.   Suppose I fell into the hands of the Germans!
It was a large notebook, filled with much information.
I could never swallow the thing, as officers are sup-
posed to swallow the password slips in case of capture.
After a time the general spy alarm got into my blood.
I regarded the boy who brought my morning coffee
with suspicion, and slept with my notes under my pil-
low.   And nothing happened!

I had secured my passport *visé* at the French and
Belgian Consulates, and at the latter legation was able
also to secure a letter asking the civil and military
authorities to facilitate my journey.   The letter had
been requested for me by Colonel Depage.

It was almost miraculously easy to get out of England.   It was almost suspiciously easy.   My passport
frankly gave the object of my trip as "literary work."
Perhaps the keen eyes of the inspectors who passed me
onto the little channel boat twinkled a bit as they examined it.

The general opinion as to the hopelessness of my
trying to get nearer than thirty miles to the front had
so communicated itself to me that had I been turned
back there on the quay at Folkstone, I would have been
angry, but hardly surprised.

Not until the boat was out in the channel did I feel
sure that I was to achieve even this first leg of the
journey.

Even then, all was not well.   With Folkstone and
the war office well behind, my mind turned to submarines as a sunflower to the sun.   Afterward I found
that the thing to do is not to think about submarines.
To think of politics, or shampoos, or of people one
does not like, but not of submarines.   They are like
ghosts in that respect.   They are perfectly safe and

entirely innocuous as long as one thinks of something else.

And something went wrong almost immediately.

It was imperative that I get to Calais. And the boat, which had intended making Calais, had had a report of submarines and headed for Boulogne. This in itself was upsetting. To have, as one may say, one's teeth set for Calais, and find one is biting on Boulogne, is not agreeable. I did not want Boulogne. My pass was from Calais. I had visions of waiting in Boulogne, of growing old and grey waiting, or of trying to walk to Calais and being turned back, of being locked in a cow stable and bedded down on straw. For fear of rousing hopes that must inevitably be disappointed, again nothing happened.

There were no other women on board: only British officers and the turbaned and imposing Indians. The day was bright, exceedingly cold. The boat went at top speed, her lifeboats slung over the sides and ready for lowering. There were lookouts posted everywhere. I did not think they attended to their business. Every now and then one lifted his head and looked at the sky or at the passengers. I felt that I should report him. What business had he to look away from the sea? I went out to the bow and watched for periscopes. There were black things floating about. I decided that they were not periscopes, but mines. We went very close to them. They proved to be buoys marking the Channel.

I hated to take my eyes off the sea, even for a moment. If you have ever been driven at sixty miles an hour over a bad road, and felt that if you looked away the car would go into the ditch, and if you will multiply that by the exact number of German submarines and then add the British Army, you will know how I felt.

Afterward I grew accustomed to the Channel crossing. I made it four times. It was necessary for me to cross twice after the eighteenth of February, when the blockade began. On board the fated Arabic, later sunk by a German submarine, I ran the blockade again to return to America. It was never an enjoyable thing to brave submarine attack, but one develops a sort of philosophy. It is the same with being under fire. The first shell makes you jump. The second you speak of, commenting with elaborate carelessness on where it fell. This is a gain over shell number one, when you cannot speak to save your life. The third shell you ignore, and the fourth you forget about—if you can.

Seeing me alone the captain asked me to the canvas shelter of the bridge. I proceeded to voice my protest at our change of destination. He apologised, but we continued to Boulogne.

"What does a periscope look like?" I asked. "I mean, of course, from this boat?"

"Depends on how much of it is showing. Sometimes it's only about the size of one of those gulls. It's hard to tell the difference."

I rather suspect that captain now. There were many gulls sitting on the water. I had been looking for something like a hitching post sticking up out of the water. Now my last vestige of pleasure and confidence was gone. I went almost mad trying to watch all the gulls at once.

"What will you do if you see a submarine?'

"Run it down," said the captain calmly. "That's the only chance we've got. That is, if we see the boat itself. These little Channel steamers make about twenty-six knots, and the submarine, submerged, only about half of that. Sixteen is the best they can do on the surface. Run them down and sink them, that's my motto."

"What about a torpedo?"

"We can see them coming. It will be hard to torpedo this boat—she goes too fast."

Then and there he explained to me the snowy wake of the torpedo, a white path across the water; the mechanism by which it is kept true to its course; the detonator that explodes it. From nervousness I shifted to enthusiasm. I wanted to see the white wake. I wanted to see the Channel boat dodge it. My sporting blood was up. I was willing to take a chance. I felt that if there was a difficulty this man would escape it. I turned and looked back at the khaki-coloured figures on the deck below.

Taking a chance! They were all taking a chance. And there was one, an officer, with an empty right sleeve. And suddenly what for an enthusiastic moment, in that bracing sea air, had seemed a game, became the thing that it is, not a game, but a deadly and cruel war. I never grew accustomed to the tragedy of the empty sleeve. And as if to accentuate this thing toward which I was moving so swiftly, the British Red Cross ship, from Boulogne to Folkstone, came in sight, hurrying over with her wounded, a great white boat, garnering daily her harvest of wounded and taking them "home."

Land now—a grey-white line that is the sand dunes at Ambleteuse, north of Boulogne. I knew Ambleteuse. It gave a sense of strangeness to see the old tower at the water's edge loom up out of the sea. The sight of land was comforting, but vigilance was not relaxed. The attacks of submarines have been mostly made not far outside the harbours, and only a few days later that very boat was to make a sensational escape just outside the harbour of Boulogne.

All at once it was twilight, the swift dusk of the sea. The boat warped in slowly. I showed my passport, and at last I was on French soil. North and east, beyond the horizon, lay the thing I had come to see.

CHAPTER II

"SOMEWHERE IN FRANCE"

MANY people have seen Boulogne and have written of what they have seen: the great hotels that are now English hospitals; the crowding of transport wagons; the French signs, which now have English signs added to them; the mixture of uniforms —English khaki and French blue; the white steamer waiting at the quay, with great Red Crosses on her snowy funnels. Over everything, that first winter of the war, hung the damp chill of the Continental winter, that chill that sinks in and never leaves, that penetrates fur and wool and eats into the spirit like an acid.

I got through the customs without much difficulty. I had a large package of cigarettes for the soldiers, for given his choice, food or a smoke, the soldier will choose the latter. At last after much talk I got them in free of duty. And then I was footfree.

Here again I realise that I should have encountered great difficulties. I should at least have had to walk to Calais, or to have slept, as did one titled English-woman I know, in a bathtub. I did neither. I took a first-class ticket to Calais, and waited round the station until a train should go.

And then I happened on one of the pictures that will stand out always in my mind. Perhaps it was because I was not yet inured to suffering; certainly I was to see many similar scenes, much more of the flotsam and jetsam of the human tide that was sweeping back and forward over the flat fields of France and Flanders.

A hospital train had come in, a British train. The twilight had deepened into night. Under the flickering arc lamps, in that cold and dismal place, the train came to a quiet stop. Almost immediately it began to unload. A door opened and a British nurse alighted. Then slowly and painfully a man in a sitting position slid forward, pushing himself with his hands, his two bandaged feet held in the air. He sat at the edge of the doorway and lowered his feet carefully until they hung free.

"Frozen feet from the trenches," said a man standing beside me.

The first man was lifted down and placed on a truck, and his place was filled immediately by another. As fast as one man was taken another came. The line seemed endless. One and all, their faces expressed keen apprehension, lest some chance awkwardness should touch or jar the tortured feet. Ten at a time they were wheeled away. And still they came and came, until perhaps two hundred had been taken off. But now something else was happening. Another car of badly wounded was being unloaded. Through the windows could be seen the iron framework on which the stretchers, three in a tier, were swung.

Halfway down the car a wide window was opened, and two tall lieutenants, with four orderlies, took their places outside. It was very silent. Orders were given in low tones. The muffled rumble of the trucks carrying the soldiers with frozen feet was all that broke the quiet, and soon they, too, were gone; and there remained only the six men outside, receiving with hands as gentle as those of women the stretchers so caūtiously worked over the window sill to them. One by one the stretchers came; one by one they were added to the lengthening line that lay prone on the stone flooring beside the train. There was not a jar, not an unnecessary motion. One great officer, very young, took the weight of the end as it came toward him, and lowered it with marvellous gentleness as the others took hold. He had a trick of the wrist that enabled him to reach up, take hold and lower the stretcher, without freeing his hands. He was marvellously strong, marvellously tender.

The stretchers were laid out side by side. Their occupants did not speak or move. It was as if they had reached their limit of endurance. They lay with closed eyes, or with impassive, upturned faces, swathed in their brown blankets against the chill. Here and there a knitted neck scarf had been loosely wrapped about a head. All over America women were knitting just such scarfs.

And still the line grew. The car seemed inexhaustible of horrors. And still the young lieutenant with the tender hands and the strong wrists took the onus of the burden, the muscles of his back swelling under his khaki tunic. If I were asked to typify the attitude of the British Army and of the British people toward their wounded, I should point to that boy. Nothing that I know of in history can equal the care the English are taking of their wounded in this, the great war. They have, of course, the advantage of the best nursing system in Europe.

France is doing her best, but her nursing had always been in the hands of nuns, and there are not nearly

enough nuns in France to-day to cope with the situation.   Belgium, with some of the greatest surgeons in the world, had no organised nursing system when war broke out.   She is largely dependent
apparently on the notable work of her priests, and on
English and Dutch nurses.

When my train drew out, the khaki-clad lieutenant
and his assistants were still at work.   One car was
emptied.   They moved on to a second.   Other willing
hands were at work on the line that stretched along
the stone flooring, carrying the wounded to ambulances, but the line seemed hardly to shrink.   Always
the workers inside the train brought another stretcher
and yet another.   The rumble of the trucks had ceased.
It was very cold.   I could not look any longer.

It took three hours to go the twenty miles to Calais,
from six o'clock to nine.   I wrapped myself in my fur
coat.   Two men in my compartment slept comfortably.   One clutched a lighted cigarette.   It burned
down close to his fingers.   It was fascinating to watch.
But just when it should have provided a little excitement he wakened.   It was disappointing.

We drifted into conversation, the gentleman of the
cigarette and I.   He was an Englishman from a London newspaper.   He was counting on his luck to get
him into Calais and his wit to get him out.   He told
me his name.   Just before I left France I heard of a
highly philanthropic and talented gentleman of the
same name who was unselfishly going through the
hospitals as near the front as he could, giving a mov-
ing-picture entertainment to the convalescent soldiers.
I wish him luck; he deserves it.   And I am sure he is
giving a good entertainment.   His wit had got him
out of Calais!

Calais at last, and the prospect of food.   Still greater comfort, here my little card became operative. I was no longer a refugee, fleeing and hiding from the stern eyes of Lord Kitchener and the British War Office.   I had come into my own, even to supper.

I saw no English troops that night.   The Calais station was filled with French soldiers.   The first impression, after the trim English uniform, was not particularly good.   They looked cold, dirty, unutterably weary.   Later, along the French front, I revised my early judgment.   But I have never reconciled myself to the French uniform, with its rather slovenly cut, or to the tendency of the French private soldier to allow his beard to grow.   It seems a pity that both French and Belgians, magnificent fighters that they are, are permitted this slackness in appearance.   There are no smarter officers anywhere than the French and Belgian officers, but the appearance of their troops *en masse* is not imposing.

Later on, also, a close inspection of the old French uniform revealed it as made of lighter cloth than the English, less durable, assuredly less warm.   The new grey-blue uniform is much heavier, but its colour is questionable.   It should be almost invisible in the early morning mists, but against the green of spring and summer, or under the magnesium flares—called by the English "starlights"—with which the Germans illuminate the trenches of the Allies during the night, it appeared to me that it would be most conspicuous.

I have before me on my writing table a German fatigue cap.   Under the glare of my electric lamp it fades, loses colour and silhouette, is eclipsed.   I have tried it in sunlight against grass.   It does the same thing.   A piece of the same efficient management that has distributed white smocks and helmet covers among the German troops fighting in the rigours of Poland, to render them invisible against the snow!

Calais then, with food to get and an address to find. For Doctor Depage had kindly arranged a haven for me. Food, of a sort, I got at last. The hotel dining room was full of officers. Near me sat fourteen members of the aviation corps, whose black leather coats bore, either on left breast or left sleeve, the outspread wings of the flying division. There were fifty people, perhaps, and two waiters, one a pale and weary boy. The food was bad, but the crisp French bread was delicious. Perhaps nowhere in the world is the bread average higher than in France—just as in America, where fancy breads are at their best, the ordinary wheat loaf is, taking the average, exceedingly poor.

Calais was entirely dark. The Zeppelin attack, which took place four or five weeks later, was anticipated, and on the night of my arrival there was a general feeling that the birthday of the German Emperor the next day would produce something spectacular in the way of an air raid. That explained, possibly, the presence .so far from the front—fifty miles from the nearest point—of so many flying men.

As my French conversational powers are limited, I had some difficulty in securing a vehicle. This was explained later by the discovery the next day that no one is allowed on the streets of Calais after ten o'clock. Nevertheless I secured a hack, and rode blithely and unconsciously to the house where I was to spend the night. I have lost the address of that house. I wish I could remember it, for I left there a perfectly good and moderately expensive pair of field glasses. I have been in Calais since, and have had the wild idea of driving about the streets until I find it and my glasses. But a close scrutiny of the map of Calais has deterred me. Age would overtake me, and I should still be threading the maze of those streets, seeking an old house in an old garden, both growing older all the time.

A very large house it was, large and cold. I found that I was expected; but an air of unreality hung over everything. I met three or four most kindly Belgian people of whom I knew nothing and who knew nothing of me. I did not know exactly why I was there, and I am sure the others knew less. I went up to my room in a state of bewilderment. It was a huge room without a carpet, and the tiny fire refused to light. There was a funeral wreath over the bed, with the picture of the deceased woman in the centre. It was bitterly cold, and there was a curious odor of disinfectants in the air.

By a window was a narrow black iron bed without a mattress. It looked sinister. Where was the mattress? Had its last occupant died and the mattress been burned? I sniffed about it; the odour of disinfectant unmistakably clung to it. I do not yet know the story of that room or of that bed. Perhaps there is no story. But I think there is. I put on my fur coat and went to bed, and the lady of the wreath came in the night and talked French to me.

I rose in the morning at seven degrees Centigrade and dressed. At breakfast part of the mystery was cleared up. The house was being used as a residence by the chief surgeon of the Ambulance Jeanne d'Arc, the Belgian Red Cross hospital in Calais, and by others interested in the Red Cross work. It was a dormitory also for the English nurses from the ambulance. This

explained, naturally, my being sent there, the somewhat casual nature of the furnishing and the odour of
disinfectants. It does not, however, explain the lady
of the wreath or the black iron bed.

After breakfast some of the nurses came in from
night duty at the ambulance. I saw their bedroom,
one directly underneath mine, with four single beds
and no pretence at comfort. It was cold, icy cold.

"You are very courageous," I said. "Surely this is
not very comfortable. I should think you might at
least have a fire."

"We never think of a fire," a nurse said simply.
"The best we can do seems so little to what the men
are doing, doesn't it?"

She was not young. Some one told me she had a
son, a boy of nineteen, in the trenches. She did not
speak of him. But I have wondered since what she
must feel during those grisly hours of the night when
the ambulances are giving up their wounded at the
hospital doors. No doubt she is a tender nurse, for in
every case she is nursing vicariously that nineteen-
year-old boy of hers in the trenches.

That morning I visited the various Calais hospitals.
It was a bright morning, sunny and cold. Lines of
refugees with packs and bundles were on their way
to the quay.

The frightful congestion of the autumn of 1914 was
over, but the hospitals were all full. They were surgical hospitals, typhoid hospitals, hospitals for injured
civilians, hospital boats. One and all they were preparing as best they could for the mighty conflict of the
spring, when each side expected to make its great onward movement.

As it turned out, the terrible fighting of the spring

failed to break the deadlock, but the preparations made by the hospitals were none too great for the sad by-products of war.

The Belgian hospital question was particularly grave. To-day, several months later, it is still a matter for anxious thought. In case the Germans retire from Belgium the Belgians will find themselves in their own land, it is true, but a land stripped of everything. It is for this contingency that the Allies are preparing. In whichever direction the line moves, the arrangements that have served during the impasse of the past year will no longer answer. Portable field hospital pavilions, with portable equipment, will be required. The destructive artillery fire, with its great range, will leave no buildings intact near the battle line.

One has only to follow the present line, fringed as it is with destroyed or partially destroyed towns, to realise what the situation will be if a successful offensive movement on the part of the Allies drives the battle line back. Artillery fire leaves no buildings standing. Even the roads become impassable,—masses of broken stone with gaping holes, over which ambulances travel with difficulty.

CHAPTER III

LA PANNE

FROM Calais to La Panne is fifty miles. Calais is under military law. It is difficult to enter, almost impossible to leave in the direction in which I wished to go. But here again the Belgian Red Cross achieved the impossible. I was taken before the authorities, sharply questioned, and in the end a pink slip was passed over to the official of the Red Cross who was to take me to the front. I wish I could have secured that pink slip, if only because of its apparent fragility and its astounding wearing qualities. All told, between Calais and La Panne it was inspected—texture, weight and reading matter, front and reverse sides, upside down and under glass—by some several hundred sentries, officials and petty highwaymen. It suffered everything but attack by bayonet. I found myself repeating that way to madness of Mark Twain's:

> *Punch, brothers, punch with care,*
> *Punch in the presence of the passenjaire,*
> *A pink trip slip for a five-cent fare—*

and so on.

Northeast then, in an open grey car with "Belgian Red Cross" on each side of the machine. Northeast in a bitter wind, into a desolate and almost empty country of flat fields, canals and roads bordered by endless rows of trees bent forward like marching men. Northeast through Gravelines, once celebrated of the Armada and now a manufacturing city. It is curious to think that a part of the Armada went ashore at Gravelines, and that, by the shifting of the English Channel, it is now two miles inland and connected with the sea by a ship canal. Northeast still, to Dunkirk.

From Calais to Gravelines there had been few signs of war—an occasional grey lorry laden with supplies for the front; great ambulances, also grey, and with a red cross on the top as a warning to aëroplanes; now and then an armoured car. At Gravelines the country took on a more forbidding appearance. Trenches flanked the roads, which were partly closed here and there by overlapping earthworks, so that the car must turn sharply to the left and then to the right to get through. At night the passage is closed by barbed wire. In one place a bridge was closed by a steel rope, which a sentry lowered after another operation on the pink slip.

The landscape grew more desolate as the daylight began to fade, more desolate and more warlike. There were platforms for lookouts here and there in the trees, prepared during the early days of the war before the German advance was checked. And there were barbed-wire entanglements in the fields. I had always thought of a barbed-wire entanglement as probably breast high. It was surprising to see them only from eighteen inches to two feet in height. It was odd, too, to think that most of the barbed wire had been made in America. Barbed wire is playing a tremendous part in this war. The English say that

the Boers originated this use for it in the South
African War. Certainly much tragedy and an occasional bit of grim humour attach to its present use.

With the fortified town of Dunkirk—or Dunkerque
—came the real congestion of war. The large square
of the town was filled with soldiers and marines. Here
again were British uniforms, British transports and
ambulances. As a seaport for the Allied Armies in
the north, it was bustling with activity. The French
and Belgians predominated, with a sprinkling of
Spahis on horseback and Turcos. An air of activity,
of rapid coming and going, filled the town. Despatch
riders on motor cycles, in black leather uniforms with
black leather hoods, flung through the square at reckless speed. Battered automobiles, their glass shattered
by shells, mud guards crumpled, coated with clay and
riddled with holes, were everywhere, coming and going at the furious pace I have since learned to associate
with war.

And over all, presiding in heroic size in the centre
of the Square, the statue of Jean Bart, Dunkirk's
privateer and pirate, now come into his own again, was
watching with interest the warlike activities of the
Square. Things have changed since the days of Jean
Bart, however. The cutlass that hangs by his side
would avail him little now. The aëroplane bombs that
drop round him now and then, and the processions of
French "seventy-five" guns that rumble through the
Square, must puzzle him. He must feel rather a
piker in this business of modern war.

Dunkirk is generally referred to as the "front." It
is not, however. It is near enough for constant visits
from German aëroplanes, and has been partially de-

stroyed by German guns, firing from a distance of more than twenty miles. But the real line begins fifteen miles farther along the coast at Nieuport.

So we left Dunkirk at once and continued toward La Panne. A drawbridge in the wall guards the road out of the city in that direction. And here for the first time the pink slip threatened to fail us. The Red Cross had been used by spies sufficiently often to cover us with cold suspicion. And it was worse than that. Women were not allowed, under any circumstances, to go in that direction—a new rule, being enforced with severity. My little card was produced and eyed with hostility.

My name was assuredly of German origin. I got out my passport and pointed to the picture on it. It had been taken hastily in Washington for passport purposes, and there was a cast in the left eye. I have no cast in the left eye. Timid attempts to squint with that eye failed.

But at last the officer shrugged his shoulders and let us go. The two sentries who had kept their rifles pointed at me lowered them to a more comfortable angle. A temporary sense of cold down my back retired again to my feet, whence it had risen. We went over the ancient drawbridge, with its chains by which it may be raised, and were free. But our departure was without enthusiasm. I looked back. Some eight sentries and officers were staring after us and muttering among themselves.

Afterward I crossed that bridge many times. They grew accustomed to me, but they evidently thought me quite mad. Always they protested and complained, until one day the word went round that the American lady had been received by the King. After that I was covered with the mantle of royalty. The sentries saluted as I passed. I was of the elect.

There were other sentries until the Belgian frontier was passed. After that there was no further challenging. The occasional distant roar of a great gun could be heard, and two French aëroplanes, winging home after a reconnaissance over the German lines, hummed overhead. Where between Calais and Dunkirk there had been an occasional peasant's cart in the road or labourer in the fields, now the country was deserted, save for long lines of weary soldiers going to their billets, lines that shuffled rather than marched. There was no drum to keep them in step with its melancholy throbbing. Two by two, heads down, laden with intrenching tools in addition to their regular equipment, grumbling as the car forced them off the road into the mud that bordered it, swathed beyond recognition against the cold and dampness, in the twilight those lines of shambling men looked grim, determined, sinister.

"We are going through Furnes," said my companion. "It has been shelled all day, but at dusk they usually stop. It is out of our way, but you will like to see it."

I said I was perfectly willing, but that I hoped the Germans would adhere to their usual custom. I felt all at once that, properly conserved, a long and happy lift might lie before me. I mentioned that I was a person of no importance, and that my death would be of no military advantage. And, as if to emphasise my peaceful fireside at home, and dinner at seven o'clock with candles on the table, the fire re-commenced.

"Artillery," I said with conviction, "seems to me barbarous and unnecessary. But in a moving automobile——"

It was a wrong move. He hastened to tell me of people riding along calmly in automobiles, and of the next moment there being nothing but a hole in the road. Also he told me how shrapnel spread, scattering death over large areas. If I had had an idea of dodging anything I saw coming it vanished.

We went into the little town of Furnes. Nothing happened. Only one shell was fired, and I have no idea where it fell. The town was a dead town, its empty streets full of brick and glass. I grew quite calm and expressed some anxiety about the tires. Although my throat was dry, I was able to enunciate clearly! We dared not light the car lamps, and our progress was naturally slow.

Furnes is not on the coast, but three miles inland. So we turned sharp to the left toward La Panne, our destination, a small seaside resort in times of peace, but now the capital of Belgium. It was dark now, and the roads were congested with the movements of troops, some going to the trenches, those out of the trenches going back to their billets for twenty-four hours' rest, and the men who had been on rest moving up as pickets or reserves. Even in the darkness it was easy to tell the rested men from the ones newly relieved. Here were mostly Belgians, and the little Belgian soldier is a cheery soul. He asks very little, is never surly. A little food, a little sleep—on straw, in a stable or a church—and he is happy again. Over and over, as I saw the Belgian Army, I was impressed with its cheerfulness under unparalleled conditions.

Most of them have been fighting since Liège. Of

a hundred and fifty thousand men only fifty thousand remain. Their ration is meagre compared with the English and the French, their clothing worn and ragged. They are holding the inundated district between Nieuport and Dixmude, a region of constant struggle for water-soaked trenches, where outposts at the time I was there were being fought for through lakes of icy water filled with barbed wire, where their wounded fall and drown. And yet they are inveterately cheerful. A brave lot, the Belgian soldiers, brave and uncomplaining! It is no wonder that the King of Belgium loves them, and that his eyes are tragic as he looks at them.

La Panne at last, a straggling little town of one street and rows of villas overlooking the sea. La Panne, with the guns of Nieuport constantly in one's ears, and the low, red flash of them along the sandy beach; with ambulances bringing in their wounded now that night covers their movements; with English gunboats close to the shore and a searchlight playing over the sea. La Panne, with just over the sand dunes the beginning of that long line of trenches that extends south and east and south again, four hundred and fifty miles of death.

It was two weeks and four days since I had left America, and less than thirty hours since I boarded the one-o'clock train at Victoria Station, London. Later on I beat the thirty-hour record twice, once going from the Belgian front to England in six hours, and another time leaving the English lines at Béthune, motoring to Calais, and arriving in my London hotel the same night. Cars go rapidly over the French roads, and the distance, measured by miles, is not great. Measured by difficulties, it is a different story.

CHAPTER IV

" 'TWAS A FAMOUS VICTORY"

From My Journal:

La Panne, January 25th, 10 p.m.

I AM at the Belgian Red Cross hospital to-night. Have had supper and have been given a room on the top floor, facing out over the sea.

This is the base hospital for the Belgian lines. The men come here with the most frightful injuries. As I entered the building to-night the long tiled corridor was filled with the patient and quiet figures that are the first fruits of war. They lay on portable cots, waiting their turn in the operating rooms, the white coverings and bandages not whiter than their faces.

11 p.m. The Night Superintendent has just been in to see me. She says there is a baby here from Furnes with both legs off, and a nun who lost an arm as she was praying in the garden of her convent. The baby will live, but the nun is dying.

She brought me a hot-water bottle, for I am still chilled from my long ride, and sat down for a moment's talk. She is English, as are most of the nurses. She told me with tears in her eyes of a Dutch Red Cross nurse who was struck by a shell in Furnes, two days ago, as she crossed the street to her hospital, which was being evacuated. She was brought here.

"Her leg was shattered," she said. "So young and

so pretty she was, too! One of the surgeons was in love with her. It seemed as if he could not let her die."

How terrible! For she died.

"But she had a casket," the Night Superintendent hastened to assure me. "The others, of course, do not. And two of the nurses were relieved to-day to go with her to the grave."

I wonder if the young surgeon went. I wonder——

The baby is near me. I can hear it whimpering.

Midnight. A man in the next room has started to moan. Good God, what a place! He has shell in both lungs, and because of weakness had to be operated on without an anæsthetic.

2 A.M. I cannot sleep. He is trying to sing "Tipperary."

English battleships are bombarding the German batteries at Nieuport from the sea. The windows rattle all the time.

6 A.M. A new day now. A grey and forbidding dawn. Sentries every hundred yards along the beach under my window. The gunboats are moving out to sea. A number of French aëroplanes are scouting overhead.

The man in the next room is quiet.

Imagine one of our great seaside hotels stripped of its bands, its gay crowds, its laughter. Paint its many windows white, with a red cross in the centre of each one. Imagine its corridors filled with wounded men, its courtyard crowded with ambulances, its parlours occupied by convalescents who are blind or hopelessly maimed, its card room a chapel trimmed with the panoply of death. For bathchairs and bathers on the sands substitute long lines of weary soldiers drilling in the rain and cold. And over all imagine the unceasing roar of great guns. Then, but feebly, you will have visualised the Ambulance Ocean at La Panne as I saw it that first winter of the war.

The town is built on the sand dunes, and is not unlike Ostend in general situation; but it is hardly more than a village. Such trees as there are grow out of the sand, and are twisted by the winds from the sea. Their trunks are green with smooth moss. And over the dunes is long grass, then grey and dry with winter, grass that was beaten under the wind into waves that surge and hiss.

The beach is wide and level. There is no surf. The sea comes in in long, flat lines of white that wash unheralded about the feet of the cavalry horses drilling there. Here and there a fisherman's boat close to the line of villas marks the limit of high tide; marks more than that; marks the fisherman who has become a soldier; marks the end of the peaceful occupations of the little town; marks the change from a sea that was a livelihood to a sea that has become a menace and a hidden death.

The beach at La Panne has its story. There are guns there now, waiting. The men in charge of them wait, and, waiting, shiver in the cold. And just a few minutes away along the sands there was a house built by a German, a house whose foundation was a cemented site for a gun. The house is destroyed now. It had been carefully located, strategically, and built long before the war began. A gun on that foundation would have commanded Nieuport.

Here, in six villas facing the sea, live King Albert and Queen Elisabeth and their household, and here the

Queen, grief-stricken at the tragedy that has overtaken her innocent and injured people, visits the hospital daily.

La Panne has not been bombarded. Hostile aëroplanes are always overhead. The Germans undoubtedly know all about the town; but it has not been
touched. I do not believe that it will be. For one
thing, it is not at present strategically valuable. Much
more important, Queen Elisabeth is a Bavarian prin-
cess by birth. Quite aside from both reasons, the out-
cry from the civilised world which would result from
injury to any member of the Belgian royal house, with
the present world-wide sympathy for Belgium, would
make such an attack inadvisable.

And yet who knows? So much that was considered
fundamental in the ethics of modern warfare has gone
by the board; so certainly is this war becoming one of
reprisals, of hate and venom, that before this is published La Panne may have been destroyed, or its evacuation by the royal family have been decided.

The contrast between Brussels and La Panne is the
contrast between Belgium as it was and as it is. The
last time I was in Belgium, before this war, I was in
Brussels. The great modern city of three-quarters of
a million people had grown up round the ancient
capital of Brabant. Its name, which means "the dwell-
ing on the marsh," dates from the tenth century. The
huge Palais de Justice is one of the most remarkable
buildings in the world.

Now in front of that great building German guns
are mounted, and the capital of Belgium is a fishing
village on the sand dunes. The King of Belgium has
exchanged the magnificent Palais du Roi for a small
and cheaply built house—not that the democratic

young King of Belgium cares for palaces. But the contrast of the two pictures was impressed on me that winter morning as I stood on the sands at La Panne and looked at the royal villa. All round were sentries. The wind from the sea was biting. It set the long grey grass to waving, and blew the fine sand in clouds about the feet of the cavalry horses filing along the beach.

I was quite unmolested as I took photographs of the stirring scenes about. It was the first daylight view I had had of the Belgian soldiers. These were men on their twenty-four hours' rest, with a part of the new army that was being drilled for the spring campaign. The Belgian system keeps a man twenty-four hours in the trenches, gives him twenty-four hours for rest well back from the firing line, and then, moving him up to picket or reserve duty, holds him another twenty-four hours just behind the trenches. The English system is different. Along the English front men are four days in the trenches and four days out. All movements, of course, are made at night.

The men I watched that morning were partly on rest, partly in reserve. They were shabby, cold and cheery. I created unlimited surprise and interest. They lined up eagerly to be photographed. One group I took was gathered round a sack of potatoes, paring raw potatoes and eating them. For the Belgian soldier is the least well fed of the three armies in the western field. When I left, a good Samaritan had sent a case or two of canned things to some of the regiments, and a favoured few were being initiated into the joys of American canned baked beans. They were a new sensation. To watch the soldiers eat them was a joy and a delight.

I wish some American gentleman, tiring of storing up his treasures only in heaven, would send a can or a case or a shipload of baked beans to the Belgians. This is alliterative, but earnest. They can heat them in the trenches in the cans; they can thrive on them and fight on them. And when the cans are empty they can build fires in them or hang them, filled with stones, on the barbed-wire entanglements in front of the trenches, so that they ring like bells on a herd of cows to warn them of an impending attack.

And while we are on this subject, I wish some of the women who are knitting scarfs would stop,* now that winter is over, and make jelly and jam for the brave and cheerful little Belgian army. I am aware that it is less pleasant than knitting. It cannot be taken to lectures or musicales. One cannot make jam between the courses of a luncheon or a dinner party, or during the dummy hand at bridge. But the men have so little—unsweetened coffee and black bread for breakfast; a stew of meat and vegetables at mid-day, taken to them, when it can be taken, but carried miles from where it is cooked, and usually cold. They pour off the cold liquor and eat the unpalatable residue. Supper is like breakfast with the addition of a ration of minced meat and potatoes, also cold and not attractive at the best.

Sometimes they have bully beef. I have eaten bully beef, which is a cooked and tinned beef, semi-gelatinous. The Belgian bully beef is drier and tougher

---

* This was written in the spring. By the time this book is published knitted woollens will be again in demand. Socks and mittens, abdominal belts and neck scarfs are much liked. A soldier told me he liked his scarf wide, and eight feet long, so he can carry it around his body and fasten it in the back.

than the English. It is not bad; indeed, it is quite good. But the soldier needs variety. The English know this. Their soldiers have sugar, tea, jam and cheese.

If I were asked to-day what the Belgian army needs, now that winter is over and they need no longer shiver in their thin clothing, I should say, in addition to the surgical supplies that are so terribly necessary, port- able kitchens, to give them hot and palatable food. Such kitchens may be bought for two hundred and fifty dollars, with a horse to draw them. They are really sublimated steam cookers, with the hot water used to make coffee when they reach the trenches. I should say, then, surgical supplies and hospital equip- ment, field kitchens, jams of all sorts, canned beans, cigarettes and rubber boots! A number of field kitch- ens have already been sent over. A splendid English- man attached to the Belgian Army has secured funds for a few more. But many are needed. I have seen a big and brawny Belgian officer, with a long record of military bravery behind him, almost shed tears over the prospect of one of these kitchens for his men.

I took many pictures that morning—of dogs, three abreast, hauling *mitrailleuse,* the small and deadly quick-firing guns, from the word *mitraille,* a hail of balls; of long lines of Belgian lancers on their un- clipped and shaggy horses, each man carrying an eight-foot lance at rest; of men drilling in broken boots, in wooden shoes stuffed with straw, in carpet slippers. I was in furs from head to foot—the same fur coat that has been, in turn, lap robe, bed clothing and pillow—and I was cold. These men, smiling into my camera, were thinly dressed, with bare, ungloved hands. But they were smiling.

Afterward I learned that many of them had no underclothing, that the blue tunics and trousers were all they had. Always they shivered, but often also they smiled. Many of them had fought since Liège; most of them had no knowledge of their families on the other side of the line of death. When they return to their country, what will they go back to? Their homes are gone, their farm buildings destroyed, their horses and cattle killed.

But they are a courageous people, a bravely cheery people. For every one of them that remained there, two had gone, either to death, captivity or serious injury. They were glad to be alive that morning on the sands of La Panne, under the incessant roaring of the guns. The wind died down; the sun came out. It was January. In two months, or three, it would be spring and warm. In two months, or three, they confidently expected to be on the move toward their homes again.

What mattered broken boots and the mud and filth of their trenches? What mattered the German aëroplane overhead? Or cold and insufficient food? Or the wind? Nothing mattered but death, and they still lived. And perhaps, beyond the line——

That afternoon, from the Ambulance Ocean, a young Belgian officer was buried.

It was a bright, sunny afternoon, but bitterly cold. Troops were lined up before the hospital in the square; a band, too, holding its instruments with blue and ungloved fingers.

He had been a very brave officer, and very young. The story of what he had done had been told about. So, although military funerals are many, a handful of civilians had gathered to see him taken away to the crowded cemetery. The three English gunboats were patrolling the sea. Tall Belgian generals, in high blue-and-gold caps and great cape overcoats, met in the open space and conferred.

The dead young officer lay in state in the little chapel of the hospital. Ten tall black standards round him held burning candles, the lights of faith. His uniform, brushed of its mud and neatly folded, lay on top of the casket, with his pathetic cap and with the sword that would never lead another charge. He had fought very hard to live, they said at the hospital. But he had died.

The crowd opened, and the priest came through. He wore a purple velvet robe, and behind him came his deacons and four small acolytes in surplices. Up the steps went the little procession. And the doors of the hospital closed behind it.

The civilians turned and went away. The soldiers stood rigid in the cold sunshine, and waited. A little boy kicked a football over the sand. The guns at Nieuport crashed and hammered.

After a time the doors opened again. The boy picked up his football and came closer. The musicians blew on their fingers to warm them. The dead young officer was carried out. His sword gleamed in the sun. They carried the casket carefully, not to disorder the carefully folded tunic or the pathetic cap. The body was placed in an ambulance. At a signal the band commenced to play and the soldiers closed in round the ambulance.

The path of glory, indeed!

But it was not this boyish officer's hope of glory that had brought this scene to pass. He died fighting a defensive war, to save what was left to him of the country he loved. He had no dream of empire, no vision of commercial supremacy, no thrill of conquest as an invaded and destroyed country bent to the inevitable. For months since Liège he had fought a losing fight, a fight that Belgium knew from the beginning must be a losing fight, until such time as her allies could come to her aid. Like the others, he had nothing to gain by this war and everything to lose.

He had lost. The ambulance moved away.

I was frequently in La Panne after that day. I got to know well the road from Dunkirk, with its bordering of mud and ditch, its heavy transports, its grey gunboats in the canals that followed it on one side, its long lines of over-laden soldiers, its automobiles that travelled always at top speed. I saw pictures that no artist will ever paint—of horrors and beauties, of pathos and comedy; of soldiers washing away the filth of the trenches in the cold waters of canals and ditches; of refugees flying by day from the towns, and returning at night to their ruined houses to sleep in the cellars; of long processions of Spahis, Arabs from Algeria, silhouetted against the flat sky line against a setting sun, their tired horses moving slowly, with drooping heads, while their riders, in burnoose and turban, rode with loose reins; of hostile aëroplanes sailing the afternoon breeze like lazy birds, while shells from the anti-aircraft guns burst harmlessly below them in small balloon-shaped clouds of smoke.

But never in all that time did I overcome the sense of unreality, and always I was obsessed by the injustice, the wanton waste and cost and injustice of it all. The baby at La Panne—why should it go through life on stumps instead of legs? The boyish officer—why should he have died? The little sixteen-year-old soldier who had been blinded and who sat all day by the phonograph, listening to Madame Butterfly, Tipperary, and Harry Lauder's A Wee Deoch-an'-Doris—why should he never see again what I could see from the window beside him, the winter sunset over the sea, the glistening white of the sands, the flat line of the surf as it crept in to the sentries' feet? Why? Why?

All these wrecks of boys and men, where are they to go? What are they to do? Blind and maimed, weak from long privation followed by great suffering, what is to become of them when the hospital has fulfilled its function and they are discharged "cured"? Their occupations, their homes, their usefulness are gone. They have not always even clothing in which to leave the hospital. If it was not destroyed by the shell or shrapnel that mutilated them it was worn beyond belief and redemption. Such ragged uniforms as I have seen! Such tragedies of trousers! Such absurd and heart-breaking tunics!

When, soon after, I was presented to the King of the Belgians, these very questions had written lines in his face. It is easy to believe that King Albert of Belgium has buried his private anxieties in the common grief and stress of his people.

CHAPTER V

A TALK WITH THE KING OF THE BELGIANS

THE letter announcing that I was to have an audience with the King of the Belgians reached me at Dunkirk, France, on the evening of the day before the date set. It was brief and to the effect that the King would receive me the next afternoon at two o'clock at the Belgian Army headquarters.

The object of my visit was well known; and, because I wished an authoritative statement to give to America, I had requested that the notes of my conversation with His Majesty should be officially approved. This request was granted. The manuscript of the interview that follows was submitted to His Majesty for approval. It is published as it occurred, and nothing has been added to the record.

A general from the Ministry of War came to the Hôtel des Arcades, in Dunkirk, and I was taken in a motor car to the Belgian Army headquarters some miles away. As the general who conducted me had influenza, and I was trying to keep my nerves in good order, it was rather a silent drive. The car, as are all military cars—and there are no others—was driven by a soldier-chauffeur by whose side sat the general's orderly. Through the narrow gate, with its drawbridge guarded by many sentries, we went out into the open country.

The road, considering the constant traffic of heavy transports and guns, was very fair.   It is under constant repair.   At first, during this severe winter, on account of rain and snow, accidents were frequent. The road, on both sides, was deep in mud and prolific of catastrophe; and even now, with conditions much better, there are numerous accidents.   Cars all travel at frightful speed.   There are no restrictions, and it is nothing to see machines upset and abandoned in the low-lying fields that border the road.

Conditions, however, are better than they were. Part of the conservation system has been the building of narrow ditches at right angles to the line of the road, to lead off the water.   Every ten feet or so there is a gutter filled with fagots.

I had been in the general's car before.   The red-haired Fleming with the fierce moustache who drove it was a speed maniac, and passing the frequent sentries was only a matter of the password.   A signal to slow down, given by the watchful sentry, a hoarse whisper of the password as the car went by, and on again at full speed.   There was no bothering with papers.

On each side of the road were trenches, barbed-wire entanglements, earthen barriers, canals filled with barges.   And on the road were lines of transports and a file of Spahis on horseback, picturesque in their flowing burnouses, bearded and dark-skinned, riding their unclipped horses through the roads under the single rows of trees.   We rode on through a village where a pig had escaped from a slaughterhouse and was being pursued by soldiers—and then, at last, army headquarters and the King of the Belgians.

There was little formality.   I was taken in charge

by the King's equerry, who tapped at a closed door.
I drew a long breath.

"Madame Rinehart!" said the equerry, and stood
aside.

There was a small screen in front of the door. I
went round it. Standing alone before the fire was
Albert I, King of the Belgians. I bowed; then we
shook hands and he asked me to sit down.

It was to be a conversation rather than an interview;
but as it was to be given as accurately as possible to
the American people, I was permitted to make careful
notes of both questions and answers. It was to be, in
effect, a statement of the situation in Belgium as the
King of the Belgians sees it.

I spoke first of a message to America.

"I have already sent a message to America," he
informed me; "quite a long message. We are, of
course, intensely appreciative of what Americans have
done for Belgium."

"They are anxious to do what they can. The general feeling is one of great sympathy."

"Americans are both just and humane," the King
replied; "and their system of distribution is excellent.
I do not know what we should have done without the
American Relief Committees."

"Is there anything further Your Majesty can suggest?"

"They seem to have thought of everything," the
King said simply. "The food is invaluable—particularly the flour. It has saved many from starvation."

"But there is still need?"

"Oh, yes—great need."

It was clear that the subject was a tragic one. The
King of the Belgians loves his people, as they love

him, with a devotion that is completely unselfish. That he is helpless to relieve so much that they are compelled to endure is his great grief.

His face clouded. Probably he was seeing, as he must always see, the dejected figures of the peasants in the fields; the long files of his soldiers as they made their way through wet and cold to the trenches; the destroyed towns; the upheaval of a people.

"What is possible to know of the general condition of affairs in that part of Belgium occupied by the Germans?" I asked. "I do not mean in regard to food only, but the general condition of the Belgian people."

"It is impossible to say," was the answer. "During the invasion it was very bad. It is a little better now, of course; but here we are on the wrong side of the line to form any ordered judgment. To gain a real conception of the situation it would be necessary to go through the occupied portions from town to town, almost from house to house. Have you been in the other part of Belgium?"

"Not yet; I may go."

"You should do that—see Louvain, Aerschot, Antwerp—see the destroyed towns for yourself. No one can tell you. You must see them."

I was not certain that I should be permitted to make such a journey, but the King waved my doubts aside with a gesture.

"You are an American," he said. "It would be quite possible and you would see just what has happened. You would see open towns that were bombarded; other towns that were destroyed after occupation! You would see a country ruthlessly devastated; our wonderful monuments destroyed; our archi-

tectural and artistic treasures sacrificed without reason
—without any justification."

"But as a necessity of war?" I asked.

"Not at all. The Germans have saved buildings
when it suited their convenience to do so. No military
necessity dictated the destruction of Louvain. It was
not bombarded. It was deliberately destroyed. But,
of course, you know that."

"The matter of the violation of Belgium's neutrality
still remains an open question," I said. "I have seen
in American facsimile copies of documents referring
to conversations between staff officers of the British
and Belgian armies—documents that were found in
the ministerial offices at Brussels when the Germans
occupied that city last August. Of course I think most
Americans realise that, had they been of any real
importance, they would have been taken away. There
was time enough. But there are some, I know, who
think them significant."

The King of the Belgians shrugged his shoulders.

"They were of an unofficial character and entirely
without importance. The German Staff probably
knew all about them long before the declaration of
war. They themselves had, without doubt, discussed
and recorded similar probabilities in case of war with
other countries. It is a common practice in all army
organisations to prepare against different contingen-
cies. It is a question of military routine only."

"There was no justification, then, for the violation
of Belgian neutrality?" I inquired.

"None whatever! The German violation of Belgian neutrality was wrong," he said emphatically.
"On the fourth of August their own chancellor admitted it. Belgium had no thought of war. The Belgians

are a peace-loving people, who had every reason to believe in the friendship of Germany."

The next question was a difficult one. I inquired as to the behaviour of the Germans in the conquered territory; but the King made no sweeping condemnation of the German Army.

"Fearful things have been done, particularly during the invasion," he said, weighing his words carefully; "but it would be unfair to condemn the whole German Army. Some regiments have been most humane; but others behaved very badly. Have you seen the government report?"

I said I had not seen it, though I had heard that a careful investigation had been made.

"The government was very cautious," His Majesty said. "The investigation was absolutely impartial and as accurate as it could be made. Doubts were cast on all statements—even those of the most dependable witnesses—until they could be verified."

"They were verified?"

"Yes; again and again."

"By the victims themselves?"

"Not always. The victims of extreme cruelty do not live to tell of it; but German soldiers themselves have told the story. We have had here many hundreds of journals, taken from dead or imprisoned Germans, furnishing elaborate details of most atrocious acts. The government is keeping these journals. They furnish powerful and incontrovertible testimony of what happened in Belgium when it was swept over by a brutal army. That was, of course, during the invasion—such things are not happening now so far as we know."

He had spoken quietly, but there was a new note of

strain in his voice. The burden of the King of the Belgians is a double one. To the horror of war has been added the unnecessary violation and death of noncombatants.

The King then referred to the German advance through Belgian territory.

"Thousands of civilians have been killed without reason. The execution of noncombatants is not war, and no excuse can be made for it. Such deeds cannot be called war."

"But if the townspeople fired on the Germans?" I asked.

"All weapons had been deposited in the hands of the town authorities. It is unlikely that any organised attack by civilians could have been made. However, if in individual cases shots were fired at the German soldiers, this may always be condoned in a country suffering invasion. During an occupation it would be different, naturally. No excuse can be offered for such an action in occupied territory."

"Various Belgian officers have told me of seeing crowds of men, women and children driven ahead of the German Army to protect the troops. This is so incredible that I must ask whether it has any foundation of truth."

"It is quite true. It is a barbarous and inhuman system of protecting the German advance. When the Belgian soldiers fired on the enemy they killed their own people. Again and again innocent civilians of both sexes were sacrificed to protect the invading army during attacks. A terrible slaughter!"

His Majesty made no effort to conceal his great grief and indignation. And again, as before, there seemed to be nothing to say.

"Even now," I said, "when the Belgians return the German artillery fire they are bombarding their own towns."

"That is true, of course; but what can we do? And the civilian population is very brave. They fear invasion, but they no longer pay any attention to bombs. They work in the fields quite calmly, with shells dropping about. They must work or starve."

He then spoke of the morale of the troops, which is excellent, and of his sympathy for their situation.

"Their families are in Belgium," he said. "Many of them have heard nothing for months. But they are wonderful. They are fighting for life and to regain their families, their homes and their country. Christmas was very sad for them."

"In the event of the German Army's retiring from Belgium, do you believe, as many do, that there will be more destruction of cities? Brussels, for instance?"

"I think not."

I referred to my last visit to Belgium, when Brussels was the capital; and to the contrast now, when La Panne a small seaside resort hardly more than a village, contains the court, the residence of the King and Queen, and of the various members of his household. It seemed to me unlikely that La Panne would be attacked, as the Queen of the Belgians is a Bavarian.

"Do you think La Panne will be bombarded?" I asked.

"Why not?"

"I thought that possibly, on account of Your Majesty and the Queen being there, it would be spared.

"They are bombarding Furnes, where I go every day," he replied. "And there are German aëroplanes overhead all the time."

The mention of Furnes brought to my mind the flooded district near that village, which extends from Nieuport to Dixmude.

"Belgium has made a great sacrifice in flooding her lowlands," I said. "Will that land be as fertile as before?"

"Not for several years. The flooding of the productive land in the Yser district was only carried out as a military necessity. The water is sea water, of course, and will have a bad effect on the soil. Have you seen the flooded district?"

I told His Majesty that I had been to the Belgian trenches, and then across the inundated country to one of the outposts; a remarkable experience—one I should never forget.

The conversation shifted to America and her point of view; to American women who have married abroad. His Majesty mentioned especially Lady Curzon. Two children of the King were with Lord Curzon, in England, at the time. The Crown Prince, a boy of fourteen, tall and straight like his father, was with the King and Queen.

The King had risen and was standing in his favourite attitude, his elbow on the mantelpiece. I rose also.

"I was given some instructions as to the ceremonial of this audience," I said. "I am afraid I have not followed them!"

"What were you told to do?" said His Majesty, evidently amused. Then, without waiting for a reply:

"We are very democratic—we Belgians," he said. "More democratic than the Americans. The President of the United States has great power—very great power. He is a czar."

He referred to President Wilson in terms of great

esteem—not only as the President but as a man. He spoke, also, with evident admiration of Mr. Roosevelt and Mr. McKinley, both of whom he had met.

I looked at the clock. It was after three and the interview had begun at two. I knew it was time for me to go, but I had been given no indication that the interview was at an end. Fragments of the coaching I had received came to my mind, but nothing useful; so I stated my difficulty frankly, and again the King's serious face lighted up with a smile.

"There is no formality here; but if you are going we must find the general for you."

So we shook hands and I went out; but the beautiful courtesy of the soldier King of the Belgians brought him out to the doorstep with me.

That is the final picture I have of Albert I, King of the Belgians—a tall young man, very fair and blue-eyed, in the dark blue uniform of a lieutenant-general of his army, wearing no orders or decorations, standing bareheaded in the wind and pointing out to me the direction in which I should go to find the general who had brought me.

He is a very courteous gentleman, with the eyes of one who loves the sea, for the King of the Belgians is a sailor in his heart; a tragic and heroic figure but thinking himself neither—thinking of himself not at all, indeed; only of his people, whose griefs are his to share but not to lighten; living day and night under the rumble of German artillery at Nieuport and Dixmude in that small corner of Belgium which remains to him.

He is a King who, without suspicion of guilt, has lost his country; who has seen since August of 1914 two-thirds of his army lost, his beautiful and ancient towns destroyed, his fertile lands thrown open to the sea.

I went on. The guns were still at work. At Nieuport, Dixmude, Furnes, Pervyse—all along that flat, flooded region—the work of destruction was going on. Overhead, flying high, were two German aëroplanes—the eyes of the war.

*   *   *   *   *   *

Not politically, but humanely, it was time to make to America an authoritative statement as to conditions in Belgium.

The principle of non-interference in European politics is one of national policy and not to be questioned. But there can be no justification for the destruction of property and loss of innocent lives in Belgium. Germany had plead to the neutral nations her necessity, and had plead eloquently. On the other hand, the English and French authorities during the first year of the war had preserved a dignified silence, confident of the justice of their cause.

And official Belgium had made no complaint. She had bowed to the judgment of her allies, knowing that a time would come, at the end of the war, to speak of her situation and to demand justifiable redress.

But a million homeless Belgians in England and Holland proclaimed and still proclaim their wretchedness broadcast. The future may bring redress, but the present story of Belgium belongs to the world. America, the greatest of the neutral countries, has a right to know now the suffering and misery of this patient, hard-working people.

This war may last a long time; the western armies

are at a deadlock. Since November of 1914 the line
has varied only slightly here and there; has been pushed
out or back only to straighten again.

Advances may be counted by feet. From Nieuport
to Ypres attacks are waged round solitary farms
which, by reason of the floods, have become tiny
islands protected by a few men, mitrailleuses, and entanglements of barbed wire. Small attacking bodies
capture such an outpost, wading breast-deep—drowning when wounded—in the stagnant water. There
are no glorious charges here, no contagion of courage;
simply a dogged and desperate struggle—a gain which
the next day may see forfeited. The only thing that
goes on steadily is the devastating work of the heavy
guns on each side.

Meantime, both in England and in France, there has
been a growing sentiment that the government's policy
of silence has been a mistake. The cudgel of public
opinion is a heavy one. The German propaganda in
America has gone on steadily. There is no argument
where one side only is presented. That splendid and
solid part of the American people, the German population, essentially and naturally patriotic, keeping their
faith in the Fatherland, is constantly presenting its
case; and against that nothing official has been offered.

England is fighting heroically, stoically; but her
stoicism is a vital mistake. This silence has nothing
whatever to do with military movements, their success
or their failure. It is more fundamental, an inherent
characteristic of the English character, founded on
reserve—perhaps tinged with that often misunder-
stood conviction of the Britisher that other persons
cannot be really interested in what is strictly another's
affairs.

The Allies are beginning to realise, however, that
this war is not their own affair alone.   It affects the
world too profoundly.   Mentally, morally, spiritually
and commercially, it is an upheaval in which all must
suffer.

And the English people, who have sent and are sending the very flower of their country's manhood to the
front, are beginning to regret the error in judgment
that has left the rest of the English-speaking world in
comparative ignorance of the true situation.

They are sending the best they have—men of high
ideals, who, as volunteers, go out to fight for what
they consider a just cause.   The old families, in which
love of country and self-sacrifice are traditions, have
suffered heavily.

The crux of the situation is Belgium—the violation
of her neutrality; the conduct of the invading army;
her unnecessary and unjustifiable suffering.   And Belgium has felt that the time to speak has come.

CHAPTER VI

THE CAUSE

THE Belgian Red Cross may well be proud of the hospital at La Panne. It is modern, thoroughly organised, completely equipped. Within two weeks of the outbreak of the war it was receiving patients. It was not at the front then. But the German tide has forced itself along until now it is almost on the line.

Generally speaking, order had taken the place of the early chaos in the hospital situation when I was at the front. The British hospitals were a satisfaction to visit. The French situation was not so good. The isolated French hospitals were still in need of everything, even of anæsthetics. The lack of an organised nursing system was being keenly felt.

But the early handicaps of unpreparedness and overwhelming numbers of patients had been overcome to a large extent. Scientific management and modern efficiency had stepped in. Things were still capable of improvement. Gentlemen ambulance drivers are not always to be depended on. Nurses are not all of the same standard of efficiency. Supplies of one sort exceeded the demand, while other things were entirely lacking. Food of the kind that was needed by the very ill was scarce, expensive and difficult to secure at any price.

But the things that have been done are marvellous. Surgery has not failed. The stereoscopic X-ray and antitetanus serum are playing their active part. Once out of the trenches a soldier wounded at the front has as much chance now as a man injured in the pursuit of a peaceful occupation.

Once out of the trenches! For that is the question. The ambulances must wait for night. It is not in the hospitals but in the ghastly hours between injury and darkness that the case of life or death is decided. That is where surgical efficiency fails against the brutality of this war, where the Red Cross is no longer respected, where it is not possible to gather in the wounded under the hospital flag, where there is no armistice and no pity. This is war, glorious war, which those who stay at home say smugly is good for a nation.

But there are those who are hurt, not in the trenches but in front of them. In that narrow strip of No Man's Land between the confronting armies, and extending four hundred and fifty miles from the sea through Belgium and France, each day uncounted numbers of men fall, and, falling, must lie. The terrible thirst that follows loss of blood makes them faint; the cold winds and snows and rains of what has been a fearful winter beat on them; they cannot have water or shelter. The lucky ones die, but there are some that live, and live for days. This too is war, glorious war, which is good for a nation, which makes its boys into men, and its men into these writhing figures that die so slowly and so long.

I have seen many hospitals. Some of the makeshifts would be amusing were they not so pathetic. Old chapels with beds and supplies piled high before

the altar; kindergarten rooms with childish mottoes
on the walls, from which hang fever charts; nuns'
cubicles thrown open to doctors and nurses as living
quarters.

At La Panne, however, there are no makeshifts.
There are no wards, so called. But many of the large
rooms hold three beds. All the rooms are airy and
well lighted. True, there is no lift, and the men must
be carried down the staircases to the operating rooms
on the lower floor, and carried back again. But the
carrying is gently done.

There are two operating rooms, each with two modern operating tables. The floors are tiled, the walls,
ceiling and all furnishings white. Attached to the
operating rooms is a fully equipped laboratory and
an X-ray room. I was shown the stereoscopic X-ray
apparatus by which the figure on the plate stands out
in relief, like any stereoscopic picture. Every large
hospital I saw had this apparatus, which is invaluable
in locating bullets and pieces of shell or shrapnel.
Under the X-ray, too, extraction frequently takes
place, the operators using long-handled instruments
and gloves that are soaked in a solution of lead and
thus become impervious to the rays so destructive to
the tissues.

Later on I watched Doctor DePage operate at this
hospital. I was put into a uniform, and watched a
piece of shell taken from a man's brain and a great
blood clot evacuated. Except for the red cross on
each window and the rattle of the sash under the
guns, I might have been in one of the leading American hospitals and war a century away. There were
the same white uniforms on the surgeons; the same
white gauze covering their heads and swathing their

faces to the eyes; the same silence, the same care as to sterilisation; the same orderly rows of instruments on a glass stand; the same nurses, alert and quiet; the same clear white electric light overhead; the same rubber gloves, the same anæsthetists and assistants.

It was twelve minutes from the time the operating surgeon took the knife until the wound was closed. The head had been previously shaved by one of the assistants, and painted with iodine. In twelve minutes the piece of shell lay in my hand. The stertorous breathing was easier, bandages were being adjusted, the next case was being anæsthetised and prepared.

I wish I could go further. I wish I could follow that peasant-soldier to recovery and health. I wish I could follow him back to his wife and children, to his little farm in Belgium. I wish I could even say he recovered. But I cannot. I do not know. The war is a series of incidents with no beginning and no end. The veil lifts for a moment and drops again.

I saw other cases brought down for operation at the Ambulance Ocean. One I shall never forget. Here was a boy again, looking up with hopeful, fully conscious eyes at the surgeons. He had been shot through the spine. From his waist down he was inert, helpless. He smiled. He had come to be operated on. Now all would be well. The great surgeons would work over him, and he would walk again.

When after a long consultation they had to tell him they could not operate, I dared not look at his eyes.

Again, what is he to do? Where is he to go? He is helpless, in a strange land. He has no country, no people, no money. And he will live, think of it!

I wish I could leaven all this with something cheerful. I wish I could smile over the phonograph playing again and again A Wee Deoch-an'-Doris in that room for convalescents that overlooks the sea. I wish I could think that the baby with both legs off will grow up without missing what it has never known. I wish I could be reconciled because the dead young officer had died the death of a patriot and a soldier. or that the boy I saw dying in an upper room, from shock and loss of blood following an amputation, is only a pawn in the great chess game of empires. I wish I could believe that the two women on the floor below, one with both arms gone, another with one arm off and her back ripped open by a shell, are the legitimate fruits of a holy war. I cannot. I can see only greed and lust of battle and ambition.

In a bright room I saw a German soldier. He had the room to himself. He was blue eyed and yellow haired, with a boyish and contagious smile. He knew no more about it all than I did. It must have bewildered him in the long hours that he lay there alone. He did not hate these people. He never had hated them. It was clear, too, that they did not hate him. For they had saved a gangrenous leg for him when all hope seemed ended. He lay there, with his white coverlet drawn to his chin, and smiled at the surgeon. They were evidently on the best of terms.

"How goes it?" asked the surgeon cheerfully in German.

"*Sehr gut*," he said, and eyed me curiously.

He was very proud of the leg, and asked that I see it. It was in a cast. He moved it about triumphantly. Probably all over Germany, as over France and this corner of Belgium, just such little scenes occur daily, hourly.

The German peasant, like the French and the Belgian, is a peaceable man. He is military but not militant. He is sentimental rather than impassioned. He loves Christmas and other feast days. He is not ambitious. He fights bravely, but he would rather sing or make a garden.

It is over the bent shoulders of these peasants that the great Continental army machines must march. The German peasant is poor, because for forty years he has been paying the heavy tax of endless armament. The French peasant is poor, because for forty years he has been struggling to recover from the drain of the huge war indemnity demanded by Germany in 1871. The Russian peasant toils for a remote government, with which his sole tie is the tax-gatherer; toils with childish faith for The Little Father, at whose word he may be sent to battle for a cause of which he knows nothing.

Germany's militarism, England's navalism, Russia's autocracy, France, graft-ridden in high places and struggling for rehabilitation after a century of war—and, underneath it all, bearing it on bent shoulders, men like this German prisoner, alone in his room and puzzling it out! It makes one wonder if the result of this war will not be a great and overwhelming individualism, a protest of the unit against the mass; if Socialism, which has apparently died of an ideal, will find this ideal but another name for tyranny, and rise from its grave a living force.

Now and then a justifiable war is fought, for liberty perhaps, or like our Civil War, for a great principle. There are wars that are inevitable. Such wars are frequently revolutions and have their origins in the disaffection of a people.

But here is a world war about which volumes are

being written to discover the cause. Here were prosperous nations, building wealth and culture on a basis of peace. Europe was apparently more in danger of revolution than of international warfare. It is not only war without a known cause, it is an unexpected war. Only one of the nations involved showed any evidence of preparation. England is not yet ready. Russia has not yet equipped the men she has mobilised.

Is this war, then, because the balance of power is so nicely adjusted that a touch turns the scale, whether that touch be a Kaiser's dream of empire or the eyes of a Czar turned covetously toward the South?

I tried to think the thing out during the long nights when the sound of the heavy guns kept me awake. It was hard, because I knew so little, nothing' at all of European politics, or war, or diplomacy. When I tried to be logical, I became emotional. Instead of reason I found in myself only a deep resentment.

I could see only that blue-eyed German in his bed, those cheery and cold and ill-equipped Belgians drilling on the sands at La Panne.

But on one point I was clear. Away from all the imminent questions that filled the day, the changing ethics of war, its brutalities, its hideous necessities, one point stood out clear and distinct. That the real issue is not the result, but the cause of this war. That the world must dig deep into the mire of European diplomacy to find that cause, and having found it must destroy it. That as long as that cause persists, be it social or political, predatory or ambitious, there will be more wars. Again it will be possible for a handful of men in high place to overthrow a world.

And one of the first results of the discovery of that

cause will be a demand of the people to know what their representatives are doing. Diplomacy, instead of secret whispering, a finger to its lips, must shout from the housetops. Great nations cannot be governed from cellars. Diplomats are not necessarily conspirators. There is such a thing as walking in the sunlight.

There is no such thing in civilisation as a warlike people. There are peaceful people, or aggressive people, or military people. But there are none that do not prefer peace to war, until, inflamed and roused by those above them who play this game of empires, they must don the panoply of battle and go forth.

CHAPTER VII

THE STORY WITH AN END

I N its way that hospital at La Panne epitomised the whole tragedy of the great war. Here were women and children, innocent victims when the peaceful near-by market town of Furnes was being shelled; here was a telegraph operator who had stuck to his post under furious bombardment until both his legs were crushed. He had been decorated by the king for his bravery. Here were Belgian aristocrats without extra clothing or any money whatever, and women whose whole lives had been shielded from pain or discomfort. One of them, a young woman whose father is among the largest landowners in Belgium, is in charge of the villa where the uniforms of wounded soldiers are cleaned and made fit for use again. Over her white uniform she wore, in the bitter wind, a thin tan raincoat. We walked together along the beach. I protested.

"You are so thinly clad," I said. "Surely you do not go about like that always!"

She shrugged her shoulders.

"It is all I have," she said philosophically. "And I have no money—none. None of us has."

A titled Belgian woman with her daughter had just escaped from Brussels. She was very sad, for she had lost her only boy. But she smiled a little as she told me of their having nothing but what they wore, and that the night before they had built a fire in their room, washed their linen, and gone to bed, leaving it until morning to dry.

Across the full width of the hospital stretched the great drawing-room of the hotel, now a recreation place for convalescent soldiers. Here all day the phonograph played, the nurses off duty came in to write letters, the surgeons stopped on their busy rounds to speak to the men or to watch for a few minutes the ever-changing panorama of the beach, with its background of patrolling gunboats, its engineers on rest playing football, its occasional aëroplanes, carrying each two men—a pilot and an observer.

The men sat about. There were boys with the stringy beards of their twenty years. There were empty sleeves, many crutches, and some who must be led past the chairs and tables—who will always have to be led.

They were all cheerful. But now and then, when the bombardment became more insistent, some of them would raise their heads and listen, with the strained faces of those who see a hideous picture.

The young woman who could not buy a heavy coat showed me the villa adjoining the hospital, where the clothing of wounded soldiers is cared for. It is placed first in a fumigating plant in the basement and thoroughly sterilised. After that it is brushed of its encrusted mud and blood stains are taken out by soaking in cold water. It is then dried and thoroughly sunned. Then it is ready for the second floor.

Here tailors are constantly at work mending garments apparently unmendable, pressing, steaming, patching, sewing on buttons. The ragged uniforms come out of that big bare room clean and whole, ready to be tied up in new burlap bags, tagged, and placed in racks of fresh white cedar. There is no odour in this room, although innumerable old garments are stored in it.

In an adjoining room the rifles and swords of the injured men stand in racks, the old and unserviceable rifles with which Belgium was forced to equip so many of her soldiers side by side with the new and scientific German guns. Along the wall are officers' swords, and above them, on shelves, the haversacks of the common soldiers, laden with the things that comprise their whole comfort.

I examined one. How few the things were and how worn! And yet the haversack was heavy. As he started for the trenches, this soldier who was carried back, he had on his shoulders this haversack of hide tanned with the hair on. In it he had two pairs of extra socks, worn and ragged, a tattered and dirty undershirt, a photograph of his wife, rags for cleaning his gun, a part of a loaf of dry bread, the remnant of what had been a pair of gloves, now fingerless and stiff with rain and mud, a rosary, a pair of shoes that the woman of the photograph would have wept and prayed over, some extra cartridges and a piece of leather. Perhaps he meant to try to mend the shoes.

And here again I wish I could finish the story. I wish I could tell whether he lived or died—whether he carried that knapsack back to battle, or whether he died and its pitiful contents were divided among those of his comrades who were even more needy than he had been. But the veil lifts for a moment and drops again.

Two incidents stand out with distinctness from those first days in La Panne, when, thrust with amazing rapidity into the midst of war, my mind was a chaos of interest, bewilderment and despair.

One is of an old abbé, talking earnestly to a young Belgian noblewoman who had recently escaped from Brussels with only the clothing she wore.

The abbé was round of face and benevolent. I had met him before, at Calais, where he had posed me in front of a statue and taken my picture. His enthusiasm over photography was contagious. He had made a dark room from a closet in an old convent, and he owned a little American camera. With this carefully placed on a tripod and covered with a black cloth, he posed me carefully, making numerous excursions under the cloth. In that cold courtyard, under the marble figure of Joan of Arc, he was a warm and human and most alive figure, in his flat black shoes, his long black soutane with its woollen sash, his woollen muffler and spectacles, with the eternal cigarette, that is part and parcel of every Belgian, dangling loosely from his lower lip.

The surgeons and nurses who were watching the operation looked on with affectionate smiles. They loved him, this old priest, with his boyishness, his enthusiasms, his tiny camera, his cigarette, his beautiful faith. He has promised me the photograph and what he promises he fulfils. But perhaps it was a failure. I hope not. He would be so disappointed—and so would I.

So I was glad to meet him again at La Panne— glad and surprised, for he was fifty miles north of where we had met before. But the abbé was changed. He was without the smile, without the cigarette. And he was speaking beseechingly to the smiling young refugee. This is what he was saying:

"I am glad, daughter, to help you in every way that I can. I have bought for you in Calais everything that you requested. But I implore you, daughter, do not ask me to purchase any more ladies' underlinen. It is most embarrassing."

"But, father——"

"No underlinen," he repeated firmly. But it hurt him to refuse. One could see that. One imagined, too, that in his life of service there were few refusals. I left them still debating. The abbé's eyes were desperate but his posture firm. One felt that there would be no surrender.

Another picture, and I shall leave La Panne for a time.

I was preparing to go. A telephone message to General Melis, of the Belgian Army, had brought his car to take me to Dunkirk. I was about to leave the protection of the Belgian Red Cross and place myself in the care of the ministry of war. I did not know what the future would bring, and the few days at La Panne and the Ambulance Ocean had made friends for me there. Things move quickly in war time. The conventions with which we bind up our souls in ordinary life are cut away. La Panne was already familiar and friendly territory.

I went down the wide staircase. An ambulance had stopped and its burden was being carried in. The bearers rested the stretcher gently on the floor, and a nurse was immediately on her knees beside it.

"Shell!" she said.

The occupant was a boy of perhaps nineteen—a big boy. Some mother must have been very proud of him. He was fully conscious, and he looked up from his stained bandages with the same searching glance that now I have seen so often—the glance that would read its chances in the faces of those about. With his uninjured arm he threw back the blanket. His right arm was wounded, broken in two places, but not shattered.

"He'll do nicely," said the nurse. "A broken jaw and the arm."

His eyes were on me, so I bent over.

"The nurse says you will do nicely," I assured him. "It will take time, but you will be very comfortable here, and——"

The nurse had been making further investigations. Now she turned back the other end of the blanket. His right leg had been torn off at the hip.

That story has an end; for that boy died.

The drive back to Dunkirk was a mad one. Afterward I learned to know that red-headed Flemish chauffeur, with his fiercely upcurled moustache and his contempt of death. Rather, perhaps, I learned to know his back. It was a reckless back. He wore a large army overcoat with a cape and a cap with a tassel. When he really got under way at anything from fifty miles an hour to the limit of the speedometer, which was ninety miles, the gilt tassel, which in the Belgian cap hangs over and touches the forehead, had a way of standing up; the cape overcoat blew out in the air, cutting off my vision and my last hope.

I regard that chauffeur as a menace on the high road. Certainly he is not a lady's chauffeur. He never will be. Once at night he took me—and the car—into an iron railroad gate, and bent the gate into a V. I was bent into the whole alphabet.

The car was a limousine. After that one cold ride

from Calais to La Panne I was always in a limousine —always, of course, where a car could go at all. There may be other writers who have been equally fortunate, but most of the stories are of frightful hardships. I was not always comfortable. I was frequently in danger. But to and from the front I rode soft and warm and comfortable. Often I had a bottle of hot coffee and sandwiches. Except for the two carbines strapped to the speedometer, except for the soldier-chauffeur and the orderly who sat together outside, except for the eternal consulting of maps and showing of passes, I might have been making a pleasure tour of the towns of Northern France and Belgium. In fact, I have toured abroad during times of peace and have been less comfortable.

I do not speak Flemish, so I could not ask the chauffeur to desist, slow down, or let me out to walk. I could only sit tight as the machine flew round corners, elbowed transports, and threw a warning shriek to armoured cars. I wondered what would happen if we skidded into a wagon filled with high explosives. I tried to remember the conditions of my war insurance policy at Lloyd's. Also I recalled the unpleasant habit the sentries have of firing through the back of any car that passes them.

I need not have worried. Except that once we killed a brown chicken, and that another time we almost skidded into the canal, the journey was uneventful, almost calm. One thing cheered me—all the other machines were going as fast as mine. A car that eased up its pace would be rammed from behind probably. I am like the English—I prefer a charge to a rearguard engagement.

My pass took me into Dunkirk.

It was dusk by that time. I felt rather lost and alone. I figured out what time it was at home. I wished some one would speak English. And I hated being regarded as a spy every mile or so, and depending on a slip of paper as my testimonial of respectability. The people I knew were lunching about that time, or getting ready for bridge or the matinée. I wondered what would happen to me if the pass blew out of the orderly's hands and was lost in the canal.

The chauffeur had been instructed to take me to the *Mairie,* a great dark building of stone halls and stairways, of sentries everywhere, of elaborate officers and much ceremony. But soon, in a great hall of the old building piled high with army supplies, I was talking to General Melis, and my troubles were over. A kindly and courteous gentleman, he put me at my ease at once. More than that, he spoke some English. He had received letters from England about me, and had telegraphed that he would meet me at Calais. He had, indeed, taken the time out of his busy day to go himself to Calais, thirty miles by motor, to meet me.

I was aghast. "The boat went to Boulogne," I explained. "I had no idea, of course, that you would be there."

"Now that you are here," he said, "it is all right. But—exactly what can I do for you?"

So I told him. He listened attentively. A very fine and gallant soldier he was, sitting in that great room in the imposing uniform of his rank; a busy man, taking a little time out of his crowded day to see an American woman who had come a long way alone to see this tragedy that had overtaken his country. Orderlies and officers came and went; the *Mairie* was a hive of seething activities. But he listened patiently.

"Where do you want to go?" he asked when I had finished.

"I should like to stay here, if I may. And from here, of course, I should like to get to the front."

"Where?"

"Can I get to Ypres?"

"It is not very safe."

I proclaimed instantly and loudly that I was as brave as a lion; that I did not know fear. He smiled. But when the interview was over it was arranged that I should have a *permis de séjour* to stay in Dunkirk, and that on the following day the general himself and one of his officers having an errand in that direction would take me to Ypres.

That night the town of Dunkirk was bombarded by some eighteen German aëroplanes.

CHAPTER VIII

THE NIGHT RAID ON DUNKIRK

I FOUND that a room had been engaged for me at the Hotel des Arcades. It was a very large room looking out over the public square and the statue of Jean Bart. It was really a princely room. No wonder they showed it to me proudly, and charged it to me royally. It was an upholstered room. Even the doors were upholstered. And because it was upholstered and expensive and regal, it enjoyed the isolation of greatness. The other people in the hotel slept above or underneath.

There were times when I longed for neighbours, when I yearned for some one to occupy the other royal apartment next door. But except for a Russian prince who stayed two days, and who snored in Russian and kept two *valets de chambre* up all night in the hall outside my door polishing his boots and cleaning his uniform, I was always alone in that part of the hotel.

At my London hotel I had been lodged on the top floor, and twice in the night the hall porter had telephoned me to say that German Zeppelins were on their way to London. So I took care to find that in the Hotel des Arcades there were two stories and two layers of Belgian and French officers overhead.

I felt very comfortable—until the air raid. Then

two stories seemed absurd, inadequate. I would not have felt safe in the subcellar of the Woolworth Building.

There were no women in the hotel at that time, with the exception of a hysterical lady manager, who sat in a boxlike office on the lower floor, and two chambermaids. A boy made my bed and brought me hot water. For several weeks at intervals he knocked at the door twice a day and said: "Et wat." I always thought it was Flemish for "May I come in?" At last I discovered that he considered this the English for "hot water." The waiters in the café were too old to be sent to war, but I think the cook had gone. There was no cook. Some one put the food on the fire, but he was not a cook.

Dunkirk had been bombarded several times, I learned.

"They come in the morning," said my informant. "Every one is ordered off the streets. But they do little damage. One or two machines come and drop a bomb or two. That is all. Very few are killed."

I protested. I felt rather bitter about it. I expected trouble along the lines, I explained. I knew I would be quite calm when I was actually at the front, and when I had my nervous system prepared for trouble. But in Dunkirk I expected to rest and relax. I needed sleep after La Panne. I thought something should be done about it.

My informant shrugged his shoulders. He was English, and entirely fair.

"Dunkirk is a fortified town," he explained. "It is quite legitimate. But you may sleep to-night. The raids are always daylight ones."

So I commenced dinner calmly. I do not remember

anything about that dinner. The memory of it has gone. I do recall looking about the dining room, and feeling a little odd and lonely, being the only woman. Then a gun boomed somewhere outside, and an alarm bell commenced to ring rapidly almost overhead. Instantly the officers in the room were on their feet, and every light went out.

The *maître d'hôtel*, Emil, groped his way to my table and struck a match.

"Aëroplanes!" he said.

There was much laughing and talking as the officers moved to the door. The heavy velvet curtains were drawn. Some one near the door lighted a candle.

"Where shall I go?" I asked.

Emil, unlike the officers, was evidently nervous.

"Madame is as safe here as anywhere," he said. "But if she wishes to join the others in the cellar——"

I wanted to go to the cellar or to crawl into the office safe. But I felt that, as the only woman and the only American about, I held the reputation of America and of my sex in my hands. The waiters had gone to the cellar. The officers had flocked to the café on the ground floor underneath. The alarm bell was still ringing. Over the candle, stuck in a saucer, Emil's face looked white and drawn.

"I shall stay here," I said. "And I shall have coffee."

The coffee was not bravado. I needed something hot.

The gun, which had ceased, began to fire again. And then suddenly, not far away, a bomb exploded. Even through the closed and curtained windows the noise was terrific. Emil placed my coffee before me with shaking hands, and disappeared.

Another crash, and another, both very close!

There is nothing that I know of more hideous than an aërial bombardment. It requires an entire mental readjustment. The sky, which has always symbolised peace, suddenly spells death. Bombardment by the big guns of an advancing army is not unexpected. There is time for flight, a chance, too, for a reprisal. But against these raiders of the sky there is nothing. One sits and waits. And no town is safe. One moment there is a peaceful village with war twenty, fifty miles away. The next minute hell breaks loose. Houses are destroyed. Sleeping children die in their cradles. The streets echo and reëcho with the din of destruction. The reply of the anti-aircraft guns is feeble, and at night futile. There is no bustle of escape. The streets are empty and dead, and in each house people, family groups, noncombatants, folk who ask only the right to work and love and live, sit and wait with blanched faces.

More explosions, nearer still. They were trying for the *Mairie,* which was round the corner.

In the corridor outside the dining room a candle was lighted, and the English officer who had reassured me earlier in the evening came in.

"You need not be alarmed," he said cheerfully. "It is really nothing. But out in the corridor it is quite safe and not so lonely."

I went out. Two or three Belgian officers were there, gathered round a table on which was a candle stuck in a glass. They were having their after-dinner liqueurs and talking of many things. No one spoke of what was happening outside. I was given a corner, as being out of the draft.

The explosions were incessant now. With each

one the landlady downstairs screamed. As they came closer, cries and French adjectives came up the staircase beside me in a nerve-destroying staccato of terror.

At nine-thirty, when the aëroplanes had been overhead for three-quarters of an hour, there came a period of silence. There were no more explosions.

"It is over," said one of the Belgian officers, smiling. "It is over, and madame lives!"

But it was not over.

I took advantage of the respite to do the forbidden thing and look out through one of the windows. The moon had come up and the square was flooded with light. All around were silent houses. No ray of light filtered through their closed and shuttered windows. The street lamps were out. Not an automobile was to be seen, not a hurrying human figure, not a dog. No night prowler disturbed that ghastly silence. The town lay dead under the clear and peaceful light of the moon. The white paving stones of the square gleamed, and in the centre, saturnine and defiant, stood uninjured the statue of Jean Bart, privateer and private of Dunkirk.

Crash again! It was not over. The attack commenced with redoubled fury. If sound were destructive the little town of Dunkirk would be off the map of Northern France to-day. Sixty-seven bombs were dropped in the hour or so that the Germans were overhead.

The bombardment continued. My feet were very cold, my head hot. The lady manager was silent; perhaps she had fainted. But Emil reappeared for a moment, his round white face protruding above the staircase well, to say that a Zeppelin was reported on the way.

Then at last silence, broken soon by the rumble of ambulances as they started on their quest for the dead and the wounded. And Emil was wrong. There was no Zeppelin. The night raid on Dunkirk was history.

The lights did not come on again. From that time on for several weeks Dunkirk lay at night in darkness. Houses showing a light were fined by the police. Automobiles were forbidden the use of lamps. One crept along the streets and the roads surrounding the town in a mysterious and nerve-racking blackness broken only by the shaded lanterns of the sentries as they stepped out with their sharp command to stop.

The result of the raid? It was largely moral, a part of that campaign of terrorisation which is so strangely a part of the German system, which has set its army to burning cities, to bombarding the unfortified coast towns of England, to shooting civilians in conquered Belgium, and which now sinks the pitiful vessels of small traders and fishermen in the submarine-infested waters of the British Channel. It gained no military advantage, was intended to gain no military advantage. Not a soldier died. The great stores of military supplies were not wrecked. The victims were, as usual, women and children. The houses destroyed were the small and peaceful houses of noncombatants. Only two men were killed. They were in a side street when the first bomb dropped, and they tried to find an unlocked door, an open house, anything for shelter. It was impossible. Built like all French towns, without arcades or sheltering archways, the flat façades of the closed and barricaded houses refused them sanctuary. The second bomb killed them both.

Through all that night after the bombardment I could hear each hour the call of the trumpet from the great overhanging tower, a double note at once thin and musical, that reported no enemy in sight in the sky and all well. From far away, at the gate in the wall, came the reply of the distant watchman's horn softened by distance.

"All well here also," it said.

Following the trumpets the soft-toned chimes of the church rang out a hymn that has chimed from the old tower every hour for generations, extolling and praising the Man of Peace.

The ambulances had finished their work. The dead lay with folded hands, surrounded by candles, the lights of faith. And under the fading moon the old city rested and watched.

CHAPTER IX

NO MAN'S LAND

I HAVE just had this conversation with the little French chambermaid at my hotel. "You have not gone to mass, Mademoiselle?"

"I? No."

"But here, so near the lines, I should think——"

"I do not go to church. There is no God." She looked up with red-rimmed, defiant eyes. "My husband has been killed," she said. "There is no God. If there was a God, why should my husband be killed? He had done nothing."

This afternoon at three-thirty I am to start for the front. I am to see everything. The machine leaves the *Mairie* at three-thirty.

Do you recall the school map on which the state of Texas was always pink and Rhode Island green? And Canada a region without colour, and therefore without existence?

The map of Europe has become a battle line painted in three colours: yellow for the Belgian Army, blue for the British and red for the French. It is really a double line, for the confronting German Army is drawn in black. It is a narrow line to signify what it does—not only death and wanton destruction, but the end of the myth of civilisation; a narrow line to prove that the brotherhood of man is a dream, that modern science is but an improvement on fifth-century barbarity; that right, after all, is only might.

It took exactly twenty-four hours to strip the shirt off the diplomacy of Europe and show the coat of mail underneath.

It will take a century to hide that coat of mail. It will take a thousand years to rebuild the historic towns of Belgium. But not years, nor a reclothed diplomacy, nor the punishment of whichever traitor to the world brought this thing to pass, nor anything but God's great eternity, will ever restore to one mother her uselessly sacrificed son; will quicken one of the figures that lie rotting along the battle line; will heal this scar that extends, yellow and blue and red and black, across the heart of Western Europe.

It is a long scar—long and irregular. It begins at Nieuport, on the North Sea, extends south to the region of Soissons, east to Verdun, and then irregularly southeast to the Swiss border.

The map from which I am working was coloured and marked for me by General Foch, commander of the French Army of the North, at his headquarters. It is a little map, and so this line, which crosses empires and cuts civilisation in half, is only fourteen inches long, although it represents a battle line of over four hundred miles. Of this the Belgian front is one-half inch, or approximately one-twenty-eighth. The British front is a trifle more than twice as long. All the rest of that line is red—French.

That is the most impressive thing about the map, the length of the French line.

With the arrival of Kitchener's army this last spring

the blue portion grew somewhat. The yellow remained as it was, for the Belgian casualties have been two-thirds of her army. There have been many tragedies in Belgium. That is one of them.

In the very north then, yellow; then a bit of red; below that blue; then red again in that long sweeping curve that is the French front. Occasionally the line moves a trifle forward or back, like the shifting record of a fever chart; but in general it remains the same. It has remained the same since the first of November. A movement to thrust it forward in any one place is followed by a counter-attack in another place. The reserves must be drawn off and hurried to the threatened spot. Automatically the line straightens again.

The little map is dated the twenty-third of February. All through the spring and summer the line has remained unchanged. There will be no change until one side or the other begins a great offensive movement. After that it will be a matter of the irresistible force and the immovable body, a question not of maps but of empires.

Between the confronting lines lies that tragic strip of No Man's Land, which has been and is the scene of so much tragedy. No Man's Land is of fixed length but of varying width. There are places where it is very narrow, so narrow that it is possible to throw across a hand grenade or a box of cigarettes, depending on the nearness of an officer whose business is war. Again it is wide, so that friendly relations are impossible, and sniping becomes a pleasure as well as an art.

It was No Man's Land that I was to visit the night of the entry in my journal.

From the neighbourhood of Ypres to the Swiss border No Man's Land varies. The swamps and flat ground give way to more rolling country, and this to hills. But in the north No Man's Land is a series of shallow lakes, lying in flat, unprotected country.

For Belgium, in desperation, last October opened the sluices and let in the sea. It crept in steadily, each high tide advancing the flood farther. It followed the lines of canal and irrigation ditches mile after mile till it had got as far south as Ypres, beyond Ypres indeed. To the encroachment of the sea was added the flooding resulting from an abnormally rainy winter. Ordinarily the ditches have carried off the rain; now even where the inundation does not reach it lies in great ponds. Belgium's fertile sugar-beet fields are under salt water.

The method was effectual, during the winter, at least, in retarding the German advance. Their artillery destroyed the towns behind the opposing trenches of the Allies, but their attempts to advance through the flood failed.

Even where the floods were shallow—only two feet or so—they served their purpose in masking the character of the land. From a wading depth of two feet, charging soldiers stepped frequently into a deep ditch and drowned ignominiously.

It is a noble thing, war! It is good for a country! It unites its people and develops national spirit!

Great poems have been written about charges. Will there ever be any great poems about these men who have been drowned in ditches? Or about the soldiers who have been caught in the barbed wire with which these inland lakes are filled? Or about the wounded who fall helpless into the flood?

The inland lakes that ripple under the wind from
the sea, or gleam silver in the light of the moon, are
beautiful, hideous, filled with bodies that rise and
float, face down. And yet here and there the situation is not without a sort of grim humour. Brilliant
engineers on one side or the other are experimenting
with the flood. Occasionally trenches hitherto dry and
fairly comfortable find themselves unexpectedly filling
with water, as the other side devises some clever
scheme for turning the flood from a menace into a
military asset.

In No Man's Land are the outposts.

The fighting of the winter has mystified many noncombatants, with its advances and retreats, which have
yet resulted in no definite change of the line. In
many instances this sharp fighting has been a matter
of outposts, generally farms, churches or other isolated buildings, sometimes even tiny villages. In the
inundated portion of Belgium these outposts are buildings which, situated on rather higher land, a foot or
two above the flood, have become islands. Much of
the fighting in the north has been about these island
outposts. Under the conditions, charges must be made
by relatively small bodies of men. The outposts can
similarly house but few troops.

They are generally defended by barbed wire and a
few quick-firing guns. Their purpose is strategical;
they are vantage points from which the enemy may
be closely watched. They change sides frequently;
are won and lost, and won again.

Here and there the side at the time in command of
the outpost builds out from its trenches through the
flood a pathway of bags of earth, topped by fascines
or bundles of fagots tied together. Such a path pays

a tribute of many lives for every yard of advance. It is built under fire; it remains under fire. It is destroyed and reconstructed.

When I reached the front the British, Belgian and French troops in the north had been fighting under these conditions for four months. My first visit to the trenches was made under the auspices of the Belgian Ministry of War. The start was made from the *Mairie* in Dunkirk, accompanied by the necessary passes and escorted by an attaché of the Military Cabinet.

I was taken in an automobile from Dunkirk to the Belgian Army Headquarters, where an officer of the headquarters staff, Captain F——, took charge. The headquarters had been a brewery.

Stripped of the impedimenta of its previous occupation, it now housed the officers of the staff.

Since that time I have frequently visited the headquarters staffs of various armies or their divisions. I became familiar with the long, bare tables stacked with papers, the lamps, the maps on the walls, the telephones, the coming and going of dispatch riders in black leather. I came to know something of the chafing restlessness of these men who must sit, well behind the firing line, and play paper battles on which lives and empires hang.

But one thing never ceased to puzzle me.

That night, in a small kitchen behind the Belgian headquarters rooms, a French peasant woman was cooking the evening meal. Always, at all the headquarters that were near the front, somewhere in a back room was a resigned-looking peasant woman cooking a meal. Children hung about the stove or stood in corners looking out at the strange new life that sur-

rounded them. Peasants too old for war, their occupations gone, sat listlessly with hanging hands, their
faces the faces of bewildered children; their clean
floors were tracked by the muddy boots of soldiers;
their orderly lives disturbed, uprooted; their once tidy
farmyards were filled with transports; their barns
with army horses; their windmills, instead of housing
sacks of grain, were occupied by *mitrailleuses.*

What were the thoughts of these people? What
are they thinking now?—for they are still there.
What does it all mean to them? Do they ever glance
at the moving cord of the war map on the wall? Is
this war to them only a matter of a courtyard or a
windmill? Of mud and the upheaval of quiet lives?
They appear to be waiting—for spring, probably,
and the end of hostilities; for spring and the planting of crops, for quiet nights to sleep and days to
labour.

The young men are always at the front. They who
are left express confidence that these their sons and
husbands will return. And yet in the spring many of
them ploughed shallow over battlefields.

It had been planned to show me first a detail map
of the places I was to visit, and with this map before
me to explain the present position of the Belgian line
along the embankment of the railroad from Nieuport
to Dixmude. The map was ready on a table in the
officers' mess, a bare room with three long tables of
planks, to which a flight of half a dozen steps led from
the headquarters room below.

Twilight had fallen by that time. It had commenced to rain. I could see through the window
heavy drops that stirred the green surface of the moat
at one side of the old building. On the wall hung

the advertisement of an American harvester, a reminder of more peaceful days. The beating of the rain kept time to the story Captain F—— told that night, bending over the map and tracing his country's ruin with his forefinger.

Much of it is already history. The surprise and fury of the Germans on discovering that what they had considered a contemptible military force was successfully holding them back until the English and French Armies could get into the field; the policy of systematic terrorism that followed this discovery; the unpreparedness of Belgium's allies, which left this heroic little army practically unsupported for so long against the German tidal wave.

The great battle of the Yser is also history. I shall not repeat the dramatic recital of the Belgian retreat to this point, fighting a rear-guard engagement as they fell back before three times their number; of the fury of the German onslaught, which engaged the entire Belgian front, so that there was no rest, not a moment's cessation. In one night at Dixmude the Germands made fifteen attacks. Is it any wonder that two-thirds of Belgium's Army is gone?

They had fought since the third of August. It was on the twenty-first of October that they at last retired across the Yser and two days later took up their present position at the railway embankment. On that day, the twenty-third of October, the first French troops arrived to assist them, some eighty-five hundred reaching Nieuport.

It was the hope of the Belgians that, the French taking their places on the line, they could retire for a time as reserves and get a little rest. But the German attack continuing fiercely against the combined armies of the Allies, the Belgians were forced to go into action again, weary as they were, at the historic curve of the Yser, where was fought the great battle of the war. At British Headquarters later on I was given the casualties of that battle, when the invading German Army flung itself again and again, for nineteen days, against the forces of the Allies: The English casualties for that period were forty-five thousand; the French, seventy thousand; the German, by figures given out at Berlin, two hundred and fifty thousand. The Belgian I do not know.

"It was after that battle," said Captain F——, "that the German dead were taken back and burned, to avoid pestilence."

The Belgians had by this time reached the limit of their resources. It was then that the sluices were opened and their fertile lowlands flooded.

On the thirty-first of October the water stopped the German advance along the Belgian lines. As soon as they discovered what had been done the Germans made terrific and furious efforts to get forward ahead of it. They got into the towns of Ramscappelle and Pervyse, where furious street fighting occurred.

Pervyse was taken five times and lost five times. But all their efforts failed. The remnant of the Belgian Army had retired to the railroad embankment. The English and French lines held firm.

For the time, at least, the German advance was checked.

That was Captain F——'s story of the battle of the Yser.

When he had finished he drew out of his pocket the diary of a German officer killed at the Yser during the first days of the fighting, and read it aloud. It is

a great human document. I give here as nearly as possible a literal translation.

It was written during the first days of the great
battle. For fifteen days after he was killed the German offensive kept up. General Foch, who commanded the French Army of the North during that
time, described their method to me. "The Germans
came," he said, "like the waves of the sea!"

The diary of a German officer, killed at the Yser:—

Twenty-fourth of October, 1914:

"The battle goes on—we are trying to effect a crossing of the Yser. Beginning at 5:45 P.M. the engineers
go on preparing their bridging materials. Marching
quickly over the country, crossing fields and ditches,
we are exposed to continuous heavy fire. A spent
bullet strikes me in the back, just below the coat collar, but I am not wounded.

"Taking up a position near Vandewonde farm, we
are able to obtain a little shelter from the devastating
fire of the enemy's artillery. How terrible is our
situation! By taking advantage of all available cover
we arrive at the fifth trench, where the artillery is in
action and rifle fire is incessant. We know nothing of
the general situation. I do not know where the enemy
is, or what numbers are opposed to us, and there seems
no way of getting the desired information.

"Everywhere along the line we are suffering heavy
losses, altogether out of proportion to the results
obtained. The enemy's artillery is too well sheltered,
too strong; and as our own guns, fewer in number,
have not been able to silence those of the enemy, our

infantry is unable to make any advance. We are suffering heavy and useless losses.

"The medical service on the field has been found very wanting. At Dixmude, in one place, no less than forty frightfully wounded men were left lying uncared for. The medical corps is kept back on the other side of the Yser without necessity. It is equally impossible to receive water and rations in any regular way.

"For several days now we have not tasted a warm meal; bread and other things are lacking; our reserve rations are exhausted. The water is bad, quite green, indeed; but all the same we drink it—we can get nothing else. Man is brought down to the level of the brute beast. Myself, I have nothing left to eat; I left what I had with me in the saddlebags on my horse. In fact, we were not told what we should have to do on this side of the Yser, and we did not know that our horses would have to be left on the other side. That is why we could not arrange things.

"I am living on what other people, like true comrades, are willing to give me, but even then my share is only very small. There is no thought of changing our linen or our clothes in any way. It is an incredible situation! On every hand farms and villages are burning. How sad a spectacle, indeed, to see this magnificent region all in ruins, wounded and dead lying everywhere all round."

Twenty-fifth of October, 1914:

"A relatively undisturbed night. The safety of the bridge over the Yser has been assured for a time. The battle has gone on the whole day long. We have not been given any definite orders. One would not think this is Sunday. The infantry and artillery combat is incessant, but no definite result is achieved. Nothing but losses in wounded and killed. We shall try to get into touch with the sixth division of the Third Reserve Army Corps on our right."

Twenty-sixth of October, 1914:

"What a frightful night has gone by! There was a terrible rainstorm. I felt frozen. I remained standing knee-deep in water. To-day an uninterrupted fusillade meets us in front. We shall throw a bridge across the Yser, for the enemy's artillery has again destroyed one we had previously constructed.

"The situation is practically unchanged. No progress has been made in spite of incessant fighting, in spite of the barking of the guns and the cries of alarm of those human beings so uselessly killed. The infantry is worthless until our artillery has silenced the enemy's guns. Everywhere we must be losing heavily; our own company has suffered greatly so far. The colonel, the major, and, indeed, many other officers are already wounded; several are dead.

"There has not yet been any chance of taking off our boots and washing ourselves. The Sixth Division is ready, but its help is insufficient. The situation is no clearer than before; we can learn nothing of what is going on. Again we are setting off for wet trenches. Our regiment is mixed up with other regiments in an inextricable fashion. No battalion, no company, knows anything about where the other units of the regiment are to be found. Everything is jumbled under this terrible fire which enfilades from all sides.

"There are numbers of *francs-tireurs.* Our second

battalion is going to be placed under the order of the Cyckortz Regiment, made up of quite diverse units. Our old regiment is totally broken up. The situation is terrible. To be under a hail of shot and shell, without any respite, and know nothing whatever of one's own troops!

"It is to be hoped that soon the situation will be improved. These conditions cannot be borne very much longer. I am hopeless. The battalion is under the command of Captain May, and I am reduced to acting as *Fourier*. It is not at all an easy thing to do in our present frightful situation. In the black night soldiers must be sent some distance in order to get and bring back the food so much needed by their comrades. They have brought back, too, cards and letters from those we love. What a consolation in our cheerless situation! We cannot have a light, however, so we are forced to put into our pockets, unread, the words of comfort sent by our dear ones—we have to wait till the following morning.

"So we spend the night again on straw, huddled up close one to another in order to keep warm. It is horribly cold and damp. All at once a violent rattle of rifle fire raises us for the combat; hastily we get ready, shivering, almost frozen."

Twenty-seventh of October, 1914:

"At dawn I take advantage of a few moments' respite to read over the kind wishes which have come from home. What happiness! Soon, however, the illusion leaves me. The situation here is still all confusion; we cannot think of advancing——"

The last sentence is a broken one. For he died.

Morning came and he read his letters from home. They cheered him a little; we can be glad of that, at least. And then he died.

That record is a great human document. It is absolutely genuine. He was starving and cold. As fast as they built a bridge to get back it was destroyed. From three sides he and the others with him were being shelled. He must have known what the inevitable end would be. But he said very little. And then he died.

There were other journels taken from the bodies of other German officers at that terrible battle of the Yser. They speak of it as a "hell"—a place of torment and agony impossible to describe. Some of them I have seen. There is nowhere in the world a more pitiful or tragic or thought-compelling literature than these diaries of German officers thrust forward without hope and waiting for the end.

At six o'clock it was already entirely dark and raining hard. Even in the little town the machine was deep in mud. I got in and we started off again, moving steadily toward the front. Captain F—— had brought with him a box of biscuits, large, square, flaky crackers, which were to be my dinner until some time in the night. He had an electric flash and a map. The roads were horrible; it was impossible to move rapidly. Here and there a sentry's lantern would show him standing on the edge of a flooded field. The car careened, righted itself and kept on. As the roads became narrower it was impossible to pass another vehicle. The car drew out at crossroads here and there to allow transports to get by.

CHAPTER X

THE IRON DIVISION

IT was bitterly cold, and the dead officer's diary weighed on my spirit. The two officers in the machine pored over the map; I sat huddled in my corner. I had come a long distance to do the thing I was doing. But my enthusiasm for it had died. I wished I had not heard the diary.

"At dawn I take advantage of a few moments' respite to read over the kind wishes which have come from home. What happiness!" And then he died.

The car jolted on.

The soldier and the military chauffeur out in front were drenched. The wind hurled the rain at them like bullets. We were getting close to the front. There were shellholes now, great ruts into which the car dropped and pulled out again with a jerk.

Then at last a huddle of dark houses and a sentry's challenge. The car stopped and we got out. Again there were seas of mud, deeper even than before. I had reached the headquarters of the Third Division of the Belgian Army, commonly known as the Iron Division, so nicknamed for its heroic work in this war.

The headquarters building was ironically called the "château." It had been built by officers and men, of fresh boards and lined neatly inside with newspapers. Some of them were illustrated French papers. It had much the appearance of a Western shack during the early days of the gold fever. On one of the walls was a war map of the Eastern front, the line a cord fastened into place with flag pins. The last time I had seen such a map of the Eastern front was in the Cabinet Room at Washington.

A large stove in the centre of the room heated the building, which was both light and warm. Some fifteen officers received us. I was the only woman who had been so near the front, for out here there are no nurses. One by one they were introduced and bowed. There were fifteen hosts and extremely few guests!

Having had telephone notice of our arrival, they showed me how carefully they had prepared for it. The long desk was in beautiful order; floors gleamed snow white; the lamp chimneys were polished. There were sandwiches and tea ready to be served.

In one room was the telephone exchange, which connected the headquarters with every part of the line. In another, a long line of American typewriters and mimeographing machines wrote out and copied the orders which were regularly distributed to the front.

"Will you see our museum?" said a tall officer, who spoke beautiful English. His mother was an Englishwoman. So I was taken into another room and shown various relics of the battlefield—pieces of shells, rifles and bullets.

"Early German shells," said the officer who spoke English, "were like this. You see how finely they splintered. The later ones are not so good; the material is inferior, and here is an aluminum nose which shows how scarce copper is becoming in Germany today."

I have often thought of that visit to the "château,"

of the beautiful courtesy of those Belgian officers, their hospitality, their eagerness to make an American woman comfortable and at home. And I was to have still further proof of their kindly feeling, for when toward daylight I came back from the trenches they were still up, the lamps were still burning brightly, the stove was red hot and cheerful, and they had provided food for us against the chill of the winter dawn. Out through the mud and into the machine again. And now we were very near the trenches. The car went without lights and slowly. A foot off the centre of the road would have made an end to the excursion.

We began to pass men, long lines of them standing in the drenching rain to let us by. They crowded close against the car to avoid the seas of mud. Sometimes they grumbled a little, but mostly they were entirely silent. That is the thing that impressed me always about the lines of soldiers I saw going to and from the trenches—their silence. Even their feet made no noise. They loomed up like black shadows which the night swallowed immediately.

The car stopped again. We had made another leg of the journey. And this time our destination was a church. We were close behind the trenches now and our movements were made with extreme caution. Captain F—— piloted me through the mud.

"We will go quietly," he said. "Many of them are doubtless sleeping; they are but just out of the trenches and very tired."

Now and then one encounters in this war a picture that cannot be painted. Such a picture is that little church just behind the Belgian lines at L——. There are no pews, of course, in Continental churches.

The chairs had been piled up in a corner near the altar, and on the stone floor thus left vacant had been spread quantities of straw. Lying on the straw and covered by their overcoats were perhaps two hundred Belgian soldiers. They lay huddled close together for warmth; the mud of the trenches still clung to them. The air was heavy with the odour of damp straw.

The high vaulted room was a cave of darkness. The only lights were small flat candles here and there, stuck in saucers or on haversacks just above the straw. These low lights, so close to the floor, fell on the weary faces of sleeping men, accentuating the shadows, bringing pinched nostrils into relief, showing lines of utter fatigue and exhaustion.

But the picture was not all sombre. Here were four men playing cards under an image of Our Lady, which was just overhead. They were muffled against the cold and speaking in whispers. In a far corner a soldier sat alone, cross-legged, writing by the light of a candle. His letter rested on a flat loaf of bread, which was his writing table. Another soldier had taken a loaf of bread for his pillow and was comfortably asleep on it.

Captain F—— led the way through the church. He stepped over the men carefully. When they roused and looked up they would have risen to salute, but he told them to lie still.

It was clear that the relationship between the Belgian officers and their troops was most friendly. Not only in that little church at midnight, but again and again I have seen the same thing. The officers call their men their "little soldiers," and eye them with affection.

One boy insisted on rising and saluting. He was very young, and on his chin was the straggly beard of his years. The Captain stooped, and lifting a candle held it to his face.

"The handsomest beard in the Belgian Army!" he said, and the men round chuckled.

And so it went, a word here, a nod there, an apology when we disturbed one of the sleepers.

"They are but boys," said the Captain, and sighed. For each day there were fewer of them who returned to the little church to sleep.

On the way back to the car, making our way by means of the Captain's electric flash through the crowded graveyard, he turned to me.

"When you write of this, madame," he said, "you will please not mention the location of this church. So far it has escaped—perhaps because it is small. But the churches always suffer."

I regretted this. So many of the churches are old and have the interest of extreme age, even when they are architecturally insignificant. But I found these officers very fair, just as I had found the King of the Belgians disinclined to condemn the entire German Army for the brutalities of a part of it.

"There is no reason why churches should not be destroyed if they are serving military purposes," one of them said. "When a church tower shelters a gun, or is used for observations, it is quite legitimate that it be subject to artillery fire. That is a necessity of war."

We moved cautiously. Behind the church was a tiny cluster of small houses. The rain had ceased, but the electric flashlight showed great pools of water, through which we were obliged to walk. The hamlet was very silent—not a dog barked. There were no dogs.

I do not recall seeing any dogs at any time along the front, except at La Panne. What has become of them? There were cats in the destroyed towns, cats even in the trenches. But there were no dogs. It is not because the people are not fond of dogs. Dunkirk was full of them when I was there. The public square resounded with their quarrels and noisy playing. They lay there in the sun and slept, and ambulances turned aside in their headlong career to avoid running them down. But the villages along the front were silent.

I once asked an officer what had become of the dogs.

"The soldiers eat them!" he said soberly.

I heard the real explanation later. The strongest dogs had been commandeered for the army, and these brave dogs of Flanders, who have always laboured, are now drawing *mitrailleuses,* as I saw them at L——. The little dogs must be fed, and there is no food to spare. And so the children, over whose heads passes unheeded the real significance of this drama that is playing about them, have their own small tragedies these days.

We got into the car again and it moved off. With every revolution of the engine we were advancing toward that sinister line that borders No Man's Land. We were very close. The road paralleled the trenches, and shelling had begun again.

It was not close, and no shells dropped in our vicinity. But the low, horizontal red streaks of the German guns were plainly visible.

With the cessation of the rain had begun again the throwing over the Belgian trenches of the German magnesium flares, which the British call starlights. The French call them *fusées*. Under any name I do not like them. One moment one is advancing in a comfortable obscurity. The next instant it is the Fourth of July, with a white rocket bursting overhead. There is no noise, however. The thing is miraculously beautiful, silent and horrible. I believe the light floats on a sort of tiny parachute. For perhaps sixty seconds it hangs low in the air, throwing all the flat landscape into clear relief.

I do not know if one may read print under these *fusées*. I never had either the courage or the print for the experiment. But these eyes of the night open and close silently all through the hours of darkness. They hang over the trenches, reveal the movements of troops on the roads behind, shine on ammunition trains and ambulances, on the righteous and the unrighteous. All along the German lines these *fusées* go up steadily. I have seen a dozen in the air at once. Their silence and the eternal vigilance which they reveal are most impressive. On the quietest night, with only an occasional shot being fired, the horizon is ringed with them.

And on the horizon they are beautiful. Overhead they are distinctly unpleasant.

"They are very uncomfortable," I said to Captain F——. "The Germans can see us plainly, can't they?"

"But that is what they are for," he explained. "All movements of troops and ammunition trains to and from the trenches are made during the night, so they watch us very carefully."

"How near are we to the trenches?" I asked.

"Very near, indeed."

"To the first line?"

For I had heard that there were other lines behind, and with the cessation of the rain my courage was rising. Nothing less than the first line was to satisfy me.

"To the first line," he said, and smiled.

The wind which had driven the rain in sheets against the car had blown the storm away. The moon came out, a full moon. From the car I could see here and there the gleam of the inundation. The road was increasingly bad, with shell holes everywhere. Buildings loomed out of the night, roofless and destroyed. The *fusées* rose and burst silently overhead; the entire horizon seemed encircled with them. We were so close to the German lines that we could see an electric signal sending its message of long and short flashes, could even see the reply. It seemed to me most unmilitary.

"Any one who knew telegraphy and German could read that message," I protested.

"It is not so simple as that. It is a cipher code, and is probably changed daily."

Nevertheless, the officers in the car watched the signalling closely, and turning, surveyed the country behind us. In so flat a region, with trees and shrubbery cut down and houses razed, even a pocket flash can send a signal to the lines of the enemy. And such signals are sent. The German spy system is thorough and far-reaching.

I have gone through Flanders near the lines at various times at night. It is a dead country apparently. There are destroyed houses, sodden fields, ditches lipful of water. But in the most amazing fashion lights spring up and disappear. Follow one of these lights and you find nothing but a deserted farm, or a ruined barn, or perhaps nothing but a field of sugar beets dying in the ground.

Who are these spies? Are they Belgians and French, driven by the ruin of everything they possess to selling out to the enemy? I think not. It is much more probable that they are Germans who slip through the lines in some uncanny fashion, wading and swimming across the inundation, crawling flat where necessary, and working, an inch at a time, toward the openings between the trenches. Frightful work, of course. Impossible work, too, if the popular idea of the trenches were correct—that is, that they form one long, communicating ditch from the North Sea to Switzerland! They do not, of course. There are blank spaces here and there, fully controlled by the trenches on either side, and reënforced by further trenches behind. But with a knowledge of where these openings lie it is possible to work through.

Possible, not easy. And there is no mercy for a captured spy.

The troops who had been relieved were moving out of the trenches. Our progress became extremely slow. The road was lined with men. They pressed their faces close to the glass of the car and laughed and talked a little among themselves. Some of them were bandaged. Their white bandages gleamed in the moonlight. Here and there, as they passed, one blew on his fingers, for the wind was bitterly cold.

"In a few moments we must get out and walk," I was told. "Is madame a good walker?"

I said I was a good walker. I had a strong feeling that two or three people might walk along that road under those starlights much more safely and inconspicuously than an automobile could move. For automobiles at the front mean generals as a rule, and are always subject to attack.

Suddenly the car stopped and a voice called to us sharply. There were soldiers coming up a side road. I was convinced that we had surprised an attack, and were in the midst of the German advance. One of the officers flung the door open and looked out.

But we were only on the wrong road, and must get into reverse and turn the machine even closer to the front. I know now that there was no chance of a German attack at that point, that my fears were absurd. Nevertheless, so keen was the tension that for quite ten minutes my heart raced madly.

On again. The officers in the car consulted the map and, having decided on the route, fell into conversation. The officer of the Third Division, whose mother had been English, had joined the party. He had been on the staff of General Leman at the time of the capture of Liège, and he told me of the sensational attempt made by the Germans to capture the General.

"I was upstairs with him at headquarters," he said, "when word came up that eight Englishmen had just entered the building with a request to see him. I was suspicious and we started down the staircase together. The 'Englishmen' were in the hallway below. As we appeared on the stairs the man in advance put his hand in his pocket and drew a revolver. They were dressed in civilians' clothes, but I saw at once that they were German.

"I was fortunate in getting my revolver out first, and shot down the man in advance. There was a struggle, in which the General made his escape and all of the eight were either killed or taken prisoners. They were uhlans, two officers and six privates."

"It was very brave," I said. "A remarkable exploit."

"Very brave indeed," he agreed with me. "They are all very brave, the Germans."

Captain F—— had been again consulting his map. Now he put it away.

"Brave but brutal," he said briefly. "I am of the Third Division. I have watched the German advance protected by women and children. In the fighting the civilians fell first. They had no weapons. It was terrible. It is the German system," he went on, "which makes everything of the end, and nothing at all of the means. It is seen in the way they have sacrificed their own troops."

"They think you are equally brutal," I said. "The German soldiers believe that they will have their eyes torn out if they are captured."

I cited a case I knew of, where a wounded German had hidden in the inundation for five days rather than surrender to the horrors he thought were waiting for him. When he was found and taken to a hospital his long days in the water had brought on gangrene and he could not be saved.

"They have been told that to make them fight more savagely," was the comment. "What about the official German order for a campaign of 'frightfulness' in Belgium?"

And here, even while the car is crawling along toward the trenches, perhaps it is allowable to explain the word "frightfulness," which now so permeates the literature of the war. Following the scenes of the German invasion into Belgium, where here and there some maddened civilian fired on the German troops and precipitated the deaths of his townsmen,* Berlin issued, on August twenty-seventh, a declaration, of which this paragraph is a part:

"The only means of preventing surprise attacks from the civil population has been to interfere with unrelenting severity and to create examples which, by their frightfulness, would be a warning to the whole country."

A Belgian officer once quoted it to me, with a comment.

"This is not an order to the army. It is an attempt at justification for the very acts which Berlin is now attempting to deny!"

That is how "frightfulness" came into the literature of the war.

Captain F—— stopped the car. Near the road was a ruin of an old church.

"In that church," he said, "our soldiers were sleeping when the Germans, evidently informed by a spy, began to shell it. The first shot smashed that house there, twenty-five yards away; the second shot came through the roof and struck one of the supporting pillars, bringing the roof down. Forty-six men were killed and one hundred and nine wounded."

He showed me the grave from a window of the car, a great grave in front of the church, with a wooden cross on it. It was too dark to read the inscription, but he told me what it said:

"Here lie forty-six *chasseurs.*" Beneath are the names, one below the other in two columns, and underneath all: *"Morts pour la Patrie."*

* The Belgians contend that, in almost every case, such firing by civilians was the result of attack on their women.

We continued to advance. Our lamps were out, but the *fusées* made progress easy. And there was the moon. We had left behind us the lines of the silent men. The scene was empty, desolate. Suddenly we stopped by a low brick house, a one-story building with overhanging eaves. Sentries with carbines stood under the eaves, flattened against the wall for shelter from the biting wind.

CHAPTER XI

AT THE HOUSE OF THE BARRIER

A NARROW path led up to the house. It was flanked on both sides by barbed wire, and progress through it was slow. The wind caught my rain cape and tore it against the barbs. I had to be disentangled. The sentries saluted, and the low door, through which the officers were obliged to stoop to enter, was opened by an orderly from within.

We entered The House of the Mill of Saint ——.

The House of the Mill of Saint —— was less pretentious than its name. Even at its best it could not have been imposing. Now, partially destroyed and with its windows carefully screened inside by grain sacks nailed to the frames for fear of a betraying ray of light, it was not beautiful. But it was hospitable. A hanging lamp in its one livable room, a great iron stove, red and comforting, and a large round table under the lamp made it habitable and inviting. It was Belgian artillery headquarters, and I was to meet here Colonel Jacques, one of the military idols of Belgium, the hero of the Congo, and now in charge of Belgian batteries. In addition, since it was midnight, we were to sup here.

We were expected, and Colonel Jacques himself waited inside the living-room door. A tall man, as are almost all the Belgian officers—which is curious, considering that the troops seem to be rather under average size—he greeted us cordially. I fancied that behind his urbanity there was the glimmer of an amused smile. But his courtesy was beautiful. He put me near the fire and took the next chair himself.

I had a good chance to observe him. He is no longer a young man, and beyond a certain military erectness and precision in his movements there is nothing to mark him the great soldier he has shown himself to be.

"We are to have supper," he said smilingly in French. "Provided you have brought something to eat with you!"

"We have brought it," said Captain F——.

The officers of the staff came in and were formally presented. There was much clicking of heels, much deep and courteous bowing. Then Captain F—— produced his box of biscuits, and from a capacious pocket of his army overcoat a tin of bully beef. The House of the Mill of Saint —— contributed a bottle of thin white native wine and, triumphantly, a glass. There are not many glasses along the front.

There was cheese too. And at the end of the meal Colonel Jacques, with great *empressement,* laid before me a cake of sweet chocolate.

I had to be shown the way to use the bully beef. One of the hard flat biscuits was split open, spread with butter and then with the beef in a deep layer. It was quite good, but what with excitement and fatigue I was not hungry. Everybody ate; everybody talked; and, after asking my permission, everybody smoked. I sat near the stove and dried my steaming boots.

Afterward I remembered that with all the conversation there was very little noise. Our voices were subdued.   Probably we might have cheered in that closed and barricaded house without danger.   But the sense of the nearness of the enemy was over us all, and the business of war was not forgotten.   There were men who came, took orders and went away. There were maps on the walls and weapons in every corner.   Even the sacking that covered the windows bespoke caution and danger.

Here it was too near the front for the usual peasant family huddled round its stove in the kitchen, and looking with resignation on these strange occupants of their house.   The humble farm buildings outside were destroyed.

I looked round the room; a picture or two still hung on the walls, and a crucifix.   There is always a crucifix in these houses.   There was a carbine just beneath this one.

Inside of one of the picture frames one of the Colonel's medals had been placed, as if for safety.

Colonel Jacques sat at the head of the table and beamed at us all.   He has behind him many years of military service.   He has been decorated again and again for bravery.   But, perhaps, when this war is over and he has time to look back he will smile over that night supper with the first woman he had seen for months, under the rumble of his own and the German batteries.

It was time to go to the advance trenches.   But before we left one of the officers who had accompanied me rose and took a folded paper from a pocket of his tunic.   He was smiling.

"I shall read," he said, "a little tribute from one of Colonel Jacques' soldiers to him."

So we listened.   Colonel Jacques sat and smiled;

but he is a modest man, and his fingers were beating a
nervous tattoo on the table. The young officer stood
and read, glancing up now and then to smile at his
chief's embarrassment. The wind howled outside,
setting the sacks at the windows to vibrating.

This is a part of the poem:

III

"Comme chef nous avons l'homme à la hauteur
Un homme aimé et adoré de tous
L'Colonel Jacques; de lui les hommes sont fous
En lui nous voyons l'emblème de l'honneur.
Des campagnes il en a des tas: En Afrique
Haecht et Dixmude, Ramsdonck et Sart-Tilmau
Et toujours premier et toujours en avant
Toujours en têt' de son beau régiment,
     Toujours railleur
     Chef au grand cœur.

REFRAIN

"L'Colo du 12me passe
Regardez ce vaillant
Quand il crie dans l'espace
Joyeus'ment 'En avant!'
Ses hommes, la mine heureuse
Gaîment suivent sa trace
Sur la route glorieuse.
Saluez-le, l'Colo du 12me passe.

  "AD. DAUVISTER,

        "Sous-Lieutenant."

We applauded. It is curious to remember how
cheerful we were, how warm and comfortable, there

at the House of the Mill of Saint ——, with war only a step away now. Curious, until we think that, of all the created world, man is the most adaptable. Men and horses! Which is as it should be now, with both men and horses finding themselves in strange places, indeed, and somehow making the best of it.

The copy of the poem, which had been printed at the front, probably on an American hand press, was given to me with Colonel Jacques' signature on the back, and we prepared to go. There was much donning of heavy wraps, much bowing and handshaking. Colonel Jacques saw us out into the wind-swept night. Then the door of the little house closed again, and we were on our way through the barricade.

Until now our excursion to the trenches, aside from the discomfort of the weather and the mud, had been fairly safe, although there was always the chance of a shell. To that now was to be added a fresh hazard— the sniping that goes on all night long.

Our car moved quietly for a mile, paralleling the trenches. Then it stopped. The rest of the journey was to be on foot.

All traces of the storm had passed, except for the pools of mud, which, gleaming like small lakes, filled shell holes in the road. An ammunition lorry had drawn up in the shadow of a hedge and was cautiously unloading. Evidently the night's movement of troops was over, for the roads were empty.

A few feet beyond the lorry we came up to the trenches. We were behind them, only head and shoulders above.

There was no sign of life or movement, except for the silent *fusées* that burst occasionally a little to our right. Walking was bad. The Belgian blocks of the

road were coated with slippery mud, and from long
use and erosion the stones themselves were rounded,
so that our feet slipped over them. At the right was
a shallow ditch three or four feet wide. Immediately
beyond that was the railway embankment where, as
Captain F—— had explained, the Belgian Army had
taken up its position after being driven back across
the Yser.

The embankment loomed shoulder high, and between
it and the ditch were the trenches. There was no sound
from them, but sentries halted us frequently. On such
occasions the party stopped abruptly—for here sentries
are apt to fire first and investigate afterward—and one
officer advanced with the password.

There is always something grim and menacing about
the attitude of the sentry as he waits on such occasions.
His carbine is not over his shoulder, but in his hands,
ready for use. The bayonet gleams. His eyes are
fixed watchfully on the advance. A false move, and
his overstrained nerves may send the carbine to his
shoulder.

We walked just behind the trenches in the moonlight for a mile. No one said anything. The wind
was icy. Across the railroad embankment it chopped
the inundation into small crested waves. Only by
putting one's head down was it possible to battle ahead.
From Dixmude came the intermittent red flashes of
guns. But the trenches beside us were entirely silent.

At the end of a mile we stopped. The road turned
abruptly to the right and crossed the railroad embankment, and at this crossing was the ruin of what had
been the House of the Barrier, where in peaceful times
the crossing tender lived.

It had been almost destroyed. The side toward the

German lines was indeed a ruin, but one room was fairly whole. However, the door had been shot away. To enter, it was necessary to lift away an extemporised one of planks roughly nailed together, which leaned against the aperture.

The moving of the door showed more firelight, and a very small, shaded and smoky lamp on a stand. There were officers here again. The little house is slightly in front of the advanced trenches, and once inside it was possible to realise its exposed position. Standing as it does on the elevation of the railroad, it is constantly under fire. It is surrounded by barbed wire and flanked by trenches in which are *mitrailleuses*.

The walls were full of shell holes, stuffed with sacks of straw or boarded over. What had been windows were now jagged openings, similarly closed. The wind came through steadily, smoking the chimney of the lamp and making the flame flicker.

There was one chair.

I wish I could go farther. I wish I could say that shells were bursting overhead, and that I sat calmly in the one chair and made notes. I sat, true enough, but I sat because I was tired and my feet were wet. And instead of making notes I examined my new six-guinea silk rubber rain cape for barbed-wire tears. Not a shell came near. The German battery across had ceased firing at dusk that evening, and was playing pinochle four hundred yards away across the inundation. The snipers were writing letters home.

It is true that any time an artilleryman might lose a game and go out and fire a gun to vent his spleen or to keep his hand in. And the snipers might begin to notice that the rain was over, and that there was suspicious activity at the House of the Barrier. And, to take away the impression of perfect peace, big guns were busy just north and south of us. Also, just where we were the Germans had made a terrific charge three nights before to capture an outpost. But the fact remains that I brought away not even a bullet hole through the crown of my soft felt hat.

CHAPTER XII

NIGHT IN THE TRENCHES

WHEN I had been thawed out they took me into the trenches. Because of the inundation directly in front, they are rather shallow, and at this point were built against the railroad embankment with earth, boards, and here and there a steel rail from the track. Some of them were covered, too, but not with bombproof material. The tops were merely shelters from the rain and biting wind.

The men lay or sat in them—it was impossible to stand. Some of them were like tiny houses into which the men crawled from the rear, and by placing a board, which served as a door, managed to keep out at least a part of the bitter wind.

In the first trench I was presented to a bearded major. He was lying flat and apologised for not being able to rise. There was a machine gun beside him. He told me with some pride that it was an American gun, and that it never jammed. When a machine gun jams the man in charge of it dies and his comrades die, and things happen with great rapidity. On the other side of him was a cat, curled up and sound asleep. There was a telephone instrument there. It was necessary to step over the wire that was stretched along the ground.

All night long he lies there with his gun, watching

for the first movement in the trenches across. For here, at the House of the Barrier, has taken place some of the most furious fighting of this part of the line.

In the next division of the trench were three men. They were cleaning and oiling their rifles round a candle.

The surprise of all of these men at seeing a woman was almost absurd. Word went down the trenches that a woman was visiting. Heads popped out and cautious comments were made. It was concluded that I was visiting royalty, but the excitement died when it was discovered that I was not the Queen. Now and then, when a trench looked clean and dry, I was invited in. It was necessary to get down and crawl in on hands and knees.

Here was a man warming his hands over a tiny fire kindled in a tin pail. He had bored holes in the bottom of the pail for air, and was shielding the glow carefully with his overcoat.

Many people have written about the trenches—the mud, the odours, the inhumanity of compelling men to live under such foul conditions. Nothing that they have said can be too strong. Under the best conditions the life is ghastly, horrible, impossible.

That night, when from a semi-shielded position I could look across to the German line, the contrast between the condition of the men in the trenches and the beauty of the scenery was appalling. In each direction, as far as one could see, lay a gleaming lagoon of water. The moon made a silver path across it, and here and there on its borders were broken and twisted winter trees.

"It is beautiful," said Captain F——, beside me, in a low voice. "But it is full of the dead. They are taken out whenever it is possible; but it is not often possible."

"And when there is an attack the attacking side must go through the water?"

"Not always, but in many places."

"What will happen if it freezes over?"

He explained that it was salt water, and would not freeze easily. And the cold of that part of the country is not the cold of America in the same latitude. It is not a cold of low temperature; it is a damp, penetrating cold that goes through garments of every weight and seems to chill the very blood in a man's body.

"How deep is the water?" I asked.

"It varies—from two to eight feet. Here it is shallow."

"I should think they would come over."

"The water is full of barbed wire," he said grimly. "And some, a great many, have tried—and failed."

As of the trenches, many have written of the stenches of this war. But the odour of that beautiful lagoon was horrible. I do not care to emphasize it. It is one of the things best forgotten. But any lingering belief I may have had in the grandeur and glory of war died that night beside that silver lake—died of an odour, and will never live again.

And now came a discussion.

The road crossing the railroad embankment turned sharply to the left and proceeded in front of the trenches. There was no shelter on that side of the embankment. The inundation bordered the road, and just beyond the inundation were the German trench. ..

There were no trees, no shrubbery, no houses; just a flat road, paved with Belgian blocks, that gleamed in the moonlight.

At last the decision was made. We would go along the road, provided I realised from the first that it was dangerous. One or two could walk there with a good chance for safety, but not more. The little group had been augmented. It must break up; two might walk together, and then two a safe distance behind. Four would certainly be fired on.

I wanted to go. It was not a matter of courage. I had simply, parrot-fashion, mimicked the attitude of mind of the officers. One after another I had seen men go into danger with a shrug of the shoulders.

"If it comes it comes!" they said, and went on. So I, too, had become a fatalist. If I was to be shot it would happen, if I had to buy a rifle and try to clean it myself to fulfil my destiny.

So they let me go. I went farther than they expected, as it turned out. There was a great deal of indignation and relief when it was over. But that is later on.

A very tall Belgian officer took me in charge. It was necessary to work through a barbed-wire barricade, twisting and turning through its mazes. The moonlight helped. It was at once a comfort and an anxiety, for it seemed to me that my khaki-coloured suit gleamed in it. The Belgian officers in their dark blue were less conspicuous. I thought they had an unfair advantage of me, and that it was idiotic of the British to wear and advocate anything so absurd as khaki. My cape ballooned like a sail in the wind. I felt at least double my ordinary size, and that even a sniper with a squint could hardly miss me. And, by way of comfort, I had one last instruction before I started:

"If a *fusée* goes up, stand perfectly still. If you move they will fire."

The entire safety of the excursion depended on a sort of tacit agreement that, in part at least, obtains as to sentries.

This is a new warfare, one of artillery, supported by infantry in trenches. And it has been necessary to make new laws for it. One of the most curious is a sort of *modus vivendi* by which each side protects its own sentries by leaving the enemy's sentries unmolested so long as there is no active fighting. They are always in plain view before the trenches. In case of a charge they are the first to be shot, of course. But long nights and days have gone by along certain parts of the front where the hostile trenches are close together, and the sentries, keeping their monotonous lookout, have been undisturbed.

No doubt by this time the situation has changed to a certain extent; there has been more active fighting, larger bodies of men are involved. The spring floods south of the inundation will have dried up. No Man's Land will have ceased to be a swamp and the deadlock may be broken.

But on that February night I put my faith in this agreement, and it held.

The tall Belgian officer asked me if I was frightened. I said I was not. This was not exactly the truth; but it was no time for the truth.

"They are not shooting," I said. "It looks perfectly safe."

He shrugged his shoulders and glanced toward the German trenches.

"They have been sleeping during the rain," he said briefly. "But when one of them wakes up, look out!"

After that there was little conversation, and what there was was in whispers.

As we proceeded the stench from the beautiful moonlit water grew overpowering. The officer told me the reason.

A little farther along a path of fascines had been built out over the inundation to an outpost halfway to the German trenches. The building of this narrow roadway had cost many lives.

Half a mile along the road we were sharply challenged by a sentry. When he had received the password he stood back and let us pass. Alone, in that bleak and exposed position in front of the trenches, always in full view as he paced back and forward, carbine on shoulder, with not even a tree trunk or a hedge for shelter, the first to go at the whim of some German sniper or at any indication of an attack, he was a pathetic, almost a tragic, figure. He looked very young too. I stopped and asked him in a whisper how old he was.

He said he was nineteen!

He may have been. I know something about boys, and I think he was seventeen at the most. There are plenty of boys of that age doing just what that lad was doing.

Afterward I learned that it was no part of the original plan to take a woman over the fascine path to the outpost; that Captain F—— ground his teeth in impotent rage when he saw where I was being taken. But it was not possible to call or even to come up to us. So, blithely and unconsciously the tall Belgian officer and I turned to the right, and I was innocently on my way to the German trenches.

After a little I realised that this was rather more

war than I had expected.   The fascines were slippery;
the path only four or five feet wide.   On each side
was the water, hideous with many secrets.

I stopped, a third of the way out, and looked back.
It looked about as dangerous in one direction as another.   So we went on.   Once I slipped and fell.   And
now, looming out of the moonlight, I could see the
outpost which was the object of our visit.

I have always been grateful to that Belgian lieutenant for his mistake.   Just how grateful I might have
been had anything untoward happened, I cannot say.
But the excursion was worth all the risk, and
more.

On a bit of high ground stands what was once the
tiny hamlet of Oudstuyvenskerke—the ruins of two
small white houses and the tower of the destroyed
church—hardly a tower any more, for only three sides
of it are standing and they are riddled with great shell
holes.

Six hundred feet beyond this tower were the German trenches.   The little island was hardly a hundred
feet in its greatest dimension.

I wish I could make those people who think that war
is good for a country see that Belgian outpost as I
saw it that night under the moonlight.   Perhaps we
were under suspicion; I do not know.   Suddenly the
fusées, which had ceased for a time, began again, and
with their white light added to that of the moon the
desolate picture of that tiny island was a picture of
the war.   There was nothing lacking.   There was the
beauty of the moonlit waters, there was the tragedy
of the destroyed houses and the church, and there was
the horror of unburied bodies.

There was heroism, too, of the kind that will make

Belgium live in history. For in the top of that church
tower for months a Capuchin monk has held his position alone and unrelieved. He has a telephone, and he
gains access to his position in the tower by means of
a rope ladder which he draws up after him.

Furious fighting has taken place again and again
round the base of the tower. The German shells assail
it constantly. But when I left Belgium the Capuchin
monk, who has become a soldier, was still on duty;
still telephoning the ranges of the gun; still notifying
headquarters of German preparations for a charge.

Some day the church tower will fall and he will go
with it, or it will be captured; one or the other is inevitable. Perhaps it has already happened; for not
long ago I saw in the newspapers that furious fighting
was taking place at this very spot.

He came down and I talked to him—a little man,
regarding his situation as quite ordinary, and looking
quaintly unpriestlike in his uniform of a Belgian officer
with its tasselled cap. Some day a great story will be
written of these priests of Belgium who have left
their churches to fight.

We spoke in whispers. There was after all very
little to say. It would have embarrassed him horribly
had any one told him that he was a heroic figure. And
the ordinary small talk is not currency in such a situation.

We shook hands and I think I wished him luck.
Then he went back again to the long hours and days
of waiting.

I passed under his telephone wires. Some day he
will telephone that a charge is coming. He will give
all the particulars calmly, concisely. Then the message
will break off abruptly. He will have sent his last

warning. For that is the way these men at the advance posts die.

As we started again I was no longer frightened. Something of his courage had communicated itself to me, his courage and his philosophy, perhaps his faith.

The priest had become a soldier; but he was still a priest in his heart. For he had buried the German dead in one great grave before the church, and over them had put the cross of his belief.

It was rather absurd on the way back over the path of death to be escorted by a cat. It led the way over the fascines, treading daintily and cautiously. Perhaps one of the destroyed houses at the outpost had been its home, and with a cat's fondness for places it remained there, though everything it knew had gone; though battle and sudden death had usurped the place of its peaceful fireside, though that very fireside was become a heap of stone and plaster, open to winds and rain.

Again and again in destroyed towns I have seen these forlorn cats stalking about, trying vainly to adjust themselves to new conditions, cold and hungry and homeless.

We were challenged repeatedly on the way back. Coming from the direction we did we were open to suspicion. It was necessary each time to halt some forty feet from the sentry, who stood with his rifle pointed at us. Then the officer advanced with the word.

Back again, then, along the road, past the youthful sentry, past other sentries, winding through the barbed-wire barricade, and at last, quite whole, to the House of the Barrier again. We had walked three miles in front of the Belgian advanced trenches, in full view of the Germans. There had been no protecting hedge or bank or tree between us and that ominous line two hundred yards across. And nothing whatever had happened.

Captain F——— was indignant. The officers in the House of the Barrier held up their hands. For men such a risk was legitimate, necessary. In a woman it was foolhardy. Nevertheless, now that it was safely over, they were keenly interested and rather amused. But I have learned that the gallant captain and the officer with him had arranged, in case shooting began, to jump into the water, and by splashing about draw the fire in their direction!

We went back to the automobile, a long walk over the shell-eaten roads in the teeth of a biting wind. But a glow of exultation kept me warm. I had been to the front. I had been far beyond the front, indeed, and I had seen such a picture of war and its desolation there in the centre of No Man's Land as perhaps no one not connected with an army had seen before; such a picture as would live in my mind forever.

I visited other advanced trenches that night as we followed the Belgian lines slowly northward toward Nieuport.

Save the varying conditions of discomfort, they were all similar. Always they were behind the railroad embankment. Always they were dirty and cold. Frequently they were full of mud and water. To reach them one waded through swamps and pools. Just beyond them there was always the moonlit stretch of water, now narrow, now wide.

I was to see other trenches later on, French and English. But only along the inundation was there that curious combination of beauty and hideousness, of rippling water with the moonlight across it in a silver path, and in that water things that had been men.

In one place a cow and a pig were standing on ground a little bit raised. They had been there for weeks between the two armies. Neither side would shoot them, in the hope of some time obtaining them for food.

They looked peaceful, rather absurd.

Now so near that one felt like whispering, and now a quarter of a mile away, were the German trenches. We moved under their *fusées,* passing destroyed towns where shell holes have become vast graves.

One such town was most impressive. It had been a very beautiful town, rather larger than the others. At the foot of the main street ran the railroad embankment and the line of trenches. There was not a house left.

It had been, but a day or two before, the scene of a street fight, when the Germans, swarming across the inundation, had captured the trenches at the railroad and got into the town itself.

At the intersection of two streets, in a shell hole, twenty bodies had been thrown for burial. But that was not novel or new. Shell-hole graves and destroyed houses were nothing. The thing I shall never forget is the cemetery round the great church.

Continental cemeteries are always crowded. They are old, and graves almost touch one another. The crosses which mark them stand like rows of men in close formation.

This cemetery had been shelled. There was not a cross in place; they lay flung about in every grotesque position. The quiet God's Acre had become a hell. Graves were uncovered; the dust of centuries exposed.

In one the cross had been lifted up by an explosion and had settled back again upside down, so that the Christ was inverted.

It was curious to stand in that chaos of destruction, that ribald havoc, that desecration of all we think of as sacred, and see, stretched from one broken tombstone to another, the telephone wires that connect the trenches at the foot of the street with headquarters and with the "château."

Ninety-six German soldiers had been buried in one shell hole in that cemetery. Close beside it there was another, a great gaping wound in the earth, half full of water from the evening's rain.

An officer beside me looked down into it.

"See," he said, "they dig their own graves!"

It was almost morning. The automobile left the pathetic ruin of the town and turned back toward the "château." There was no talking; a sort of heaviness of spirit lay on us all. The officers were seeing again the destruction of their country through my shocked eyes. We were tired and cold, and I was heartsick.

A long drive through the dawn, and then the "château."

The officers were still up, waiting. They had prepared, against our arrival, sandwiches and hot drinks.

The American typewriters in the next room clicked and rattled. At the telephone board messages were coming in from the very places we had just left—from the instrument at the major's elbow as he lay in his trench beside the House of the Barrier; from the priest who had left his cell and become a soldier; from that desecrated and ruined graveyard with its gaping shell holes that waited, open-mouthed, for—what?

When we had eaten, Captain F—— rose and made

a little speech.   It was simply done, in the words of
a soldier and a patriot speaking out of a full heart.

"You have seen to-night a part of what is happening
to our country," he said.   "You have seen what the
invading hosts of Germany have made us suffer.   But
you have seen more than that.   You have seen that the
Belgian Army still exists; that it is still fighting and
will continue to fight.   The men in those trenches
fought at Liège, at Louvain, at Antwerp, at the Yser.
They will fight as long as there is a drop of Belgian
blood to shed.

"Beyond the enemy's trenches lies our country, devastated; our national life destroyed; our people under
the iron heel of Germany.   But Belgium lives.   Tell
America, tell the world, that destroyed, injured as she
is, Belgium lives and will rise again, greater than
before!"

CHAPTER XIII

"WIPERS"

A N aëroplane man at the next table starts to-night on a dangerous scouting expedition over the German lines. In case he does not return he has given a letter for his mother to Captain T——.

It now appears quite certain that I am to be sent along the French and English lines. I shall be the first correspondent, I am told, to see the British front, as "Eyewitness," who writes for the English papers, is supposed to be a British officer.

I have had word also that I am to see Mr. Winston Churchill, the First Lord of the British Admiralty. But to-day I am going to Ypres. The Tommies call it "Wipers."

Before I went abroad I had two ambitions among others: One was to be able to pronounce Ypres; the other was to bring home and exhibit to my admiring friends the pronunciation of Przemysl. To a moderate extent I have succeeded with the first. I have discovered that the second one must be born to.

Two or three towns have stood out as conspicuous points of activity in the western field. Ypres is one of these towns. Day by day it figures in the reports from the front. The French are there, and just to the east the English line commences.* The line of trenches lies beyond the town, forming a semicircle round it.

A few days later I saw this semicircle, the flat and muddy battlefield of Ypres. But on this visit I was to see only the town, which, although completely destroyed, was still being shelled.

The curve round the town gave the invading army a great advantage in its destruction. It enabled them to shell it from three directions, so that it was raked by cross fire. For that reason the town of Ypres presents one of the most hideous pictures of desolation of the present war.

General M—— had agreed to take me to Ypres. But as he was a Belgian general, and the town of Ypres is held by the French, it was a part of the etiquette of war that we should secure the escort of a French officer at the town of Poperinghe.

For war has its etiquette, and of a most exacting kind. And yet in the end it simplifies things. It is to war what rules are to bridge—something to lead by! Frequently I was armed with passes to visit, for instance, certain batteries. My escort was generally a member of the Headquarters' Staff of that particular army. But it was always necessary to visit first the officer in command of that battery, who in his turn either accompanied us to the battlefield or deputised one of his own staff. The result was an imposing number of uniforms of various sorts, and the conviction, as I learned, among the gunners that some visiting royalty was on an excursion to the front!

It was a cold winter day in February, a grey day

* Written in May, 1915.

with a fine snow that melted as soon as it touched the ground. Inside the car we were swathed in rugs. The chauffeur slapped his hands at every break in the journey, and sentries along the road hugged such shelter as they could find.

As we left Poperinghe the French officer, Commandant D——, pointed to a file of men plodding wearily through the mud.

"The heroes of last night's attack," he said. "They are very tired, as you see."

We stopped the car and let the men file past. They did not look like heroes; they looked tired and dirty and depressed. Although our automobile generally attracted much attention, scarcely a man lifted his head to glance at us. They went on drearily through the mud under the pelting sleet, drooping from fatigue and evidently suffering from keen reaction after the excitement of the night before.

I have heard the French soldier crticised for this reaction. It may certainly be forgiven him, in view of his splendid bravery. But part of the criticism is doubtless justified. The English Tommy fights as he does everything else. There is a certain sporting element in what he does. He puts into his fighting the same fairness he puts into sport, and it is a point of honour with him to keep cool. The English gunner will admire the enemy's marksmanship while he is ducking a shell.

The French soldier, on the other hand, fights under keen excitement. He is temperamental, imaginative; as he fights he remembers all the bitterness of the past, its wrongs, its cruelties. He sees blood. There is nothing that will hold him back. The result has made history, is making history to-day.

But he has the reaction of his temperament. Who shall say he is not entitled to it?

Something of this I mentioned to Monsieur le Commandant as the line filed past.

"It is because it is fighting that gets nowhere," he replied. "If our men, after such an attack, could advance, could do anything but crawl back into holes full of water and mud, you would see them gay and smiling to-day."

After a time I discovered that the same situation holds to a certain extent in all the armies. If his fighting gets him anywhere the soldier is content. The line has made a gain. What matter wet trenches, discomfort, freezing cold? The line has made a gain. It is lack of movement that sends their spirits down, the fearful boredom of the trenches, varied only by the dropping shells, so that they term themselves, ironically, "Cannon food."

We left the victorious company behind, making their way toward whatever church bedded down with straw, or coach-house or drafty barn was to house them for their rest period.

"They have been fighting waist-deep in water," said the Commandant, "and last night was cold. The British soldier rubs his body with oil and grease before he dresses for the trenches. I hope that before long our men may do this also. It is a great protection."

I have in front of me now a German soldier's fatigue cap, taken by one of those men from a dead soldier who lay in front of the trench.

It is a pathetic cap, still bearing the crease which showed how he folded it to thrust it into his pocket. When his helmet irked him in the trenches he was allowed to take it off and put this on. He belonged to Bavarian Regiment Number Fifteen, and the cap was given him in October, 1914. There is a blood-stain on one side of it. Also it is spotted with mud inside and out. It is a pathetic little cap, because when its owner died, that night before, a thousand other Germans died with him, died to gain a trench two hundred yards from their own line, a trench to capture which would have gained them little but glory, and which, since they failed, lost them everything, even life itself.

We were out of the town by this time, and started on the road to Ypres. Between Poperinghe and Ypres were numerous small villages with narrow, twisting streets. They were filled with soldiers at rest, with tethered horses being re-shod by army blacksmiths, with small fires in sheltered corners on which an anxious cook had balanced a kettle.

In each town a proclamation had been nailed to a wall and the townspeople stood about it, gaping.

"An inoculation proclamation," explained the Commandant. "There is typhoid here, so the civilians are to be inoculated. They are very much excited about it. It appears to them worse than a bombardment."

We passed a file of Spahis, native Algerians who speak Arabic. They come from Tunis and Algeria, and, as may be imagined, they were suffering bitterly from the cold.

They peered at us with bright, black eyes from the encircling folds of the great cloaks with pointed hoods which they had drawn closely about them. They have French officers and interpreters, and during the spring fighting they probably proved very valuable. During the winter they gave me the impression of being out of place and rather forlorn. Like the Indian troops with the British, they were fighting a new warfare. For gallant charges over dry desert sands had been substituted mud and mist and bitter cold, and the stagnation of armies.

Terrible tales have been told of the ferocity of these Arabs, and of the Turcos also. I am inclined to think they are exaggerated. But certainly, met with on a lonely road, these long files of men in their quaint costumes moving silently along with heads lowered against the wind were sombre, impressive and rather alarming.

The car, going furiously, skidded, was pulled sharply round and righted itself. The conversation went on. No one appeared to notice that we had been on the edge of eternity, and it was not for me to mention it. But I made a jerky entry in my notebook:

"Very casual here about human life. Enlarge on this."

The general, who was a Belgian, continued his complaint. It was about the Belgian absentee tax.

The Germans now in control in Belgium had imposed an absentee tax of ten times the normal on all Belgians who had left the country and did not return by the fifteenth of March. The general snorted his rage and disgust.

"But," I said innocently, "I should think it would make very little difference to you. You are not there, so of course you cannot pay it."

"Not there!" he said. "Of course I am not there. But everything I own in the world is there, except this uniform that I have on my back."

"They would confiscate it?" I asked. "Not the uniform, of course; I mean your property."

He broke into a torrent of rapid French. I felt quite sure that he was saying that they would confiscate it; that they would annihilate it, reduce it to its atomic constituents; take it, acres and buildings and shade trees and vegetable garden, back to Germany. But as his French was of the ninety horsepower variety and mine travels afoot, like Bayard Taylor, and limps at that, I never caught up with him.

Later on, in a calmer moment, I had the thing explained to me.

It appears that the Germans have instituted a tax on all the Belgian refugees of ten times the normal tax; the purpose being to bring back into Belgium such refugees as wish to save the remnants of their property. This will mean bringing back people of the better class who have property to save. It will mean to the far-seeing German mind a return of the better class of Belgians to reorganise things, to put that prostrate country on its feet again, to get the poorer classes to work, to make it self-supporting.

"The real purpose, of course," said my informant, "is so that American sympathy, now so potent, will cease for both refugees and interned Belgians. If the factories start, and there is work for them, and the refugees still refuse to return, you can see what it means."

He may be right; I do not think so. I believe that at this moment Germany regards Belgium as a new but integral part of the German Empire, and that she wishes to see this new waste land of hers productive. Assuredly Germany has made a serious effort to reorganise and open again some of the great Belgian factories that are now idle.

In one instance that I know of a manufacturer was offered a large guarantee to come back and put his factory into operation again. He refused, although he knew that it spelled ruin. The Germans, unable themselves at this time to put skilled labour in his mill, sent its great machines by railroad back into Germany. I have been told that this has happened in a number of instances. Certainly it sounds entirely probable.

The factory owner in question is in America at the time I am writing this, obtaining credit and new machines against the time of the retirement of the German Army.

From the tax the conversation went on to the finances of Belgium. I learned that the British Government, through the Bank of England, is guaranteeing the payment of the Belgian war indemnity to Germany! The war indemnity is over nineteen million pounds, or approximately ninety-six millions of dollars. Of this the Belgian authorities are instructed to pay over nine million dollars each month.

The Société Générale de Belgique has been obliged by the German Government to accept the power of issuing notes, on a strict understanding that it must guarantee the note issue on the gold reserve and foreign bill book, which is at present deposited in the Bank of England at London. If the Société Générale de Belgique had not done so, all notes of the Bank of Belgium would have been declared valueless by Germany.

A very prominent Englishman, married to a Belgian lady, told me a story about this gold reserve which is amusing enough to repeat, and which has a certain appearance of truth.

When the Germans took possession of Brussels, he said, their first move was to send certain officers to the great Brussels Bank, in whose vaults the gold reserve was kept. The word had been sent ahead that they were coming, and demanding that certain high officials of the bank were to be present.

The officials went to the bank, and the German officers presented themselves promptly.

The conversation was brief.

"Take us to the vaults," said one of the German officers.

"To the vaults?" said the principal official of the bank.

"To the vaults," was the curt reply.

"I am not the vault keeper. We shall have to send for him."

The bank official was most courteous, quite bland, indeed. The officer scowled, but there was nothing to do but wait.

The vault keeper was sent for. It took some time to find him.

The bank official commented on the weather, which was, he considered, extremely warm.

At last the vault keeper came. He was quite breathless. But it seemed that, not knowing why he came, he had neglected to bring his keys. The bank official regretted the delay. The officers stamped about.

"It looks like a shower," said the bank official. "Later in the day it may be cooler."

The officers muttered among themselves.

It took the vault keeper a long time to get his keys and return, but at last he arrived. They went down and down, through innumerable doors that must be unlocked before them, through gratings and more steel doors. And at last they stood in the vaults.

The German officers stared about and then turned to the Belgian official.

"The gold!" they said furiously. "Where is the gold?"

"The gold!" said the official, much surprised. "You wished to see the gold? I am sorry. You asked for the vaults and I have shown you the vaults. The gold, of course, is in England."

We sped on, the same flat country, the same grey fields, the same files of soldiers moving across those fields toward distant billets, the same transports and ambulances, and over all the same colourless sky.

Not very long ago some inquiring British scientist discovered that on foggy days in London the efficiency of the average clerk was cut down about fifty per cent. One begins to wonder how much of this winter *impasse* is due to the weather, and what the bright and active days of early spring will bring. Certainly the weather that day weighed on me. It was easier to look out through the window of the car than to get out and investigate. The penetrating cold dulled our spirits.

A great lorry had gone into the mud at the side of the road and was being dug out. A horse neatly disembowelled lay on its back in the road, its four stark legs pointed upward.

"They have been firing at a German *Taube,*" said the Commandant, "and naturally what goes up must come down."

On the way back we saw the same horse. It was dark by that time, and some peasants had gathered round the carcass with a lantern. The hide had been cut away and lay at one side, and the peasants were carving the animal into steaks and roasts. For once fate had been good to them. They would dine that night.

Everywhere here and there along the road we had passed the small sheds that sentries built to protect themselves against the wind, little huts the size of an American patrol box, built of the branches of trees and thatched all about with straw.

Now we passed one larger than the others, a shed with the roof thatched and the sides plastered with mud to keep out the cold.

The Commandant halted the car. There was one bare little room with a wooden bench and a door. The bench and the door had just played their part in a tragedy.

I have been asked again and again whether it is true that on both sides of the line disheartened soldiers have committed suicide during this long winter of waiting. I have always replied that I do not know. On the Allied side it is thought that many Germans have done so; I daresay the Germans make the same contention. This one instance is perfectly true. But it was the result of an accident, not of discouragement.

The sentry was alone in his hut, and he was cleaning his gun. For a certain length of time he would be alone. In some way the gun exploded and blew off his right hand. There was no one to call on for help. He waited quite a while. It was night. Nobody came; he was suffering frightfully.

Perhaps, sitting there alone, he tried to think out what life would be without a right hand. In the end he decided that it was not worth while. But he could not pull the trigger of his gun with his left hand. He tried it and failed. So at last he tied a stout cord to the trigger, fastened the end of it to the door, and sitting on the bench kicked the door to. They had just taken him away.

Just back of Ypres there is a group of buildings that had been a great lunatic asylum. It is now a hospital for civilians, although it is partially destroyed.

"During the evacuation of the town," said the Commandant, "it was decided that the inmates must be taken out. The asylum had been hit once and shells were falling in every direction. So the nuns dressed their patients and started to march them back along the route to the nearest town. Shells were falling all about them; the nuns tried to hurry them, but as each shell fell or exploded close at hand the lunatics cheered and clapped their hands. They could hardly get them away at all; they wanted to stay and see the excitement."

That is a picture, if you like. It was a very large asylum, containing hundreds of patients. The nuns could not hurry them. They stood in the roads, faces upturned to the sky, where death was whining its shrill cry overhead. When a shell dropped into the road, or into the familiar fields about them, tearing great holes, flinging earth and rocks in every direction, they cheered. They blocked the roads, so that gunners with badly needed guns could not get by. And behind and all round them the nuns urged them on in vain. Some of them were killed, I believe. All about great holes in fields and road tell the story of the hell that beat about them.

Here behind the town one sees fields of graves

marked each with a simple wooden cross. Here and there a soldier's cap has been nailed to the cross.

The officers told me that in various places the French peasants had placed the dead soldier's number and identifying data in a bottle and placed it on the grave. But I did not see this myself.

Unlike American towns, there is no gradual approach to these cities of Northern France; no straggling line of suburbs. Many of them were laid out at a time when walled cities rose from the plain, and although the walls are gone the tradition of compactness for protection still holds good. So one moment we were riding through the shell-holed fields of Northern France and the next we were in the city of Ypres.

At the time of my visit few civilians had seen the city of Ypres since its destruction. I am not sure that any had been there. I have seen no description of it, and I have been asked frequently if it is really true that the beautiful Cloth Hall is gone—that most famous of all the famous buildings of Flanders.

Ypres!

What a tragedy! Not a city now; hardly a skeleton of a city. Rumour is correct, for the wonderful Cloth Hall is gone. There is a fragment left of the façade, but no repairing can ever restore it. It must all come down. Indeed, any storm may finish its destruction. The massive square belfry, two hundred and thirty feet high and topped by its four turrets, is a shell swaying in every gust of wind.

The inimitable arcade at the end is quite gone. Nothing indeed is left of either the Cloth Hall, which, built in the year 1200, was the most remarkable edifice of Belgium, or of the Cathedral behind it, erected

in 1300 to succeed an earlier edifice. General M——
stood by me as I stared at the ruins of these two great
buildings. Something of the tragedy of Belgium was
in his face.

"We were very proud of it," he said. "If we
started now to build another it would take more than
seven hundred years to give it history."

There were shells overhead. But they passed harmlessly, falling either into the open country or into
distant parts of the town. We paid no attention to
them, but my curiosity was roused.

"It seems absurd to continue shelling the town," I
said. "There is nothing left."

Then and there I had a lesson in the new warfare.
Bombardment of the country behind the enemy's
trenches is not necessarily to destroy towns. Its
strategical purpose, I was told, is to cut off communi-
cations, to prevent, if possible, the bringing up of reserve troops and transport wagons, to destroy ammunition trains. I was new to war, with everything
to learn. This perfectly practical explanation had
not occurred to me.

"But how do they know when an ammunition train
is coming?" I asked.

"There are different methods. Spies, of course, always. And aëroplanes also."

"But an ammunition train moves."

It was necessary then to explain the various
methods by which aëroplanes signal, giving ranges
and locations. I have seen since that time the charts
carried by aviators and airship crews, in which every
hedge, every ditch, every small detail of the landscape is carefully marked. In the maps I have seen
the region is divided into lettered squares, each square

made up of four small squares, numbered. Thus B 3 means the third block of the B division, and so on. By wireless or in other ways the message is sent to the batteries, and B 3, along which an ammunition train is moving, suddenly finds itself under fire. Thus ended the second lesson!

An ammunition train, having safely escaped B 3 and all the other terrors that are spread for such as it, rumbled by, going through the Square. The very vibration of its wheels as they rattled along the street set parts of the old building to shaking. Stones fell. It was not safe to stand near the belfry.

Up to this time I had found a certain philosophy among the French and Belgian officers as to the destruction of their towns. Not of Louvain, of course, or those earlier towns destroyed during the German invasion, but of the bombardment which is taking place now along the battle line. But here I encountered furious resentment.

There is nothing whatever left of the city for several blocks in each direction round the Cloth Hall. At the time it was destroyed the army of the Allies was five miles in advance of the town. The shells went over their heads for days, weeks.

So accurate is modern gunnery that given a chart of a city the gunner can drop a shell within a few yards of any desired spot. The Germans had a chart of Ypres. They might have saved the Cloth Hall, as they did save the Cathedral at Antwerp. But they were furious with thwarted ambition—the onward drive had been checked. Instead of attempting to save the Cloth Hall they focussed all their fire on it. There was nothing to gain by this wanton destruction.

It is a little difficult in America, where great structures are a matter of steel and stone erected in a year or so, to understand what its wonderful old buildings meant to Flanders. In a way they typified its history, certainly its art. The American likes to have his art in his home; he buys great paintings and puts them on the walls. He covers his floors with the entire art of a nomadic people. But on the Continent the method is different. They have built their art into their buildings; their great paintings are in churches or in structures like the Cloth Hall. Their homes are comparatively unadorned, purely places for living. All that they prize they have stored, open to the world, in their historic buildings. It is for that reason that the destruction of the Cloth Hall of Ypres is a matter of personal resentment to each individual of the nation to which it belonged. So I watched the faces of the two officers with me. There could be no question as to their attitude. It was a personal loss they had suffered. The loss of their homes they had accepted stoically. But this was much more. It was the loss of their art, their history, their tradition. And it could not be replaced.

The firing was steady, unemotional.

As the wind died down we ventured into the ruins of the Cloth Hall itself. The roof is gone, of course. The building took fire from the bombardment, and what the shells did not destroy the fire did. Melted lead from ancient gutters hung in stalactites. In one place a wall was still standing, with a bit of its mural decoration. I picked up a bit of fallen gargoyle from under the fallen tower and brought it away. It is before me now.

It is seven hundred and fifteen years since that gargoyle was lifted into its place. The Crusades were going on about that time; the robber barons were sallying out onto the plains on their raiding excursions. The Norman Conquest had taken place. From this very town of Ypres had gone across the Channel "workmen and artisans to build churches and feudal castles, weavers and workers of many crafts."

In those days the Yperlée, a small river, ran open through the town. But for many generations it has been roofed over and run under the public square.

It was curious to stand on the edge of a great shell hole and look down at the little river, now uncovered to the light of day for the first time in who knows how long.

In all that chaos, with hardly a wall intact, at the corner of what was once the cathedral, stood a heroic marble figure of Burgomaster Vandenpeereboom. It was quite untouched and as placid as the little river, a benevolent figure rising from the ruins of war.

"They have come like a pestilence," said the General. "When they go they will leave nothing. What they will do is written in what they have done."

Monsieur le Commandant had disappeared. Now he returned triumphant, carrying a great bundle in both arms.

"I have been to what was the house of a relative," he explained. "He has told me that in the cellar I would find these. They will interest you."

"These" proved to be five framed photographs of the great paintings that had decorated the walls of the great Cloth Hall. Although they had been hidden in a cellar, fragments of shell had broken and torn them. But it was still possible to gain from them a faint idea of the interior beauty of the old building before its destruction.

I examined them there in the public square, with a shell every now and then screeching above but falling harmlessly far away.

A priest joined us. He told pathetically of watching the destruction of the Arcade, of seeing one arch after another go down until there was nothing left.

"They ate it," said the priest graphically. "A bite at a time."

We walked through the town. One street after another opened up its perspective of destruction. The strange antics that shell fire plays had left doors and lintels standing without buildings, had left intact here and there pieces of furniture. There was an occasional picture on an exposed wall; iron street lamps had been twisted into travesties; whole panes of glass remained in façades behind which the buildings were gone. A part of the wooden scaffolding by which repairs were being made to the old tower of the Cloth Hall hung there uninjured by either flame or shell.

On one street all the trees had been cut off as if by one shell, about ten feet above the ground, but in another, where nothing whatever remained but piles of stone and mortar, a great elm had apparently not lost a single branch.

Much has been written about the desolation of these towns. To get a picture of it one must realise the solidity with which even the private houses are built. They are stone, or if not, the walls are of massive brick coated with plaster. There are no frame buildings; wood is too expensive for that purpose. It is only in prodigal America that we can use wood.

So the destruction of a town there means the destruction of buildings that have stood for centuries, and would in the normal course of events have stood for centuries more.

A few civilians had crept back into the town. As in other places, they had come back because they had no place else to go. At any time a shell might destroy the fragment of the building in which they were trying to reëstablish themselves. There were no shops open, because there were no shops to open. Supplies had to be brought from long distances. As all the horses and automobiles had been commandeered by the government, they had no way to get anything. Their situation was pitiable, tragic. And over them was the daily, hourly fear that the German Army would concentrate for its onward drive at some near-by point.

CHAPTER XIV

LADY DECIES' STORY

IT was growing dark; the chauffeur was preparing to light the lamps of the car. Shells were fewer. With the approach of night the activity behind the lines increased; more ammunition trains made their way over the débris; regiments prepared for the trenches marched through the square on their way to the front.

They were laden, as usual, with extra food and jars of water. Almost every man had an additional loaf of bread strapped to the knapsack at his back. They were laughing and talking among themselves, for they had had a sleep and hot food; for the time at least they were dry and fed and warm.

On the way out of the town we passed a small restaurant, one of a row of houses. It was the only undestroyed building I saw in Ypres.

"It is the only house," said the General, "where the inhabitants remained during the entire bombardment. They made coffee for the soldiers and served meals to officers. Shells hit the pavement and broke the windows; but the house itself is intact. It is extraordinary."

We stopped at the one-time lunatic asylum on our way back. It had been converted into a hospital for injured civilians, and its long wards were full of

women and children.   An English doctor was in
charge.

Some of the buildings had been destroyed, but in
the main it had escaped serious injury.   By a curious
fatality that seems to have followed the chapels and
churches of Flanders, the chapel was the only part that
was entirely gone.   One great shell struck it while it
was housing soldiers, as usual, and all of them were
killed.   As an example of the work of one shell the
destruction of that building was enormous.   There
was little or nothing left.

"The shell was four feet high," said the Doctor,
and presented me with the nose of it.

"You may get more at any moment," I said.

He shrugged his shoulders.   "What must be, must
be," he said quietly.

When the bombardment was at its height, he said,
they took their patients to the cellar and continued
operating there.   They had only a candle or two.
But it was impossible to stop, for the wards were
full of injured women and children.

I walked through some of the wards.   It was the
first time I had seen together so many of the innocent victims of this war—children blind and forever
cut off from the light of day, little girls with arms
gone, women who will never walk again.

It was twilight.   Here and there a candle gleamed,
for any bright illumination was considered unwise.

What must they think as they lie there during the
long dark hours between twilight and the late winter
morning?   Like the sentry, many of them must wonder if it is worth while.   These are people, most of
them, who have lived by their labour.   What will
they do when the war is over, or when, having made

such recovery as they may, the hospital opens its doors and must perforce turn them out on the very threshold of war?

And yet they cling to life. I met a man who crossed the Channel—I believe it was from Flushing—with the first lot of hopelessly wounded English prisoners who had been sent home to England from Germany in exchange for as many wrecked and battered Germans on their way back to the Fatherland.

One young boy was all eagerness. His home was on the cliff above the harbour which was their destination. He alternately wept and cheered.

"They'll be glad enough to see me, all right," he said. "It's six months since they heard from me. More than likely they think I'm lying over there with some of the other chaps."

He was in a wheeled chair. In his excitement the steamer rug slipped down. Both his legs were gone above the knees!

Our hands were full. The General had picked up a horseshoe on the street at Ypres and given it to me to bring me luck; the Commandant had the framed pictures. The General carried the gargoyle wrapped in a newspaper. I had the nose of the shell.

We walked through the courtyard, with its broken fountain and cracked walks, out to the machine. The password for the night was "Écosse," which means "Scotland." The General gave the word to the orderly and we went on again toward Poperinghe, where we were to have coffee.

The firing behind us had ceased. Possibly the German gunners were having coffee also. We went at our usual headlong speed through almost empty roads. Now and then a lantern waved. We checked our

headlong speed to give the password, and on again.
More lanterns; more challenges.

Since we passed, a few hours before, another car
had been wrecked by the road. One sees these cars
everywhere, lying on their sides, turned turtle in
ditches, bent and twisted against trees. No one seems
to be hurt in these accidents; at least one hears nothing of them, if they are. And now we were back
at Poperinghe again.

The Commandant had his headquarters in the
house of a notary. Except in one instance, all the
houses occupied by the headquarters' staffs that I
visited were the houses of notaries. Perhaps the notary is the important man of a French town. I do not
know.

This was a double house with a centre hall, a house
of some pretension in many ways. But it had only
one lamp. When we went from one room to another
we took the lamp with us. It was not even a hand-
some lamp. In that very comfortable house it was one
of the many anomalies of war.

One or two of the best things from the museum
at Ypres had been secured and brought back here.
On a centre table was a bronze equestrian statue
in miniature of a Crusader, a beautiful piece of work.

While we were waiting for coffee the Commandant
opened the lower drawer of a secretary and took out
a letter.

"This may interest Madame," he said. "I have
just received it. It is from General Leman, the hero
of Liège."

He held it close to the lamp and read it. I have
the envelope before me now. It is addressed in
lead pencil and indorsed as coming from General

Leman, Prisoner of War at Magdeburg, Germany.

The letter was a soldier's simple letter, written to a friend. I wish I had made a copy of it; but I remember in effect what it said. Clearly the hero of Liège has no idea that he is a hero. He said he had a good German doctor, but that he had been very ill. It is known, of course, that his foot was injured during the destruction of one of the fortresses just before he was captured.

"I have a very good German doctor," he wrote. "But my foot gives me a great deal of trouble. Gangrene set in and part of it had to be amputated. The wound refuses to heal, and in addition my heart is bad."

He goes on to ask for his family, for news of them, especially of his daughter. I saw this letter in March. He had been taken a prisoner the previous August. He had then been seven or eight months without news of his family.

"I am no longer young," he wrote in effect, for I am not quoting him exactly, "and I hope my friends will not forget me, in case of an exchange of prisoners."

He will never be forgotten. But of course he does not realise that. He is sixty-four and very ill. One read through all the restraint of the letter his longing to die among his own people. He hopes he will not be forgotten in an exchange of prisoners!

The Commandant's orderly announced that coffee was served, and we followed the lamp across the hall. An English officer made a fourth at the table.

It was good coffee, served with cream, the first I had seen for weeks. With it the Commandant served small, very thin cakes, with a layer of honey in the centre. "A specialty of the country," he said.

We talked of many things: of the attitude of America toward the war, her incredulity as to atrocities, the German propaganda, and a rumour that had reached the front of a German-Irish coalition in the House of Representatives at Washington.

From that the talk drifted to uniforms. The Commandant wished that the new French uniforms, instead of being a slaty blue, had been green, for use in the spring fighting.

I criticised the new Belgian uniform, which seemed to me much thinner than the old.

"That is wrong. It is of excellent cloth," said the General, and brought his cape up under the lamp for examination.

The uniforms of three armies were at the table— the French, the Belgian and the English. It was possible to compare them under the light of a single lamp.

The General's cloak, in spite of my criticism, was the heaviest of the three. But all of them seemed excellent. The material was like felt in body, but much softer.

All of the officers were united in thinking khaki an excellent all-round colour.

"The Turcos have been put into khaki," said the Commandant. "They disliked it at first; but their other costumes were too conspicuous. Now they are satisfied."

The Englishman offered the statement that England was supplying all of the Allies, including Russia, with cloth.

Sitting round the table under the lamp, the Commandant read a postcard taken from the body of a dead German in the attack the night before.   There was a photograph with it, autographed.   The photograph was of the woman who had written the card. It began "Beloved Otto," and was signed "Your loving wife, Hedwig."

This is the postcard:

"Beloved Otto: To-day your dear cards came, so full of anxiety for us.   So that now at last I know that you have received my letters.   I was convinced you had not.   We have sent you so many packages of things you may need.   Have you got any of them? To-day I have sent you my photograph.   I wished to send a letter also instead of this card, but I have no writing paper.   All week I have been busy with the children's clothing.   We think of you always, dear Otto.   Write to us often.   Greetings from your Hedwig and the children."

So she was making clothing for the children and sending him little packages.   And Otto lay dead under the stars that night—dead of an ideal, which is that a man must leave his family and all that he loves and follow the beckoning finger of empire.

"For king and country!"

The Commandant said that when a German soldier surrenders he throws down his gun, takes off his helmet and jerks off his shoulder straps, saying over and over, *"Pater familias."*   Sometimes, by way of emphasising that he is a family man, he holds up his fingers—two children or three children, whatever it may be.   Even boys in their teens will claim huge families.

I did not find it amusing after the postcard and

the photograph. I found it all very tragic and sad
and disheartening.

It was growing late and the General was impatient
to be off. We had still a long journey ahead of us,
and riding at night was not particularly safe.

I got into the car and they bundled in after me
the damaged pictures, the horseshoe, the piece of gargoyle from the Cloth Hall and the nose of the shell.

The orderly reported that a Zeppelin had just
passed overhead; but the General shrugged his shoulders.

"They are always seeing Zeppelins," he said. "Me,
I do not believe there is such a thing!"

That night in my hotel, after dinner, Gertrude, Lady
Decies, told me the following story:

"I had only twelve hours' notice to start for the
front. I am not a hospital nurse, but I have taken
for several years three months each summer of special training. So I felt that I would be useful if I
could get over.

"It was November and very cold. When I got
to Calais there was not a room to be had anywhere.
But at the Hotel Centrale they told me I might have
a bathroom to sleep in.

"At the last moment a gentleman volunteered to
exchange with me. But the next day he left, so that
night I slept in a bathtub with a mattress in it!

"The following day I got a train for Dunkirk. On
the way the train was wrecked. Several coaches left
the track, and there was nothing to do but to wait
until they were put back on.

"I went to the British Consul at Dunkirk and asked

him where I could be most useful. He said to go
to the railroad station at once.

"I went to the station. The situation there was horrible. Three doctors and seven dressers were working
on four-hour shifts.

"As the wounded came in only at night, that was
when we were needed. I worked all night from that
time on. My first night we had eleven hundred men.
Some of them were dead when they were lifted out
onto the stone floor of the station shed. One boy
flung himself out of the door. I caught him as he
fell and he died in my arms. He had diphtheria,
as well as being wounded.

"The station was frightfully cold, and the men
had to be laid on the stone floors with just room for
moving about between them. There was no heat of
any sort. The dead were laid in rows, one on top
of another, on cattle trucks. As fast as a man died
they took his body away and brought in another
wounded man.

"Every now and then the electric lights would go
out and leave us there in black darkness. Finally we
got candles and lamps for emergencies.

"We had no surgical dressings, but we had some
iodine. The odours were fearful. Some of the men
had not had their clothes off for five weeks. Their
garments were like boards. It was almost impossible
to cut through them. And underneath they were
coated with vermin. Their bodies were black with
them frequently.

"In many cases the wounds were green through lack
of attention. One man, I remember, had fifteen.
The first two nights I was there we had no water,
which made it terrible. There was a pump outside,

but the water was bad. At last we had a little stove set up, and I got some kettles and jugs and boiled the water.

"We were obliged to throw the bandages in a heap on the floor, and night after night we walked about in blood. My clothing and stockings were stained with blood to my knees.

"After the first five nights I kept no record of the number of wounded; but the first night we had eleven hundred; the second night, nine hundred; the third night, seven hundred and fifty; the fourth night, two thousand; the fifth night, fifteen hundred.

"The men who were working at the station were English Quakers. They were splendid men. I have never known more heroic work than they did, and the curé was a splendid fellow. There was nothing too menial for him to do. He was everywhere."

This is the story she told me that night, in her own words. I have not revised it. Better than anything I know it tells of conditions as they actually existed during the hard fighting of the first autumn of the war, and as in the very nature of things they must exist again whenever either side undertakes an offensive.

It becomes a little wearying, sometimes, this constant cry of horrors, the ever-recurring demands on America's pocketbook for supplies, for dressings, for money to buy the thousands of things that are needed.

Read Lady Decies' account again, and try to place your own son on that stone floor on the station platform. Think of that wounded boy, sitting for hours in a train, and choking to death with diphtheria.

This is the thing we call war.

CHAPTER XV

RUNNING THE BLOCKADE

FROM MY JOURNAL written during an attack of influenza at the Gare Maritime in Calais:

LAST night I left England on the first boat to cross the Channel after the blockade. I left London at midnight, with the usual formality of being searched by Scotland Yard detectives. The train was empty and very cold.

"At half-past two in the morning we reached Folkestone. I was quite alone, and as I stood shivering on the quay waiting to have my papers examined a cold wind from the harbour and a thin spray of rain made the situation wretched. At last I confronted the inspector, and was told that under the new regulations I should have had my Red Cross card viséed in Paris. It was given back to me with a shrug, but my passport was stamped.

"There were four men round the table. My papers and I were inspected by each of the four in turn. At last I was through. But to my disgust I found I was not to be allowed on the Calais boat. There was one going to Boulogne and carrying passengers, but Calais was closed up tight, except to troops and officers.

"I looked at the Boulogne boat. It was well lighted

and cheerful. Those few people who had come down from London on the train were already settling themselves for the crossing. They were on their way to Paris and peace.

"I did not want Paris and certainly I did not want peace. I had telegraphed to Dunkirk and expected a military car to meet me at Calais. Once across, I knew I could neither telegraph nor telephone to Dunkirk, all lines of communication being closed to the public. I felt that I might be going to be ill. I would not be ill in Boulogne.

"At the end of the quay, dark and sinister, loomed the Calais boat. I had one moment of indecision. Then I picked up my suitcase and started toward it in the rain. Luckily the gangway was out. I boarded the boat with as much assurance as I could muster, and was at once accosted by the chief officer.

"I produced my papers. Some of them were very impressive. There were letters from the French Ambassador in London, Monsieur Cambon, to leading French generals. There was a letter to Sir John French and another letter expediting me through the customs, but unluckily the customs at Boulogne.

"They left him cold. I threw myself on his mercy. He apologised, but continued firm. The Boulogne boat drew in its gangway. I mentioned this, and that, so to speak, I had burned my Boulogne gangway behind me. I said I had just had an interview with Mr. Winston Churchill, and that I felt sure the First Lord of the Admiralty would not approve of my standing there arguing when I was threatened with influenza. He acted as though he had never heard of the First Lord.

"At last he was called away. So I went into a

deck cabin, and closed and bolted the door. I remember that, and that I put a life preserver over my feet, in case of a submarine, and my fur coat over the rest of me, because of a chill. And that is all I do remember, until this morning in a grey, rainy dawn I opened the door to find that we were entering the harbour of Calais. If the officers of the boat were surprised to see me emerge they concealed it. No doubt they knew that with Calais under military law I could hardly slip through the fingers of the police.

"This morning I have a mild attack of what the English call 'flu.' I am still at the hotel in Calais. I have breakfasted to the extent of hot coffee, have taken three different kinds of influenza remedies, and am now waiting and aching, but at least I am in France.

"If the car from Dunkirk does not come for me to-day I shall be deported to-night.

"Two torpedo boats are coaling in the harbor. They have two large white letters which answer for their names. One is the BE; the other is the ER. As they lie side by side these tall white letters spell B-E-E-R.

"I have heard an amusing thing: that the English have built duplicates of all their great battleships, building them of wood, guns and all, over the hulls of other vessels; and that the Germans have done the same thing! What would happen if one of the 'dummy' fleets met the other? Would it be a battle of expletives? Would the German consonant triumph over the English aspirate, and both ships go down in a sea of language?

"The idea is, of course, to delude submarines into the belief that they are sinking battleships, while the real dreadnoughts are somewhere else—pure strategy, but amusing, except for the crews of these sham war flotillas."

The French Ambassador in London had given me letters to the various generals commanding the divisions of the French Army.

It was realised that America knew very little of what the French were doing in this great war. We knew, of course, that they were holding a tremendous battle line and that they were fighting bravely. Rumours we had heard of the great destruction done by the French seventy-five millimetre gun, and the names of numerous towns had become familiar to us in print, even when we could not pronounce them. The Paris omnibuses had gone to the front. Paris fashions were late in coming to us, and showed a military trend. For the first time the average American knew approximately where and what Alsace-Lorraine is, and that Paris has forts as well as shops and hotels.

But what else did we know of France and its part in the war? What does America generally know of France, outside of Paris? Very little. Since my return, almost the only question I have been asked about France is: "Is Paris greatly changed?"

Yet America owes much to her great sister republic; much encouragement in the arts, in literature, in research. For France has always extended a kindly hand and a splendid welcome to gifted and artistic Americans. But her encouragement neither begins nor ends there.

It was in France that American statesmen received the support that enabled them to rear the new republic on strong and sturdy foundations. It is curious to think of that France of Louis the Sixteenth, with its every tradition opposed to the democracy for which America was contending, sending the very flower of her chivalry to assist the new republic. It is amazing to remember that when France was in a deplorable condition financially it was yet found possible to lend America six million dollars, and to exempt us from the payment of interest for a year.

And the friendship of France was of the people, not alone of the king, for it survived the downfall of the monarchy and the rise of the French Republic. When Benjamin Franklin died the National Assembly at Paris went into three days' mourning for "the great American."

As a matter of fact, France's help to America precipitated her own great crisis. The Declaration of Independence was the spark that set her ablaze. If the king was right in America he was utterly wrong at home. Lafayette went back from America convinced that "resistance is the most sacred of duties."

The French adopted the American belief that liberty is the object of government, and liberty of the individual—that very belief which France is standing for to-day as opposed to the nationalism of Germany. The Frenchman believes, like the American, that pressure should be from within out, not from without in. In other words, his own conscience, and not the arbitrary ruling of an arbitrary government, is his dictator. To reconcile liberty and democracy, then, has been France's problem, as it has been that of America. She has faced the same problems against a handicap that America has not had—the handicap of a discontented nobility. And by sheer force and determination France has won.

It has been said that the French in their Revolution were not reckless innovators. They were confiding followers. And the star they followed was the same star which, multiplied by the number of states, is the American flag to-day—Liberty.

Because of the many ties between the two countries, I had urged on the French Ambassador the necessity of letting America know a little more intimately what was being done by the French in this war. Since that time a certain relaxation has taken place along all the Allied lines. Correspondents have been taken out on day excursions and have cabled to America what they saw. But at the time I visited the French Army of the North there had been no one there.

Those Americans who had seen the French soldier in times of peace had not been greatly impressed. His curious, bent-kneed, slouching step, so carefully taught him—so different from the stately progress of the British, for instance, but so effective in covering ground—his loose trousers and huge pack, all conspire against the *ensemble* effect of French soldiers on the march.

I have seen British regiments at ease, British soldiers at rest and in their billets. Always they are smart, always they are military. A French regiment at ease ceases to be a part of a great machine. It shows, perhaps, more humanity. The men let their muscles sag a bit. They talk, laugh, sing if they are happy. They lie about in every attitude of complete relaxation. But at the word they fall in again. They take up the slack, as it were, and move on again in

that remarkable *pas de flexion* that is so oddly tireless. It is a difference of method; probably the best
thing for men who are Gallic, temperamental. A more
lethargic army is better governed probably by rule
of thumb.

I had crossed the Channel again to see the French
and English lines. On my previous visit, which had
lasted for several weeks, I had seen the Belgian Army
at the front and the French Army in billets and on
reserve. This time I was to see the French Army in
action.

The first step to that end, getting out of Calais,
proved simple enough. The car came from Dunkirk,
and brought passes. I took more influenza medicine,
dressed and packed my bag. There was some little
regret mingled with my farewell to the hotel at the
Gare Maritime. I had had there a private bath, with
a porcelain tub. More than that, the tub had been
made in my home city. It was, I knew, my last
glimpse of a porcelain tub, probably of any tub, for
some time. There were bath towels also. I wondered
if I would ever see a bath towel again. I left a cake
of soap in that bathroom. I can picture its next occupant walking in, calm and deliberate, and then his
eye suddenly falling on a cake of soap. I can picture
his stare, his incredulity. I can see him rushing to
the corridor and ringing the fire bell and calling the
other guests and the strangers without the gates, and
the boot boy in an apron, to come and see that cake
of soap.

But not the management. They would take it
away.

The car which came for me had been at the front
all night. It was filled inside and out with mud,

so that it was necessary to cover the seat before I
got in. Of all the cars I have ever travelled in, this
was the most wrecked. Hardly a foot of the metal
body was unbroken by shell or bullet hole. The wind
shield had been torn away. Tatters of curtain
streamed out in the wind. The mud guards were
bent and twisted. Even in that region of wrecked
cars people turned to look at it.

Calais was very gay that Sunday afternoon. The
sun was out. At the end of the drawbridge a soldier
was exercising a captured German horse.

Officers in scarlet and gold, in pale blue, in green
and red, in all the picturesqueness of a Sunday back
from the front, were decked for the public eye. They
walked in groups or singly. There were no women
with them. Their wives and sweethearts were far
away. A Sunday in Calais, indifferent food at a hotel,
a saunter in the sunlight, and then—Monday and
war again, with the bright colours replaced by sombre ones, with mud and evil odours and wretchedness.

They wandered about, smoking eternal cigarettes
and watching the harbour, where ships were coaling,
and where, as my car waited, the drawbridge opened
to allow a great Norwegian merchantman to pass.
The blockade was only two days old, but already this
Norwegian boat had her name painted in letters ten
feet high along each side of her hull, flanked on both
sides by the Norwegian flag, also painted. Her crew,
leaning over the side, surveyed the quay curiously.
So this was war—this petulant horse with its soldier
rider, these gay uniforms!

It had been hoped that neutral shipping would, by
thus indicating clearly its nationality, escape the at-

tacks of submarines. That very ship was sunk three days later in the North Sea.

Convalescent soldiers limped about on crutches; babies were wheeled in perambulators in the sun; a group of young aviators in black leather costumes watched a French biplane flying low. English naval officers from the coaling boats took shore leave and walked along with the free English stride.

There were no guns; everything was gaiety and brightness. But for the limping soldiers, my own battered machine, and the ominous grey ships in the harbour, it might have been a carnival.

In spite of the appearance of the machine it went northeast at an incredible pace, its dried mud flying off like missiles, through those French villages, which are so tidy because there is nothing to waste; where there is just enough and no more—no extra paper, no extra string, or food, or tin cans, or any of the litter that goes to make the disorder of a wasteful American town; where paper and string and tin cans and old boots serve their original purpose and then, in the course of time, become flower-pots or rag carpets or soup meat, or heaven knows what; and where, having fulfilled this second destiny, they go on being useful in feeding chickens, or repairing roads, or fertilising fields.

For the first time on this journey I encountered difficulty with the sentries. My Red Cross card had lost its potency. A new rule had gone out that even a staff car might not carry a woman. Things looked very serious for a time. But at last we got through.

There were many aviators out that bright day, going to the front, returning, or merely flying about taking the air. Women walked along the roads wear-

ing bright-coloured silk aprons.   Here and there the
sentries had stretched great chains across the road,
against which the car brought up sharply.   And then
at last Dunkirk again, and the royal apartment, and
a soft bed, and—influenza.

Two days later I started for the French lines.   I
packed a small bag, got out a fresh notebook, and,
having received the proper passes, the start was made
early in the morning.   An officer was to take me to
the headquarters of the French Army of the North.
From there I was to proceed to British headquarters.

My previous excursions from Dunkirk had all been
made east and southeast.   This new route was south.
As far as the town of Bergues we followed the route
by which I had gone to Ypres.   Bergues, a little fortified town, has been at times owned by the French,
English, Spanish and Dutch.

It is odd, remembering the new alignment of the
nations, to see erected in the public square a monu-
ment celebrating the victory of the French over the
English in 1793, a victory which had compelled the
British to raise the siege of Dunkirk.

South of Bergues there was no sign of war.   The
peasants rode along the road in their high, two-
wheeled carts with bare iron hoops over the top, hoops
over which canvas is spread in wet weather.

There were trees again; windmills with their great
wings turning peacefully; walled gardens and wayside shrines; holly climbing over privet hedges; and
rows of pollard willows, their early buds a reddish
brown; and tall Lombardy poplars, yellow-green with
spring.

The road stretched straight ahead, a silver line.
Nothing could have been more peaceful, more unwar-

like. Peasants trudged along with heavy milk cans hanging from wooden neck yokes, chickens flew squawking from the onslaught of the car. There were sheep here and there.

"It is forbidden to take or kill a sheep—except in self-defence!" said the officer.

And then suddenly we turned into a small town and came on hundreds of French omnibuses, requisitioned from all parts of France and painted a dingy grey.

Out of the town again. The road rose now to Cassel, with its three windmills in a row on the top of a hill. We drove under an arch of trees, their trunks covered with moss. On each side of the highway peasants were ploughing in the mud—old peasants, bent to the plough, or very young boys, who eyed us without curiosity.

Still south. But now there were motor ambulances and an occasional long line of motor lorries. At one place in a village we came on a great three-ton lorry, driven and manned by English Tommies. They knew no French and were completely lost in a foreign land. But they were beautifully calm. They sat on the driving seat and smoked pipes and derided each other, as in turn they struggled to make their difficulty known.

"Bailleul," said the Tommies over and over, but they pronounced it "Berlue," and the villagers only laughed.

The officer in the car explained.

" 'Berlue,' " he said, "is—what do you Americans say—dotty? They are telling the villagers they want to go crazy!"

So he got out and explained. Also he found out

their road for them and sent them off, rather sheepish, but laughing.

"I never get over the surprises of this war," said the officer when he returned. "Think of those boys, with not a word of French, taking that lorry from the coast to the English lines! They'll get there too. They always do."

As we left the flat land toward the coast the country grew more and more beautiful. It rolled gently and there were many trees.

The white houses with their low thatched roofs, which ended in a bordering of red tiles, looked prosperous. But there were soldiers again. We were approaching the war zone.

CHAPTER XVI

THE MAN OF YPRES

THE sun was high when we reached the little town where General Foch, Commander of the Armies of the North, had his headquarters. It was not difficult to find the building. The French flag furled at the doorway, a gendarme at one side of the door and a sentry at the other, denoted the headquarters of the staff. But General Foch was not there at the moment. He had gone to church.

The building was near. Thinking that there might be a service, I decided to go also. Going up a steep street to where at the top stood a stone church, with an image of the Christ almost covered by that virgin vine which we call Virginia creeper, I opened the leather-covered door and went quietly in.

There was no service. The building was quite empty. And the Commander of the Armies of the North, probably the greatest general the French have in the field to-day, was kneeling there alone.

He never knew I had seen him. I left before he did. Now, as I look back, it seems to me that that great general on his knees alone in that little church is typical of the attitude of France to-day toward the war.

It is a totally different attitude from the English —not more heroic, not braver, not more resolute to an end. But it is peculiarly reverential. The enemy is on the soil of France. The French are fighting for their homes, for their children, for their country. And in this great struggle France daily, hourly, on its knees asks for help.

I went to the hotel—an ancient place, very small, very clean, very cold and shabby. The entrance was through an archway into a cobble-paved courtyard, where on the left, under the roof of a shed, the saddles of cavalry horses and gendarmes were waiting on saddle trestles. Beyond, through a glazed door, was a long dining room, with a bare, white-scrubbed floor and whitewashed walls. Its white table-cloths, white walls and ceiling and white floor, with no hint of fire, although a fine snow had commenced to fall, set me to shivering. Even the attempt at decoration of hanging baskets, of trailing vines with strings of red peppers, was hardly cheering.

From the window a steep, walled garden fell away, dreary enough under the grey sky and the snowfall. The same curious pale-green moss covered the trees, and beyond the garden wall, in a field, was a hole where a German aëroplane had dropped a bomb.

Hot coffee had been ordered, and we went into a smaller room for it. Here there was a fire, with four French soldiers gathered round it. One of them was writing at the table. The others were having their palms read.

"You have a heart line," said the palmist to one of them—"a heart line like a windmill!"

I drank my coffee and listened. I could understand only a part of it, but it was eminently cheerful. They laughed, chaffed each other, and although my presence in the hotel must have caused much curiosity in that land of no women, they did not stare at me. Indeed, it was I who did the gazing.

After a time I was given a room. It was at the end of a whitewashed corridor, from which pine doors opened on either side into bedrooms. The corridor was bare of carpet, the whole upstairs freezing cold. There were none of the amenities. My room was at the end. It boasted two small windows, with a tiny stand between them containing a tin basin and a pitcher; a bed with one side of the mattress torn open and exposing a heterogeneous content that did not bear inspection; a pine chair, a candle and a stove.

They called it a stove. It had a coal receptacle that was not as large as a porridge bowl, and one small lump of coal, pulverized, was all it held. It was lighted with a handful of straw. Turn your back and count ten, and it was out. Across the foot of the bed was one of the Continental feather comforts which cover only one's feet and let the rest freeze.

It was not so near the front as La Panne, but the windows rattled incessantly from the bombardment of Ypres. I glanced through one of the windows. The red tiles I had grown to know so well were not in evidence. Most of the roofs were blue, a weathered and mottled blue, very lovely, but, like everything else about the town, exceedingly cold to look at.

Shortly after I had unpacked my few belongings I was presented to General Foch, not at headquarters, but at the house in which he was living. He came out himself to meet me, attended by several of his officers, and asked at once if I had had *déjeuner*. I had not, so he invited me to lunch with him and with his staff.

Déjeuner was ready and we went in immediately.

A long table had been laid for fourteen. General Foch took his place at the centre of one of the long sides, and I was placed in the seat of honour directly across. As his staff is very large, only a dozen officers dine with him. The others, juniors in the service, are billeted through the town and have a separate mess.

Sitting where I did I had a very good opportunity to see the hero of Ypres, philosopher, strategist and theorist, whose theories were then bearing the supreme test of war.

Erect, and of distinguished appearance, General Foch is a man rather past middle life, with heavy iron-grey hair, rather bushy grey eyebrows and a moustache. His eyes are grey and extremely direct. His speech incisive and rather rapid.

Although some of the staff had donned the new French uniform of grey-blue, the general wore the old uniform, navy-blue, the only thing denoting his rank being the three dull steel stars on the embroidered sleeve of his tunic.

There was little ceremony at the meal. The staff remained standing until General Foch and I were seated. Then they all sat down and *déjeuner* was immediately served.

One of the staff told me later that the general is extremely punctilious about certain things. The staff is expected to be in the dining room five minutes before meals are served. A punctual man himself, he expects others to be punctual. The table must always be the epitome of neatness, the food well cooked and quietly served.

Punctuality and neatness no doubt are due to his long military training, for General Foch has always been a soldier. Many of the officers of France owe their knowledge of strategy and tactics to his teaching at the *École de Guerre.*`

General Foch led the conversation. Owing to the rapidity of his speech, it was necessary to translate much of it for me. We spoke, one may say, through a clearing house. But although he knew it was to be translated to me, he spoke, not to the interpreter, but to me, and his keen eyes watched me as I replied. And I did not interview General Foch. General Foch interviewed me. I made no pretence at speaking for America. I had no mission. But within my limitations I answered him as well as I could.

"There are many ties between America and France," said General Foch. "We wish America to know what we are doing over here, to realise that this terrible war was forced on us."

I mentioned my surprise at the great length of the French line—more than four hundred miles.

"You do not know that in America?" he asked, evidently surprised.

I warned him at once not to judge the knowledge of America by what I myself knew, that no doubt many quite understood the situation.

"But you have been very modest," I said. "We really have had little information about the French Army and what it is doing, unless more news is going over since I left."

"We are more modest than the Germans, then?"

"You are, indeed. There are several millions of German-born Americans who are not likely to let America forget the Fatherland. There are many German newspapers also."

"What is the percentage of German population?"

I told him. I think I was wrong. I think I made it too great. But I had not expected to be interviewed.

"And these German newspapers, are they neutral?"

"Not at all. Very far from it."

I told him what I knew of the German propaganda in America, and he listened intently.

"What is its effect? Is it influencing public opinion?"

"It did so undeniably for a time. But I believe it is not doing so much now. For one thing, Germany's methods on the sea will neutralise all her agents can say in her favour—that and the relaxation of the restrictions against the press, so that something can be known of what the Allies are doing."

"You have known very little?"

"Absurdly little."

There was some feeling in my tone, and he smiled.

"We wish to have America know the splendid spirit of the French Army," he said after a moment. "And the justice of its cause also."

I asked him what he thought of the future.

"There is no question about the future," he said with decision. "That is already settled. When the German advance was checked it was checked for good."

"Then you do not believe that they will make a further advance toward Paris?"

"Certainly not."

He went on to explain the details of the battle of the Marne, and how in losing that battle the invading army had lost everything.

It will do no harm to digress for a moment and explain exactly what the French did at the battle of the Marne.

All through August the Allies fell back before the onward rush of the Germans. But during all that strategic retreat plans were being made for resuming the offensive again. This necessitated an orderly retreat, not a rout, with constant counter-engagements to keep the invaders occupied. It necessitated also a fixed point of retreat, to be reached by the different Allied armies simultaneously.

When, on September fifth, the order for assuming the offensive was given, the extreme limit of the retreat had not yet been reached. But the audacity of the German march had placed it in a position favourable for attack, and at the same time extremely dangerous for the Allies and Paris if they were not checked.

On the evening of September fifth General Joffre sent this message to all the commanders of armies:

"The hour has come to advance at all costs, and do or die where you stand rather than give way."

The French did not give way. Paris was saved after a colossal battle, in which more than two million men were engaged. The army commanded by General Foch was at one time driven back by overwhelming odds, but immediately resumed the offensive, and making a flank attack forced the Germans to retreat.

Not that he mentioned his part in the battle of the Marne. Not that any member of his staff so much as intimated it. But these are things that get back.

"How is America affected by the war?"

I answered as best I could, telling him something of the paralysis it had caused in business, of the war tax, and of our anxiety as to the status of our shipping.

"From what I can gather from the newspapers, the sentiment in America is being greatly influenced by the endangering of American shipping."

"Naturally. But your press endeavours to be neutral, does it not?"

"Not particularly," I admitted. "Sooner or later our papers become partisan. It is difficult not to. In this war one must take sides."

"Certainly. One must take sides. One cannot be really neutral in this war. Every country is interested in the result, either actively now or later on, when the struggle is decided. One cannot be disinterested; one must be partisan."

The staff echoed this.

Having been interviewed by General Foch for some time, I ventured to ask him a question. So I asked, as I asked every general I met, if the German advance had been merely ruthless or if it had been barbaric.

He made no direct reply, but he said:

"You must remember that the Germans are not only fighting against an army, they are fighting against nations; trying to destroy their past, their present, even their future."

"How does America feel as to the result of this war?" he asked. "I suppose it feels no doubt as to the result."

Again I was forced to explain my own inadequacy to answer such a question and my total lack of authority to voice American sentiment. While I was confident that many Americans believed in the cause of the Allies, and had every confidence in the outcome of the war, there remained always that large and prosperous portion of the population, either German-born or of German parentage, which had no doubt of Germany's success.

"It is natural, of course," he commented. "How many French have you in the United States?"

I thought there were about three hundred thousand, and said so.

"You treat your people so well in France," I said, "that few of them come to us."

He nodded and smiled.

"What do you think of the blockade, General Foch?" I said. "I have just crossed the Channel and it is far from comfortable."

"Such a blockade cannot be," was his instant reply; "a blockade must be continuous to be effective. In a real blockade all neutral shipping must be stopped, and Germany cannot do this."

One of the staff said "Bluff!" which has apparently been adopted into the French language, and the rest nodded their approval.

Their talk moved on to aëroplanes, to shells, to the French artillery. General Foch considered that Zeppelins were useful only as air scouts, and that with the coming of spring, with short nights and early dawns, there would be no time for them to range far. The aëroplanes he considered much more valuable.

"One thing has impressed me," I said, "as I have seen various artillery duels—the number of shells used with comparatively small result. After towns are destroyed the shelling continues. I have seen a hillside where no troops had been for weeks, almost entirely covered with shell holes.

He agreed that the Germans had wasted a great deal of their ammunition.

Like all great commanders, he was intensely proud of his men and their spirit.

"They are both cheerful and healthy," said the general; "splendid men. We are very proud of them. I am glad that America is to know something of their spirit, of the invincible courage and resolution of the French to fight in the cause of humanity and justice."

Luncheon was over. It had been a good luncheon, of a mound of boiled cabbage, finely minced beef in the centre, of mutton cutlets and potatoes, of strawberry jam, cheese and coffee. There had been a bottle of red wine on the table. A few of the staff took a little, diluting it with water. General Foch did not touch it.

We rose. I had an impression that I had had my interview; but the hospitality and kindness of this French general were to go further.

In the little corridor he picked up his dark-blue cap and we set out for official headquarters, followed by several of the officers. He walked rapidly, taking the street to give me the narrow sidewalk and going along with head bent against the wind. In the square, almost deserted, a number of staff cars had gathered, and lorries lumbered through. We turned to the left, between the sentry and the gendarme, and climbing a flight of wooden stairs were in the anteroom of the general's office. Here were tables covered with papers, telephones, maps, the usual paraphernalia of such rooms. We passed through a pine door, and there was the general's room—a bare and shabby room, with a large desk in front of the two windows that overlooked the street, a shaded lamp, more papers and a telephone. The room had a fireplace, and

in front of it was a fine old chair. And on the mantelpiece, as out of place as the chair, was a marvellous
Louis-Quinze clock, under glass. There were great
maps on the walls, with the opposing battle lines shown
to the smallest detail. General Foch drew my attention at once to the clock.

"During the battle of the Yser," he said, "night
and day my eyes were on that clock. Orders were
sent. Then it was necessary to wait until they were
carried out. It was by the clock that one could know
what should be happening. The hours dragged. It
was terrible."

It must have been terrible. Everywhere I had
heard the same story. More than any of the great
battles of the war, more even than the battle of the
Marne, the great fight along the Yser, from the
twenty-first of October, 1914, to the twelfth of November, seems to have impressed itself in sheer horror
on the minds of those who know its fearfulness. At
every headquarters I have found the same feeling.

It was General Foch's army that reënforced the
British at that battle. The word had evidently been
given to the Germans that at any cost they must break
through. They hurled themselves against the British
with unprecedented ferocity. I have told a little of
that battle, of the frightful casualties, so great among
the Germans that they carried their dead back and
burned them in great pyres. The British Army was
being steadily weakened. The Germans came steadily,
new lines taking the place of those that were gone.
Then the French came up, and, after days of struggle, the line held.

General Foch opened a drawer of the desk and
showed me, day by day, the charts of the battle. They

were bound together in a great book, and each day
had a fresh page. The German Army was black. The
French was red. Page after page I lived that battle,
the black line advancing, the blue of the British wavering against overwhelming numbers and ferocity, the
red line of the French coming up. "The Man of
Ypres," they call General Foch, and well they may.

"They came," said General Foch, "like the waves
of the sea."

It was the second time I had heard the German
onslaught so described.

He shut the book and sat for a moment, his head
bent, as though in living over again that fearful time
some of its horror had come back to him.

At last: "I paced the floor and watched the clock,"
he said.

How terrible! How much easier to take a sword
and head a charge! How much simpler to lead men
to death than to send them! There in that quiet room,
with only the telephone and the ticking of the clock
for company, while his staff waited outside for orders,
this great general, this strategist on whose strategy
hung the lives of armies, this patriot and soldier at
whose word men went forth to die, paced the floor.

He walked over to the clock and stood looking
at it, his fine head erect, his hands behind him. Some
of the tragedy of those nineteen days I caught from
his face.

But the line held.

To-day, as I write this, General Foch's army in
the North and the British are bearing the brunt of
another great attack at Ypres.* The British have made

* Battle of Neuve Chapelle March, 1915.

a gain at Neuve Chapelle, and the Germans have retaliated by striking at their line, some miles farther north. If they break through it will be toward Calais and the sea. Every offensive movement in this new warfare of trench and artillery requires a concentration of reserves. To make their offensive movement the British have concentrated at Neuve Chapelle. The second move of this game of death has been made by the other side against the weakened line of the Allies. During the winter the line, in this manner, automatically straightened. But what will happen now?

One thing we know: General Foch will send out his brave men, and, having sent them, will watch the Louis-Quinze clock and wait. And other great generals will send out their men, and wait also. There will be more charts, and every fresh line of black or blue or red or Belgian yellow will mean a thousand deaths, ten thousand deaths.

They are fighting to-day at Ypres. I have seen that flat and muddy battlefield. I have talked with the men, have stood by the batteries as they fired. How many of the boys I watched playing prisoners' base round their guns in the intervals of firing are there to-day? How many remain of that little company of soldiers who gave three cheers for me because I was the only woman they had seen for months? How many of the officers who shrugged their shoulders when I spoke of danger have gone down to death?

Outside the window where I am writing this, Fifth Avenue, New York, has just left its churches and is flaunting its spring finery in the sun. Across the sea, such a little way as measured by time, people are in the churches also. The light comes through the ancient, stained-glass windows and falls, not on spring finery, not on orchids and gardenias, but on thousands of tiny candles burning before the shrine of the Mother of Pity.

It is so near. And it is so terrible. How can we play? How can we think of anything else? But for the grace of God, your son and mine lying there in the spring sunlight on the muddy battlefield of Ypres!

CHAPTER XVII

IN THE LINE OF THE "MITRAILLEUSE"

I WAS taken to see the battlefield of Ypres by Captain Boisseau, of the French War Academy, and Lieutenant René Puaux, of the staff of General Foch. It was a bright and sunny day, with a cold wind, however, that set the water in the wayside ditches to rippling.

All the night before I had wakened at intervals to heavy cannonading and the sharp cracking of *mitrailleuse*. We were well behind the line, but the wind was coming from the direction of the battle-field.

The start was made from in front of General Foch's headquarters. He himself put me in the car, and bowed an *au revoir*.

"You will see," he said, "the French soldier in the field, and you will see him cheerful and well. You will find him full also of invincible courage and resolution."

And all that he had said, I found. I found the French soldiers smiling and cheerful and ruddy in the most wretched of billets. I found them firing at the enemy, still cheerful, but with a coolness of courage that made my own shaking nerves steady themselves.

To-day, when that very part of the line I visited is,

as was expected when I was there, bearing the brunt of the German attack in the most furious fighting of the war, I wonder, of those French soldiers who crowded round to see the first woman they had beheld for months, how many are lying on that muddy battlefield? What has happened on that road, guarded by buried quick-firers, that stretched to the German trenches beyond the poplar trees? Did the "rabbit trap" do its work? Only for a time, I think, for was it not there that the Germans broke through? Did the Germans find and silence that concealed battery of seventy-five-millimetre guns under its imitation hedge? Who was in the tree lookout as the enemy swarmed across, and did he get away?

Except for the constant road repairing there was little to see during the first part of the journey. Here in a flat field, well beyond the danger zone, some of the new British Army was digging practice trenches in the mud. Their tidy uniforms were caked with dirt, their faces earnest and flushed. At last the long training at Salisbury Plain was over, and here they were, if not at the front, within hearing distance of the guns. Any day now a bit of luck would move them forward, and there would be something doing.

By now, no doubt, they have been moved up and there has been something doing. Poor lads! I watched them until even their khaki-coloured tents had faded into the haze. The tall, blonde, young officer, Lieutenant Puaux, pointed out to me a detachment of Belgian soldiers mending roads. As our car passed they leaned on their spades and looked after us.

"Belgian carabineers," he said. "They did some of the most heroic work of the war last summer and autumn. They were decorated by the King. Now they are worn out and they mend roads!"

For—and this I had to learn—a man may not fight always, even although he escapes actual injury. It is the greatest problem of commanding generals that they must be always moving forward fresh troops. The human element counts for much in any army. Nerves go after a time. The constant noise of the guns has sent men mad.

More than ever, in this new warfare, is the problem serious. For days the men suffer not only the enemy's guns but the roar of their own batteries from behind them. They cannot always tell which side they hear. Their tortured ears ache with listening. And when they charge and capture an outpost it is not always certain that they will escape their own guns. In one tragic instance that I know of this happened.

The route was by way of Poperinghe, with its narrow, crowded streets, its fresh troops just arrived and waiting patiently, heavy packs beside them, for orders. In Poperinghe are found all the troops of the Allies: British, Belgian, French, Hindus, Cingalese, Algerians, Moroccans. Its streets are a series of colourful pictures, of quaint uniforms, of a babel of tongues, of that minor confusion that is order on a great scale. The inevitable guns rumbled along with six horses and three drivers: a lead driver, a centre driver and wheel driver. Unlike the British guns, there are generally no gunners with the guns, but only an officer or two. The gunners go ahead on foot. Lines of hussars rode by, making their way slowly round a train of British Red-Cross ambulances.

At Elverdingue I was to see the men in their billets. Elverdingue was another Poperinghe—the same crowds of soldiers, the same confusion, only perhaps more emphasised, for Elverdingue is very near the front, between Poperinghe and Ypres and a little to the north, where the line that curves out about Ypres bends back again.

More guns, more hussars. It was difficult to walk across the narrow streets. We watched our chance and broke through at last, going into a house at random. As each house had soldiers billeted in it, it was certain we would find some, and I was to see not selected quarters but billets chosen at random. Through a narrow, whitewashed centre hall, with men in the rooms on either side, and through a muddy kitchen, where the usual family was huddled round a stove, we went into a tiny, brick-paved yard. Here was a shed, a roof only, which still held what remained of the winter's supply of coal.

Two soldiers were cooking there. Their tiny fire of sticks was built against a brick wall, and on it was a large can of stewing meat. One of the cooks—they were company cooks—was watching the kettle and paring potatoes in a basket. The other was reading a letter aloud. As the officers entered the men rose and saluted, their bright eyes taking in this curious party, which included, of all things, a woman!

"When did you get in from the trenches?" one of the officers asked.

"At two o'clock this morning, *Monsieur le Capitaine*."

"And you have not slept?"

"But no. The men must eat. We have cooked ever since we returned."

Further questioning elicited the facts that he would sleep when his company was fed, that he was twenty-two years old, and that—this not by questions but by investigation—he was sheltered against the cold by a large knitted muffler, an overcoat, a coat, a green sweater, a flannel shirt and an undershirt. Under his blue trousers he wore also the red ones of an old uniform, the red showing through numerous rents and holes.

"You have a letter, comrade!" said the Lieutenant to the other man.

"From my family," was the somewnat sheepis.. reply.

Round the doorway other soldiers had gathered to see what was occurring. They came, yawning with sleep, from the straw they had been sleeping on, or drifted in from the streets, where they had been smoking in the sun. They were true republicans, those French soldiers. They saluted the officers without subservience, but as man to man. And through a break in the crowd a new arrival was shoved forward. He came, smiling uneasily.

"He has the new uniform," I was informed, and he must turn round to show me how he looked in it.

We went across the street and through an alleyway to an open place where stood an old coach house. Here were more men, newly in from the front. The coach house was a ruin, far from weather-proof and floored with wet and muddy straw. One could hardly believe that that straw had been dry and fresh when the troops came in at dawn. It was hideous now, from the filth of the trenches. The men were awake, and being advised of our coming by an anxious and loud-voiced member of the company who ran ahead, they were on their feet, while others, who had been sleeping in the loft, were on their way down the ladder.

"They have been in a very bad place all night," said the Captain. "They are glad to be here, they say."

"You mean that they have been in a dangerous place?"

The men were laughing among themselves and pushing forward one of their number. Urged by their rapid French, he held out his cap to me. It had been badly torn by a German bullet. Encouraged by his example, another held out his cap. The crown had been torn almost out of it.

"You see," said Captain Boisseau, "it was not a comfortable night. But they are here, and they are content."

I could understand it, of course, but "here" seemed so pitifully poor a place—a wet and cold and dirty coach house, open to all the winds that blew; before it a courtyard stabling army horses that stood to the fetlocks in mud. For food they had what the boy of twenty-two or other cooks like him were preparing over tiny fires built against brick walls. But they were alive, and there were letters from home, and before very long they expected to drive the Germans back in one of those glorious charges so dear to the French heart. They were here, and they were content.

More sheds, more small fires, more paring of potatoes and onions and simmering of stews. The meal of the day was in preparation and its odours were savoury. In one shed I photographed the cook, paring potatoes with a knife that looked as though it belonged on the end of a bayonet. And here I was lined up by the fire and the cook—and the knife—and my picture taken. It has not yet reached me. Perhaps it went by way of England, and was deleted by the censor as showing munitions of war!

From Elverdingue the road led north and west, following the curves of the trenches. We went through Woesten, where on the day before a dramatic incident had taken place. Although the town was close to the battlefield and its church in plain view from the German lines, it had escaped bombardment. But one Sunday morning a shot was fired. The shell went through the roof of the church just above the altar, fell and exploded, killing the priest as he knelt. The hole in the roof of the building bore mute evidence to this tragedy. It was a small hole, for the shell exploded inside the building. When I saw it a half dozen planks had been nailed over it to keep out the rain.

There were trees outside Woesten, more trees than I had been accustomed to nearer the sea. Here and there a troop of cavalry horses was corralled in a grove; shaggy horses, not so large as the English ones. They were confined by the simple expedient of stretching a rope from tree to tree in a large circle.

"French horses," I said, "always look to me so small and light compared with English horses."

Then a horse moved about, and on its shaggy flank showed plainly the mark of a Western branding iron! They were American cow ponies from the plains.

"There are more than a hundred thousand American horses here," observed the Lieutenant. "They are very good horses."

Later on I stopped to stroke the soft nose of a black horse as it stood trembling near a battery of heavy guns that was firing steadily. It was American too. On its flank there was a Western brand. I gave it an additional caress, and talked a little American into one of its nervous, silky ears. We were both far from home, a trifle bewildered, a bit uneasy and frightened.

And now it was the battlefield—the flat, muddy plain of Ypres. On the right bodies of men, sheltered by intervening groves and hedges, moved about. Dispatch riders on motor cycles flew along the roads, and over the roof of a deserted farmhouse an observation balloon swung in the wind. Beyond the hedges and the grove lay the trenches, and beyond them again German batteries were growling. Their shells, however, were not bursting anywhere near us.

The balloon was descending. I asked permission to go up in it, but when I saw it near at hand I withdrew the request. It had no basket, like the ones I had seen before, but instead the observers, two of them, sat astride a horizontal bar.

The English balloons have a basket beneath, I am told. One English airship man told me that to be sent up in a stationary balloon was the greatest penalty a man could be asked to pay. The balloon jerks at the end of its rope like a runaway calf, and "the resulting nausea makes sea-sickness seem like a trip to the Crystal Palace."

So I did not go up in that observation balloon on the field of Ypres. We got out of the car, and trudged after the balloon as it was carried to its new position by many soldiers. We stood by as it rose again above the tree tops, the rope and the telephone wire hanging beneath it. But what the observers saw that afternoon from their horizontal bar I do not yet know—trenches, of course. But trenches are interesting in this war only when their occupants have left them and started forward. Batteries and ammunition trains, probably, the latter crawling along the enemy's roads. But both of these can be better and more easily located by aëroplanes.

The usefulness of the captive balloon in this war is doubtful. It serves, at the best, to take the place of an elevation of land in this flat country, is a large and tempting target, and can serve only on very clear days when there is no ground mist—a difficult thing to achieve in Flanders.

We were getting closer to the front all the time. As the automobile jolted on, drawing out for transports, for ambulances and ammunition wagons, the two French officers spoke of the heroism of their men. They told me, one after the other, of brave deeds that had come under their own observation.

"The French common soldier is exceedingly brave— quite reckless," one of them said. "Take, for instance, the case, a day or so ago, of Philibert Musillat, of the 168th Infantry. We had captured a communication trench from the Germans and he was at the end of it, alone. There was a renewal of the German attack, and they came at him along the trench. He refused to retreat. His comrades behind handed him loaded rifles, and he killed every German that appeared until they lay in a heap. The Germans threw bombs at him, but he would not move. He stood there for more than twelve hours!"

There were many such stories, such as that of the boys of the senior class of the military school of St. Cyr, who took, the day of the beginning of the war, an oath to put on gala dress, white gloves and a red, white and blue plume, when they had the honour to receive the first order to charge.

They did it, too. Theatrical? Isn't it just splendidly boyish? They did it, you see. The first of them to

die, a young sub-lieutenant, was found afterward, his
red, white and blue plume trampled in the mud, his
brave white gloves stained with his own hot young
blood. Another of these St. Cyr boys, shot in the
face hideously and unable to speak, stood still under
fire and wrote his orders to his men. It was his first
day under fire.

A boy fell injured between the barbed wire in front
of his trench and the enemy, in that No Man's Land
of so many tragedies. His comrades, afraid of hitting
him, stopped firing.

"Go on!" he called to them. "No matter about me.
Shoot at them!"

So they fired, and he writhed for a moment.

"I got one of yours that time!" he said.

The Germans retired, but the boy still lay on the
ground, beyond reach. He ceased moving, and they
thought he was dead. One may believe that they
hoped he was dead. It was more merciful than the
slow dying of No Man's Land. But after a time he
raised his head.

"Look out," he called. "They are coming again.
They are almost up to me!"

That is all of that story.

CHAPTER XVIII

FRENCH GUNS IN ACTION

THE car stopped. We were at the wireless and telephone headquarters for the French Army of the North. It was a low brick building, and outside, just off the roadway, was a high van full of telephone instruments. That it was moved from one place to another was shown when, later in the day, returning by that route, we found the van had disappeared.

It was two o'clock. The German wireless from Berlin had just come in. At three the receiving station would hear from the Eiffel Tower in Paris. It was curious to stand there and watch the operator, receivers on his ears, picking up the German message. It was curious to think that, just a little way over there, across a field or two, the German operator was doing the same thing, and that in an hour he would be receiving the French message.

All the batteries of the army corps are—or were— controlled from that little station. The colonel in charge came out to greet us, and to him Captain Boisseau gave General Foch's request to show me batteries in action.

The colonel was very willing. He would go with us himself. I conquered a strong desire to stand with the telephone building between me and the German lines, now so near, and looked about. A French aëroplane was overhead, but there was little bustle and activity along the road. It is a curious fact in this war that the nearer one is to the front the quieter things become. Three or four miles behind there is bustle and movement. A mile behind, and only an occasional dispatch rider, a few men mending roads, an officer's car, a few horses tethered in a wood, a broken gun carriage, a horse being shod behind a wall, a soldier on a lookout platform in a tree, thickets and hedges that on occasion spout fire and death—that is the country round Ypres and just behind the line, in daylight.

We were between Ypres and the Allied line, in that arc which the Germans are, as I write, trying so hard to break through. The papers say that they are shelling Ypres and that it is burning. They were shelling it that day also. But now, as then, I cannot believe it is burning. There was nothing left to burn.

While arrangements were being made to visit the batteries, Lieutenant Puaux explained to me a method they had established at that point for measuring the altitude of hostile aëroplanes for the guns.

"At some anti-aircraft batteries," he explained, "they have the telemeter for that purpose. But here there is none. So they use the system of *visée laterale,* or side sight, literally."

He explained it all carefully to me. I understood it at the time, I think.

I remember saying it was perfectly clear, and a child could do it, and a number of other things. But the system of *visée laterale* has gone into that part of my mind which contains the Latin irregular verbs, harmonies, the catechism and answers to riddles.

There is a curious feeling that comes with the firing of a large battery at an unseen enemy. One moment the air is still; there is a peaceful plain round. The sun shines, and heavy cart horses, drawing a wagon filled with stones for repairing a road, are moving forward steadily, their heads down, their feet sinking deep in the mud. The next moment hell breaks loose. The great guns stand with smoking jaws. The message of death has gone forth. Over beyond the field and that narrow line of trees, what has happened? A great noise, the furious recoiling of the guns, an upcurling of smoke—that is the firing of a battery. But over there, perhaps, one man, or twenty, or fifty men, lying still.

So I required assurance that this battery was not being fired for me. I had no morbid curiosity as to batteries. One of the officers assured me that I need have no concern. Though they were firing earlier than had been intended, a German battery had been located and it was their instructions to disable it.

The battery had been well concealed.

"No German aëroplane has as yet discovered it," explained the officer in charge.

To tell the truth, I had not yet discovered it myself. We had alighted from the machine in a sea of mud. There was mud everywhere.

A farmhouse to the left stood inaccessible in it. Down the road a few feet a tree with an observation platform rose out of it. A few chickens waded about in it. A crowd of soldiers stood at a respectful distance and watched us. But I saw no guns.

One of the officers stooped and picked up the cast shoe of a battery horse, and shaking the mud off, presented it to me.

"To bring you luck," he said, "and perhaps luck to the battery!"

We left the road, and turning to the right made a floundering progress across a field to a hedge. Only when we were almost there did I realise that the hedge was the battery.

"We built it," said the officer in charge. "We brought the trees and saplings and constructed it. Madame did not suspect?"

Madame had not suspected. There were other hedges in the neighbourhood, and the artificial one had been well contrived. Halfway through the field the party paused by a curious elevation, flat, perhaps twenty feet across and circular.

"The cyclone cellar!" some one said. "We will come here during the return fire."

But one look down the crude steps decided me to brave the return fire and die in the open. The cave below the flat roof, turf-covered against the keen eyes of aëroplanes, was full of water. The officers watched my expression and smiled.

And now we had reached the battery, and eager gunners were tearing away the trees and shrubbery that covered them. In an incredible space of time the great grey guns, sinister, potential of death, lay open to the bright sky. The crews gathered round, each man to his place. The shell was pushed home, the gunners held the lanyards.

"Open your mouth wide," said the officer in charge, and gave the signal.

The great steel throats were torn open. The monsters recoiled, as if aghast at what they had done. Their white smoke curled from the muzzles. The dull horses in the road lifted their heads.

And over there, beyond the line of poplar trees, what?

One by one they fired the great guns. Then all together, several rounds. The air was torn with noise. Other batteries, far and near, took up the echo. The lassitude of the deadlock was broken.

And then overhead the bursting shell of a German gun. The return fire had commenced!

I had been under fire before. The sound of a bursting shell was not a new one. But there had always before been a strong element of chance in my favour. When the Germans were shelling a town, who was I that a shell should pick me out to fall on or to explode near? But this was different. They were firing at a battery, and I was beside that battery. It was all very well for the officer in charge to have said they had never located his battery. I did not believe him. I still doubt him. For another shell came.

The soldiers from the farmhouse had gathered behind us in the field. I turned and looked at them. They were smiling. So I summoned a shaky smile myself and refused the hospitality of the cellar full of water.

One of the troopers stepped out from the others.

"We have just completed a small bridge," he said— "a bridge over the canal. Will madame do us the honour of walking across it? It will thus be inaugurated by the only lady at the front."

Madame would. Madame did. But without any real enthusiasm. The men cheered, and another German shell came, and everything was merry as a marriage bell.

They invited me to climb the ladder to the lookout in the tree and look at the enemy's trenches. But under the circumstances I declined. I felt that it was time to move on and get hence. The honour of being the only woman who had got to the front at Ypres began to weigh heavy on me. I mentioned the passing of time and the condition of the roads.

So at last I got into the car. The officers of the battery bowed, and the men, some fifty of them, gave me three rousing cheers. I think of them now, and there is a lump in my throat. They were so interested, so smiling and cheery, that bright late February afternoon, standing in the mud of the battlefield of Ypres, with German shells bursting overhead. Half of them, even then, had been killed or wounded. Each day took its toll of some of them, one way or another.

How many of them are left to-day? The smiling officer, so debonair, so proud of his hidden battery, where is he? The tiny bridge, has it run red this last week? The watchman in the tree, what did he see, that terrible day when the Germans got across the canal and charged over the flat lands?

The Germans claim to have captured guns at or near this place. One thing I am sure of: This battery or another, it was not taken while there were men belonging to it to defend it. The bridge would run red and the water under the bridge, the muddy field be strewn with bodies, before those cheery, cool-eyed and indomitable French gunners would lose their guns.

The car moved away, fifty feet, a hundred feet, and turned out to avoid an ammunition wagon, disabled in the road. It was fatal. We slid off into the mire and settled down. I looked back at the battery. A fresh shell was bursting high in the air.

We sat there, interminable hours that were really minutes, while an orderly and the chauffeur dug us out with spades. We conversed of other things. But it was a period of uneasiness on my part. And, as if to point the lesson and adorn the tale, away to the left, rising above the plain, was the church roof with the hole in it—mute evidence that even the mantle of righteousness is no protection against a shell.

Our course was now along a road just behind the trenches and paralleling them, to an anti-aircraft station.

I have seen a number of anti-aircraft stations at the front: English ones near the coast and again south of Ypres; guns mounted, as was this French battery, on the plain of a battlefield; isolated cannon in towers and on the tops of buildings and water tanks. I have seen them in action, firing at hostile planes. I have never yet seen them do any damage, but they serve a useful purpose in keeping the scouting machines high in the air, thus rendering difficult the work of the enemy's observer. The real weapon against the hostile aëroplane is another machine. Several times I have seen German *Taubes* driven off by French aviators, and winging a swift flight back to their lines. Not, one may be sure, through any lack of courage on the part of German aviators. They are fearless and extremely skilful. But because they have evidently been instructed to conserve their machines.

I had considerable curiosity as to the anti-aircraft batteries. How was it possible to manipulate a large field gun, with a target moving at a varying height, and at a speed velocity of, say, sixty miles an hour?

The answer was waiting on the field just north of Ypres.

A brick building by the road was evidently a storehouse for provisions for the trenches. Unloaded in front of it were sacks of bread, meal and provisions. And standing there in the sunshine was the commander of the field battery, Captain Mignot. A tall and bearded man, essentially grave, he listened while Lieutenant Puaux explained the request from General Foch that I see his battery. He turned and scanned the sky.

"We regret," he said seriously, "that at the moment there is no aëroplane in sight. We will, however, show Madame everything."

He led the way round the corner of the building to where a path, neatly banked, went out through the mud to the battery.

"Keep to the path," said a tall sign. But there was no temptation to do otherwise. There must have been fifty acres to that field, unbroken by hedge or tree. As we walked out, Captain Mignot paused and pointed his finger up and somewhat to the right.

"German shrapnel!" he said. True enough, little spherical clouds told where it had burst harmlessly.

As cannonading had been going on steadily all the afternoon, no one paid any particular attention. We walked on in the general direction of the trenches.

The gunners were playing prisoner's base just beyond the guns. When they saw us coming the game ceased, and they hurried to their stations. Boys they were, most of them. The youth of the French troops had not impressed me so forcibly as had the boyishness of the English and the Belgians. They are not so young, on an average, I believe. But also the deception of maturity is caused by a general indifference to shaving while in the field.

But Captain Mignot evidently had his own ideas of military smartness, and these lads were all cleanshaven. They trooped in from their game, under that little cloud of shrapnel smoke that still hung in the sky, for all the world a crowd of overheated and self-conscious schoolboys receiving an unexpected visit from the master of the school.

The path ended at the battery. In the centre of the guns was a raised platform of wood, and a small shelter house for the observer or officer on duty. There were five guns in pits round this focal point and forming a circle. And on the platform in the centre was a curious instrument on a tripod.

"The telemeter," explained Captain Mignot; "for obtaining the altitude of the enemy's aëroplane."

Once again we all scanned the sky anxiously, but uselessly.

"I don't care to have any one hurt," I said; "but if a plane is coming I wish it would come now. Or a Zeppelin."

The captain's serious face lighted in a smile.

"A Zeppelin!" he said. "We would with pleasure wait all the night for a Zeppelin!"

He glanced round at the guns. Every gunner was in his place. We were to have a drill.

"We will suppose," he said, "that a German aëroplane is approaching. To fire correctly we must first know its altitude. So we discover that with this." He placed his hand on the telemeter. "There are, you observe, two apertures, one for each eye. In one the aëroplane is seen right side up. In the other the image is inverted, upside down. Now! By this screw the images are made to approach, until one is superimposed exactly over the other. Immediately on the lighted dial beneath is shown the altitude, in metres."

I put my eyes to the openings, and tried to imagine an aëroplane overhead, manœuvring to drop a bomb or a dart on me while I calculated its altitude. I could not do it.

Next I was shown the guns. They were the famous seventy-five-millimetre guns of France, transformed into aircraft guns by the simple expedient of installing them in a pit with sloping sides, so that their noses pointed up and out. To swing them round, so that they pointed readily toward any portion of the sky, a circular framework of planks formed a round rim to the pit, and on this runway, heavily greased, the muzzles were swung about.

The gun drill began. It was executed promptly, skilfully. There was no bungling, not a wrong motion or an unnecessary one, as they went through the movements of loading, sighting and firing the guns. It was easy to see why French artillery has won its renown. The training of the French artilleryman is twice as severe as that of the infantryman. Each man, in addition to knowing his own work on the gun, must be able to do the work of all the eleven others. Casualties must occur, and in spite of them the work of the gun must go on.

Casualties had occurred at that station. More than half the original battery was gone. The little shelter house was splintered in a hundred places. There were shell holes throughout the field, and the breech of one gun had recently been shattered and was undergoing repair.

The drill was over and the gunners stood at attention. I asked permission to photograph the battery, and it was cheerfully given. One after the other I took the guns, until I had taken four. The gunners waited smilingly expectant. For the last gun I found I had no film, but I could not let it go at that. So I pointed the empty camera at it and snapped the shutter. It would never do to show discrimination.

Somewhere in London are all those pictures. They have never been sent to me. No doubt a watchful English government pounced on them in the mail, and, in connection with my name, based on them most unjust suspicions. They were very interesting. There was Captain Mignot, and the two imposing officers from General Foch's staff; there were smiling young French gunners; there was the telemeter, which cost, they told me, ten thousand francs, and surely deserved to have its picture taken, and there was one, not too steady, of a patch of sunny sky and a balloon-shaped white cloud, where another German shrapnel had burst overhead.

The drill was over. We went back along the path toward the road. Behind the storehouse the evening meal was preparing in a shed. The battery was to have a new ration that night for a change, bacon and codfish. Potatoes were being pared into a great kettle and there was a bowl of eggs on a stand. It appeared to me, accustomed to the meagre ration of the Belgians, that the French were dining well that night on the plains of Ypres.

In a stable near at hand a horse whinnied. I patted him as I passed, and he put his head against my shoulder.

"He recognises you!" said Captain Boisseau. "He too is American."

It was late afternoon by that time. The plan to reach the advanced trenches was frustrated by an increasing fusillade from the front. There were barbed-wire entanglements everywhere, and every field was honeycombed with trenches. One looked across the plain and saw nothing. Then suddenly as we advanced great gashes cut across the fields, and in these gashes, although not a head was seen, were men. The firing was continuous. And now, going down a road, with a line of poplar trees at the foot and the setting sun behind us throwing out faint shadows far ahead, we saw the flash of water. It was very near. It was the flooded river and the canal. Beyond, eight hundred yards or less from where we stood, were the Germans. To one side the inundation made a sort of bay.

It was along this part of the field that the Allies expected the German Army to make its advance when the spring movement commenced. And as nearly as can be learned from the cabled accounts that is where the attack was made.

A captain from General d'Urbal's staff met us at the trenches, and pointed out the strategical value of a certain place, the certainty of a German advance, and the preparations that were made to meet it.

It was odd to stand there in the growing dusk, looking across to where was the invading army, only a little over two thousand feet away. It was rather horrible to see that beautiful landscape, the untravelled road ending in the line of poplars, so very close, where were the French outposts, and the shining water just beyond, and talk so calmly of the death that was waiting for the first Germans who crossed the canal.

CHAPTER XIX

"I NIBBLE THEM"

I WENT into the trenches. The captain was very proud of them.

"They represent the latest fashion in trenches!" he explained, smiling faintly.

It seemed to me that I could easily have improved on that latest fashion. The bottom was full of mud and water. Standing in the trench, I could see over the side by making an effort. The walls were wattled —that is, covered with an interlacing of fagots which made the sides dry.

But it was not for that reason only that these trenches were called the latest fashion. They were divided, every fifteen feet or so, by a bulwark of earth about two feet thick, round which extended a communication trench.

"The object of dividing these trenches in this manner is to limit the havoc of shells that drop into them," the captain explained. "Without the earth bulwark a shell can kill every man in the trench. In this way it can kill only eight. Now stand at this end of the trench. What do you see?"

What I saw was a barbed-wire entanglement, leading into a cul-de-sac.

"A rabbit trap!" he said. "They will come over the field there, and because they cannot cross the entanglement they will follow it. It is built like a great letter V, and this is the point."

The sun had gone down to a fiery death in the west. The guns were firing intermittently. Now and then from the poplar trees came the sharp ping of a rifle. The evening breeze had sprung up, ruffling the surface of the water, and bringing afresh that ever-present and hideous odour of the battlefield. Behind us the trenches showed signs of activity as the darkness fell.

Suddenly the rabbit trap and the trench grew unspeakably loathsome and hideous to me. What a mockery, this business of killing men! No matter that beyond the canal there lurked the menace of a foe that had himself shown unspeakable barbarity and resource in plotting death. No matter if the very odour that stank in my nostrils called loud for vengeance. I thought of German prisoners I had seen, German wounded responding so readily to kindness and a smile. I saw them driven across that open space, at the behest of frantic officers who were obeying a guiding ambition from behind. I saw them herded like cattle, young men and boys and the fathers of families, in that cruel rabbit trap and shot by men who, in their turn, were protecting their country and their homes.

I have in my employ a German gardener. He has been a member of the household for years. He has raised, or helped to raise, the children, has planted the trees, and helped them, like the children, through their early weakness. All day long he works in the garden among his flowers. He coaxes and pets them, feeds them, moves them about in the sun. When guests arrive, it is Wilhelm's genial smile that greets them. When the small calamities of a household occur, it is Wilhelm's philosophy that shows us how to meet them.

Wilhelm was a sergeant in the German Army for five years. Now he is an American citizen, owning his own home, rearing his children to a liberty his own childhood never knew.

But, save for the accident of emigration, Wilhelm would to-day be in the German Army. He is not young, but he is not old. His arms and shoulders are mighty. But for the accident of emigration, then, Wilhelm, working to-day in the sun among his Delphiniums and his iris, his climbing roses and flowering shrubs, would be wearing the helmet of the invader; for his vine-covered house he would have substituted a trench; for his garden pick a German rifle.

For Wilhelm was a faithful subject of Germany while he remained there. He is a Socialist. He does not believe in war. Live and help others to live is his motto. But at the behest of the Kaiser, Wilhelm too would have gone to his appointed place.

It was of Wilhelm then, and others of his kind, that I thought as I stood in the end of the new-fashion trench, looking at the rabbit trap. There must be many Wilhelms in the German Army, fathers, good citizens, kindly men who had no thought of a place in the sun except for the planting of a garden. Men who have followed the false gods of their country with the ardent blue eyes of supreme faith.

I asked to be taken home.

On the way to the machine we passed a *mitrailleuse* buried by the roadside. Its location brought an argument among the officers. Strategically it would be valuable for a time, but there was some question as to its position in view of a retirement by the French.

I could not follow the argument. I did not try to. I was cold and tired, and the red sunset had turned to deep purple and gold. The guns had ceased. Over all the countryside brooded the dreadful peace of sheer exhaustion and weariness. And in the air, high overhead, a German plane sailed slowly home.

Sentries halted us on the way back holding high lanterns that set the bayonets of their guns to gleaming. Faces pressed to the glass, they surveyed us stolidly, making sure that we were as our passes described us. Long lines of marching men turned out to let us pass. As darkness settled down, the location of the German line, as it encircled Ypres, was plainly shown by floating *fusées*. In every hamlet reserves were lining up for the trenches, dark masses of men, with here and there a face thrown into relief as a match was held to light a cigarette. Open doors showed warm, lamp-lit interiors and the glow of fires.

I sat back in the car and listened while the officers talked together. They were speaking of General Joffre, of his great ability, of his confidence in the outcome of the war, and of his method, during those winter months when, with such steady fighting, there had been so little apparent movement. One of the officers told me that General Joffre had put his winter tactics in three words:

"I nibble them."

CHAPTER XX

DUNKIRK: FROM MY JOURNAL

I WAKENED early this morning and went to church—a great empty place, very cold but with the red light of the sanctuary lamp burning before a shrine. There were perhaps a dozen people there when I went in. Before the Mater Dolorosa two women in black were praying with upturned eyes. At the foot of the Cross crouched the tragic figure of the Mother, with her dead Son in her arms. Before her were these other mothers, praying in the light of the thin burning candles. Far away, near the altar, seven women of the Society of the Holy Rosary were conducting a private service. They were market women, elderly, plain, raising to the altar faces full of faith and devotion, as they prayed for France and for their soldier-children.

Here and there was a soldier or a sailor on his knees on a low prie-dieu, his cap dangling loose in his hands. Unlike the women, the lips of these men seldom moved in prayer; they apparently gazed in wordless adoration at the shrine. Great and swelling thoughts were theirs, no doubt, kindled by that tiny red flame: thoughts too big for utterance or even for form. To go out and fight for France, to drive back the invaders, and, please God, to come back again—that was what their faces said.

Other people came in, mostly women, who gathered silently around the Mater Dolorosa. The great empty Cross; the woman and the dead Christ at the foot of it; the quiet, kneeling people before it; over all, as the services began, the silvery bell of the Mass; the bending backs of the priests before the altar; the sound of fresh, boyish voices singing in the choir—that is early morning service in the great Gothic church at Dunkirk.

Onto this drab and grey and grieving picture came the morning sunlight, through roof-high windows of red and yellow and of that warm violet that glows like a jewel. The candles paled in the growing light. A sailor near me gathered up his cap, which had fallen unheeded to the floor, and went softly out. The private service was over; the market women picked up their baskets and, bowing to the altar, followed the sailor. The great organ pleaded and cried out. I stole out. I was an intruder, gazing at the grief of a nation.

It was a transformed square that I walked through on my way back to the hotel. It was a market morning. All week long it had been crowded with motor ambulances, lorries, passing guns. Orderlies had held cavalry horses under the shadow of the statue in the centre. The fried-potato-seller's van had exuded an appetising odour of cooking, and had gathered round it crowds of marines in tam-o'-shanters with red woollen balls in the centre, Turcos in great bloomers, and the always-hungry French and Belgian troopers.

Now all was changed. The square had become a village filled with canvas houses, the striped red-and-white booths of the market people. War had given way to peace. For the clattering of accoutrements were substituted high-pitched haggling, the cackling of geese in crates, the squawks of chickens tied by the leg.

Little boys in pink-checked gingham aprons ran about or stood, feet apart, staring with frank curiosity at tall East Indians.

There were small and carefully cherished baskets of eggs and bundles of dead Belgian hares hung by the ears, but no other fresh meats. There was no fruit, no fancy bread. The vegetable sellers had only Brussels sprouts, turnips, beets and the small round potatoes of the country. For war has shorn the market of its gaiety. Food is scarce and high. The flower booths are offering country laces and finding no buyers. The fruit sellers have only shrivelled apples to sell.

Now, at a little after midday, the market is over. The canvas booths have been taken down, packed on small handcarts and trundled away; unsold merchandise is on its way back to the farm to wait for another week and another market. Already the market square has taken on its former martial appearance, and Dunkirk is at its midday meal of rabbit and Brussels sprouts.

CHAPTER XXI

TEA WITH THE AIR-FIGHTERS

LATER: Roland Garros, the French aviator, has just driven off a German *Taube*. They both circled low over the town for some time. Then the German machine started east with Garros in pursuit. They have gone out of sight.

War is not all grey and grim and hideous. It has its lighter moments. The more terrible a situation the more keen is human nature to forget it for a time. Men play between shells in the trenches. London, suffering keenly, flocks to a comedy or a farce as a relief from strain. Wounded men, past their first agony, chaff each other in the hospitals. There are long hours behind the lines when people have tea and try to forget for a little while what is happening just ahead.

Some seven miles behind the trenches, in that vague "Somewhere in France," the British Army had established a naval air-station, where one of its dirigible airships was kept. In good weather the airship went out on reconnoissance. It was not a large airship, as such things go, and was formerly a training ship. Now it was housed in an extemporised hangar that was once a carwheel works, and made its ascent from a plain surrounded by barbed wire.

The airship men were extremely hospitable, and I

made several visits to the station. On the day of which I am about to write I was taken for an exhaustive tour of the premises, beginning with the hangar and ending with tea. Not that it really ended with tea. Tea was rather a beginning, leading to all sorts of unexpected and surprising things.

The airship was out when I arrived, and a group of young officers was watching it, a dot on the horizon near the front. They gave me the glasses, and I saw it plainly—a long, yellowish, slowly moving object that turned as I looked and headed back for the station.

The group watched the sky carefully. A German aëroplane could wreck the airship easily. But although there were planes in sight none was of the familiar German lines.

It came on. Now one could see the car below. A little closer and three dots were the men in it. On the sandy plain which is the landing field were waiting the men whose work it is to warp the great balloon into its hangar. The wind had come up and made landing difficult. It was necessary to make two complete revolutions over the field before coming down. Then the blunt yellow nose dipped abruptly. The men below caught the ropes, the engine was cut off, and His Majesty's airship, in shape and colour not unlike a great pig, was safely at home again and being led to the stable.

"Do you want to know the bravest man in all the world?" one of the young officers said. "Because here he is. The funny thing about it is he doesn't know he is brave."

That is how I met Colonel M——, who is England's greatest airship man and who is in charge of the naval air station.

"If you had come a little sooner," he said, "you could have gone out with us."

I was grateful but unenthusiastic. I had seen the officers watching the sky for German planes. I had a keen idea that a German aviator overhead, armed with a Belgian block or a bomb or a dart, could have ripped that yellow envelope open from stem to stern, and robbed American literature of one of its shining lights. Besides, even in times of peace I am afraid to look out of a third-story window.

We made a tour of the station, which had been a great factory before the war began, beginning with the hangar in which the balloon was now safely housed.

Entrance to the station is by means of a bridge over a canal. The bridge is guarded by sentries and the password of the day is necessary to gain admission. East and west along the canal are canal boats that have been painted grey and have guns mounted on them. Side by side with these gunboats are the ordinary canal boats of the region, serving as homes for that part of the populace which remains, with women knitting on the decks or hanging out lines of washing overhead.

The endless traffic of a main highroad behind the lines passes the station day and night. Chauffeurs drop in to borrow petrol or to repair their cars; visiting officers from other stations come to watch the airship perform. For England has been slow to believe in the airships, pinning her aëronautical faith to heavier-than-air machines. She has considered the great expense for building and upkeep of each of these dirigible balloons—as much as that of fifty aëroplanes—the necessity of providing hangars for them, and their vulnerability to attack, as overbalancing the advantages of long range, silence as they drift with the wind with engines cut off, and ability to hover over a given spot and thus launch aërial bombs more carefully.

There is a friendly rivalry between the two branches of the air service, and so far in this war the credit apparently goes to the aëroplanes. However, until the war is over, and Germany definitely states what part her Zeppelins have had in both sea and land attacks, it will be impossible to make any fair comparison.

The officers at the naval air station had their headquarters in the administration building of the factory, a long brick building facing the road. Here in a long room with western windows they rested and relaxed, dined and talked between their adventurous excursions to the lines.

Day by day these men went out, some in the airship for a reconnoissance, others to man observation balloons. Day by day it was uncertain who would come back.

But they were very cheerful. Officers with an hour to spare came up from the gunboats in the canal to smoke a pipe by the fire. Once in so often a woman came, stopping halfway her frozen journey to a soup kitchen or a railroad station, where she looked after wounded soldiers, to sit in the long room and thaw out; visiting officers from other parts of the front dropped in for a meal, sure of a welcome and a warm fire. As compared with the trenches, or even with the gunboats on the canal, the station represented cheer, warmth; even, after the working daylight hours, society.

There were several buildings. Outside near the bridge was the wireless building, where an operator sat all the time with his receivers over his ears. Not far from the main group was the great hangar of the airship, and to that we went first. The hangar had been a machine shop with a travelling crane. It had been partially cleared but the crane still towered at one end. High above it, reached by a ladder, was a door.

The young captain of the airship pointed up to it.

"My apartments!" he said.

"Do you mean to say that you sleep here?" I asked. For the building was bitterly cold; one end had been knocked out to admit the airship, and the wall had been replaced by great curtains of sailcloth to keep out the wind.

"Of course," he replied. "I am always within call. There are sentries also to guard the ship. It would be very easy to put it out of commission."

The construction of the great balloon was explained to me carefully. It was made of layer after layer of gold-beater's skin and contained two ballonets—a small ship compared to the Zeppelins, and non-rigid in type.

Underneath the great cigar-shaped bag hangs an aluminum car which carries a crew of three men. The pilot sits in front at a wheel that resembles the driving wheel of an automobile. Just behind him is the observer, who also controls the wireless. The engineer is the third man.

The wireless puzzled me. "Do you mean that when you go out on scouting expeditions you can communicate with the station here?" I asked.

"It is quite possible. But when the airship goes out a wireless van accompanies it, following along the roads. Messages are picked up by the van and by a telephone connection sent to the various batteries."

It may be well to mention again the airship chart system by which the entire region is numbered and lettered in small squares. Black lines drawn across the detail map of the neighbourhood divide it into lettered squares, A, B, C, and so forth, and these lettered squares are again subdivided into four small squares, 1, 2, 3, 4. Thus the direction B 4, or N 2, is a very specific one in directing the fire of a battery.

"Did you accomplish much to-day?" I inquired.

"Not as much as usual. There is a ground haze," replied Colonel M——, who had been the observer in that day's flight. "Down here it is not so noticeable, but from above it obscures everything."

He explained the difficulties of the airship builder, the expense and tendency to "pinholes" of gold-beaters' skin, the curious fact that chemists had so far failed to discover a gasproof varnish.

"But of course," he said, "those things will come. The airship is the machine of the future. Its stability, its power to carry great weights, point to that. The difference between an airship and an aëroplane is the difference between a battleship and a submarine. Each has its own field of usefulness."

All round lay great cylinders of pure hydrogen, used for inflating the balloon. Smoking in the hangar was forbidden. The incessant wind rattled the great canvas curtains and whistled round the rusting crane. From the shop next door came the hammering of machines, for the French Government has put the mill to work again.

We left the hangar and walked past the machine shop. Halfway along one of its sides a tall lieutenant pointed to a small hole in the land, leading under the building.

"The French government has sent here," he said, "the men who are unfit for service in the army. Day by day, as German aëroplanes are seen overhead, the alarm is raised in the shop. The men are panic-stricken. If there are a dozen alarms they do the same thing. They rush out like frightened rabbits, throw themselves flat on the sand, and wriggle through that hole into a cave that they have dug underneath. It is hysterically funny; they all try to get in at the same time."

I had hoped to see the thing happen myself. But when, late that afternoon, a German aëroplane actually flew over the station, the works had closed down for the day and the men were gone. It was disappointing.

Between the machine shop and the administration building is a tall water tower. On top of this are two observers who watch the sky day and night. An anti-aircraft gun is mounted there and may be swung to command any portion of the sky. This precaution is necessary, for the station has been the object of frequent attacks. The airship itself has furnished a tempting mark to numerous German airmen. Its best speed is forty miles an hour, so they are able to circle about it and attack it from various directions. As it has only two ballonets, a single shot, properly placed, could do it great damage. The Zeppelin, with its eighteen great gasbags, can suffer almost any amount of attack and still remain in the air.

"Would you like to see the trenches?" said one of the officers, smiling.

"Trenches? Seven miles behind the line?"

"Trenches certainly. If the German drive breaks through it will come along this road."

"But I thought you lived in the administration building?"

"Some of us must hold the trenches," he said solemnly. "What are six or seven miles to the German Army? You should see the letters of sympathy we get from home!"

So he showed me the trenches. They were extremely nice trenches, dug out of the sand, it is true, but almost luxurious for all that, more like rooms than ditches, with board shelves and dishes on the shelves, egg cups and rows of shining glasses, silver spoons, neat little folded napkins, and, though the beds were on the floor, extremely tidy beds of mattresses and warm blankets. The floor was boarded over. There was a chair or two, and though I will not swear to pictures on the walls there were certainly periodicals and books. Outside the door was a sort of vestibule of boards which had been built to keep the wind out.

"You see!" said the young officer with twinkling eyes. "But of course this is war. One must put up with things!"

Nevertheless it was a real trench, egg cups and rows of shining glasses and electric light and all. It was there for a purpose. In front of it was a great barbed-wire barricade. Strategically it commanded the main road over which the German Army must pass to reach the point it has been striving for. Only seven miles away along that road it was straining even then for the onward spring movement. Any day now, and that luxurious trench may be the scene of grim and terrible fighting.

And, more than that, these men at the station were not waiting for danger to come to them. Day after day they were engaged in the most perilous business of the war.

At this station some of the queer anomalies of a volunteer army were to be found. So strongly ingrained in the heart of the British youth of good family is the love of country, that when he is unable to get his commission he goes in any capacity. I heard of a little chap, too small for the regular service, who has gone to the front as a cook! His uncle sits in the House of Lords. And here, at this naval air station, there were young noncommissioned officers who were Honourables, and who were trying their best to live it down. One such youth was in charge of the great van that is the repair shop for the airship. Others were in charge of the wireless station. One met them everywhere, clear-eyed young Englishmen ready and willing to do anything, no matter what, and proving every moment of their busy day the essential democracy of the English people.

As we went into the administration building that afternoon two things happened: The observers in the water tower reported a German aëroplane coming toward the station, and a young lieutenant, who had gone to the front in a borrowed machine, reported that he had broken the wind shield of the machine. There are plenty of German aëroplanes at that British airship station, but few wind shields. The aëroplane was ignored, but the wind shield was loudly and acrimoniously discussed.

The day was cold and had turned grey and lowering. It was pleasant after our tour of the station to go into the long living room and sit by the fire. But the fire smoked. One after another those dauntless British officers attacked it, charged with poker, almost with bayonet, and retired defeated. So they closed it up finally with a curious curved fire screen and let it alone. It was ten minutes after I began looking at the fire screen before I recognised it for what it was— the hood from an automobile!

Along one side of the wall was a piano. It had been brought back from a ruined house at the front. It was rather a poor piano and no one had any music, but some of the officers played a little by ear. The top of the piano was held up by a bandage! It was a piano of German make, and the nameplate had been wrenched off!

A long table filled the centre of the room. One end formed the press censorship bureau, for it was part of the province of the station to censor and stamp letters going out. The other end was the dining table. Over the fireplace on the mantel was a baby's shoe, a little brown shoe picked up on the street of a town that was being destroyed.

Beside it lay an odd little parachute of canvas with a weighted letter-carrier beneath. One of the officers saw me examining it and presented it to me, as it was worn and past service.

"Now and then," he explained, "it is impossible to use the wireless, for one reason or another. In that case a message can be dropped by means of the parachute."

I brought the message-carrier home with me. On its weighted canvas bag is written in ink: "Urgent! You are requested to forward this at once to the inclosed address. From His Majesty's airship ——."

The sight of the press-censor stamp reminded an English officer, who had lived in Belgium, of the way letters to and from interned Belgians have been taken over the frontier into Holland and there dispatched. Men who are willing to risk their lives for money collect these letters. At one time the price was as high as two hundred francs for each one. When enough have been gathered together to make the risk worth while the bearer starts on his journey. He must slip through the sentry lines disguised as a workman, or perhaps by crawling through the barbed wire at the barrier. For fear of capture some of these bearers, working their way through the line at night, have dragged their letters behind them, so that in case of capture they could drop the cord and be found without incriminating evidence on them. For taking letters into Belgium the process is naturally reversed. But letters are sent, not to names, but to numbers. The bearer has a list of numbers which correspond to certain addresses. Thus, even if he is taken and the letters are found on him, their intended recipients will not be implicated. I saw a letter which had been received in this way by a Belgian woman. It was addressed simply to Number Twenty-eight.

The fire was burning better behind its automobile hood. An orderly had brought in tea, white bread, butter, a pitcher of condensed cream, and an English teacake. We gathered round the tea table. War seemed a hundred miles away. Except for the blue uniforms and brass buttons of the officers who belonged to the naval air service, the orderly's khaki and the bayonet from a gun used casually at the other end of the table as a paperweight, it was an ordinary English tea.

CHAPTER XXII

THE WOMEN AT THE FRONT

IT was commencing to rain outside. The rain beat on the windows and made even the reluctant fire seem cosy. Some one had had a box of candy sent from home. It was brought out and presented with a flourish.

"It is frightful, this life in the trenches!" said the young officer who passed it about.

Shortly afterward the party was increased. An orderly came in and announced that an Englishwoman, whose automobile had broken down, was standing on the bridge over the canal and asked to be admitted. She did not know the password and the sentry refused to let her pass by.

One of the officers went out and returned in a few moments with a small lady much wrapped in veils and extremely wet. She stood blinking in the doorway in the accustomed light. She was recognised at once as a well-known English novelist who is conducting a soup kitchen at a railroad station three miles behind the Belgian front.

"A car was to have picked me up," she said, "but I have walked and walked and it has not come. And I am so cold. Is that tea? And may I come to the fire?"

So they settled her comfortably, with her feet

thrust out to the blaze, and gave her hot tea and plenty of bread and butter.

"It is like the Mad Hatter's tea party in Alice in Wonderland," said one of the officers gaily. "When any fresh person drops in we just move up one place."

The novelist sipped her tea and told me about her soup kitchen.

"It is so very hard to get things to put into the soup," she said. "Of course I have no car, and now with the new law that no women are to be allowed in military cars I hardly know what to do."

"Will you tell me just what you do?" I asked. So she told me, and later I saw her soup kitchen.

"Men come in from the front," she explained, "injured and without food. Often they have had nothing to eat for a long time. We make soup of whatever meat we can find and any vegetables, and as the hospital trains come in we carry it out to the men. They are so very grateful for it."

That was to be an exceptional afternoon at the naval air-station. For hardly had the novelist been settled with her tea when two very attractive but strangely attired young women came into the room. They nodded to the officers, whom they knew, and went at once to the business which had brought them.

"Can you lend us a car?" they asked. "Ours has gone off the road into the mud, and it looks as though it would never move again."

That was the beginning of a very strange evening, almost an extraordinary evening. For while the novelist was on her way back to peace these young women were on their way home.

And home to them was one room of a shattered house directly on the firing line.

Much has been said about women at the front. As far as I know at that time there were only two women absolutely at the front. Nurses as a rule are kept miles behind the line. Here and there a soup kitchen, like that just spoken of, has held its courageous place three or four miles back along the lines of communication.

I have said that they were extraordinarily dressed. Rather they were most practically dressed. Under khaki-coloured leather coats these two young women wore khaki riding breeches with puttees and flannel shirts. They had worn nothing else for six months. They wore knitted caps on their heads, for the weather was extremely cold, and mittens.

The fire was blazing high and we urged them to take off their outer wraps. For a reason which we did not understand at the time they refused. They sat with their leather coats buttoned to the throat, and coloured violently when urged to remove them.

"But what are you doing here?" said one of the officers. "What brings you so far from P——"

They said they had had an errand, and went on drinking tea.

"What sort of an errand?" a young lieutenant demanded.

They exchanged glances.

"Shopping," they said, and took more tea.

"Shopping, for what?" He was smilingly impertinent.

They hesitated. Then: "For mutton," one of them replied. Both looked relieved. Evidently the mutton was an inspiration. "We have found some mutton." They turned to me. "It is a real festival. You have no idea how long it is since we've had anything of the sort."

"Mutton!" cried the novelist, with frankly greedy eyes. "It makes wonderful soup! Where can I get it?"

They told her, and she stood up, tied on her seven veils and departed, rejoicing, in a car that had come for her.

When she was gone Colonel M—— turned to one of the young women.

"Now," he said, "out with it. What brings you both so far from your thriving and prosperous little community?"

The irony of that was lost on me until later, when I discovered that the said community was a destroyed town with the advance line of trenches running through it, and that they lived in the only two whole rooms in the place.

"Out with it," said the colonel, and scowled ferociously.

Driven into a corner they were obliged to confess. For three hours that afternoon they had stood in a freezing wind on a desolate field, while King Albert of Belgium decorated for bravery various officers and —themselves. The jealously fastened coats were thrown open. Gleaming on the breast of each young woman was the star of the Order of Leopold!

"But why did you not tell us?" the officers demanded.

"Because," was the retort, "you have never approved of us; you have always wanted us sent back to England. The whole British Army has objected to our being where we are."

"Much good the objecting has done!" grumbled

the officers. But in their hearts they were very proud.

Originally there had been three in this valiant little group of young aristocrats who have proved as true as their brothers to the traditions of their race. The third one was the daughter of an earl. She, too, had been decorated. But she had gone to a little town near by a day or two before.

"But what do you do?" I asked one of these young women. She was drawing on her mittens ready to start for their car.

"Sick and sorry work," she said briefly. "You know the sort of thing. I wish you would come out and have dinner with us. There is to be mutton."

I accepted promptly, but it was the situation and not the mutton that appealed to me. It was arranged that they should go ahead and set things in motion for the meal, and that I should follow later.

At the door one of them turned and smiled at me.

"They are shelling the village," she said. "You don't mind, do you?"

"Not at all," I replied. And I meant it. For I was no longer so gun-shy as I had been earlier in the winter. I had got over turning pale at the slamming of a door. I was as terrified, perhaps, but my pride had come to my aid.

It was the English officers who disapproved so thoroughly who told me about them when they had gone.

"Of course they have no business there," they said. "It's a frightful responsibility to place on the men at that part of the line. But there's no question about the value of what they are doing, and if they want to stay they deserve to be allowed to. They go right into the trenches, and they take care of the wounded until the ambulances can come up at night. Wait until you see their house and you will understand why they got those medals."

And when I had seen their house and spent an evening with them I understood very well indeed.

We gathered round the fire; conversation was desultory. Muddy and weary young officers, who had been at the front all day, came in and warmed themselves for a moment before going up to their cold rooms. The owner of the broken wind shield arrived and was placated. Continuous relays of tea were coming and going. Colonel ——, who had been in an observation balloon most of the day, spoke of balloon sickness.

"I have been in balloons of one sort and another for twenty years," he said. "I never overcome the nausea. Very few airmen do."

I spoke to him about a recent night attack by German aviators.

"It is remarkable work," he commented warmly, "hazardous in the extreme; and if anything goes wrong they cannot see where they are coming down. Even when they alight in their own lines, landing safely is difficult. They are apt to wreck their machines."

The mention of German aëroplanes reminded one of the officers of an experience he had had just behind the firing line.

"I had been to the front," he said, "and a mile or so behind the line a German aëroplane overtook the automobile. He flew low, with the evident intention of dropping a bomb on us. The chauffeur, becoming excited, stalled the engine. At that moment the aviator dropped the first bomb, killing a sow and a litter of young pigs beside the car and breaking all the glass. Cranking failed to start the car. It was necessary, while the machine manœuvred to get overhead again, to lift the hood of the engine, examine a spark-plug and then crank the car. He dropped a second bomb which fell behind the car and made a hole in the road. Then at last the engine started, and it took us a very short time to get out of that neighbourhood."

The car he spoke of was the car in which I had come out to the station. I could testify that something had broken the glass!

One of the officers had just received what he said were official percentages of casualties in killed, wounded and missing among the Allies, to the first of February.

The Belgian percentage was 66 2-3, the English 33 1-3, and the French 7. I have no idea how accurate the figures were, or his authority for them. He spoke of them as official. From casualties to hospitals and nurses was but a step. I spoke warmly of the work the nurses near the front were doing. But one officer disagreed with me, although in the main his views were not held by the others.

"The nurses at the base hospitals should be changed every three months," he said. "They get the worst cases there, in incredible conditions. After a time it tells on them. I've seen it in a number of cases. They grow calloused to suffering. That's the time to bring up a new lot."

I think he is wrong. I have seen many hospitals, many nurses. If there is a change in the nurses after a time, it is that, like the soldiers in the field, they develop a philosophy which carries them through their terrible days. "What must be, must be," say the men in the trenches. "What must be, must be," say the nurses in the hospital. And both save themselves from madness.

CHAPTER XXIII

THE LITTLE "SICK AND SORRY" HOUSE

AND now it was seven o'clock, and raining. Dinner was to be at eight. I had before me a drive of nine miles along those slippery roads. It was dark and foggy, with the ground mist of Flanders turning to a fog. The lamps of the car shining into it made us appear to be riding through a milky lake. Progress was necessarily slow.

One of the English officers accompanied me.

"I shall never forget the last time I dined out here," he said as we jolted along. "There is a Belgian battery just behind the house. All evening as we sat and talked I thought the battery was firing; the house shook under tremendous concussion. Every now and then Mrs. K—— or Miss C—— would get up and go out, coming back a few moments later and joining calmly in the conversation.

"Not until I started back did I know that we had been furiously bombarded, that the noise I had heard was shells breaking all about the place. A 'coal-box,' as they call them here, had fallen in the garden and dug a great hole!"

"And when the young ladies went out, were they watching the bombs burst?" I inquired.

"Not at all," he said. "They went out to go into

the trenches to attend to the wounded. They do it all the time."

"And they said nothing about it!"

"They thought we knew. As for going into the trenches, that is what they are there to do."

My enthusiasm for mutton began to fade. I felt convinced that I should not remain calm if a shell fell into the garden. But again, as happened many times during those eventful weeks at the front, my pride refused to allow me to turn back. And not for anything in the world would I have admitted being afraid to dine where those two young women were willing to eat and sleep and have their being day and night for months.

"But of course," I said, "they are well protected, even if they are at the trenches. That is, the Germans never get actually into the town."

"Oh, don't they?" said the officer. "That town has been taken by the Germans five times and lost as many. A few nights ago they got over into the main street and there was terrific hand-to-hand fighting."

"Where do they go at such times?" I asked.

"I never thought about it. I suppose they get into the cellar. But if they do it is not at all because they are afraid."

We went on, until some five of the nine miles had been traversed.

I have said before that the activity at the front commences only with the falling of night. During the day the zone immediately back of the trenches is a dead country. But at night it wakens into activity. Soldiers leave the trenches and fresh soldiers take their places, ammunition and food are brought up, wires broken during the day by shells are replaced, ambulances come up and receive their frightful burdens.

Now we reached the zone of night activity. A travelling battery passed us, moving from one part of the line to another; the drivers, three to each gun, sat stolidly on their horses, their heads dropped against the rain. They appeared out of the mist beside us, stood in full relief for a moment in the glow of the lamps, and were swallowed up again.

At three miles from our destination, but only one mile from the German lines, it was necessary to put out the lamps. Our progress, which had been dangerous enough before, became extremely precarious. It was necessary to turn out for teams and lorries, for guns and endless lines of soldiers, and to turn out a foot too far meant slipping into the mud. Two miles and a half from the village we turned out too far.

There was a sickening side slip. The car turned over to the right at an acute angle and there remained. We were mired!

We got out. It was perfectly dark. Guns were still passing us, so that it was necessary to warn the drivers of our wrecked car. The road was full of shell holes, so that to step was to stumble. The German lines, although a mile away, seemed very near. Between the road and the enemy was not a tree or a shrub or a fence—only the line of the railway embankment which marked the Allies' trenches. To add to the dismalness of the situation the Germans began throwing the familiar magnesium lights overhead. The flares made the night alike beautiful and fearful. It was possible when one burst near to see the entire landscape spread out like a map—ditches full of water, sodden fields, shell holes in the roads which had become lakes, the long lines of poplars outlining the road ahead. At one time no less than twenty starlights hung in the air at one time. When they went out the inky night seemed blacker than ever. I stepped off the road and was almost knee-deep in mud at once.

The battery passed, urging its tired horses to such speed as was possible. After it came thousands of men, Belgian and French mostly, on their way out of the trenches.

We called for volunteers from the line to try to lift the car onto the road. But even with twenty men at the towing rope it refused to move. The men were obliged to give it up and run on to catch their companies.

Between the *fusées* the curious shuffling of feet and a deeper shadow were all that told of the passage of these troops. It was so dark that one could see no faces. But here and there one saw the light of a cigarette. The mere hardship of walking for miles along those roads, paved with round stones and covered with mud on which their feet slipped continually, must have been a great one, and agonizing for feet that had been frosted in the water of the trenches.

Afterward I inquired what these men carried. They loomed up out of the night like pack horses. I found that each soldier carried, in addition to his rifle and bayonet, a large knapsack, a canteen, a cartridge pouch, a brown haversack containing tobacco, soap, towel and food, a billy-can and a rolled blanket.

German batteries were firing intermittently as we stood there. The rain poured down. I had dressed to go out to tea and wore my one and only good hat. I did the only thing that seemed possible—I took off that hat and put it in the automobile and let the rain fall on my unprotected head. The hat had to see me through the campaign, and my hair would stand water.

At last an armoured car came along and pulled the automobile onto the road. But after a progress of only ten feet it lapsed again, and there remained.

The situation was now acute. It was impossible to go back, and to go ahead meant to advance on foot along roads crowded with silent soldiers—meant going forward, too, in a pouring rain and in high-heeled shoes. For that was another idiocy I had committed.

We started on, leaving the apologetic chauffeur by the car. A few feet and the road, curving to the right, began to near the German line. Every now and then it was necessary to call sharply to the troops, or struggling along through the rain they would have crowded us off knee-deep into the mud.

"Attention!" the officer would call sharply. And for a time we would have foot room. There were no more horses, no more guns—only men, men, men. Some of them had taken off their outer coats and put them shawl-fashion over their heads. But most of them walked stolidly on, already too wet and wretched to mind the rain.

The fog had lifted. It was possible to see that sinister red streak that follows the firing of a gun at night. The rain gave a peculiar hollowness to the concussion. The Belgian and French batteries were silent.

We seemed to have walked endless miles, and still there was no little town. We went over a bridge, and on its flat floor I stopped and rested my aching feet.

"Only a little farther now," said the British officer cheerfully.

"How much farther?"

"Not more than a mile."

By way of cheering me he told me about the town we were approaching—how the road we were on was its main street, and that the advanced line of trenches crossed at the railroad near the foot of the street.

"And how far from that are the German trenches?" I asked nervously.

"Not very far," he said blithely. "Near enough to be interesting."

On and on. Here was a barn.

"Is this the town?" I asked feebly.

"Not yet. A little farther!"

I was limping, drenched, irritable. But now and then the absurdity of my situation overcame me and I laughed. Water ran down my head and off my nose, trickled down my neck under my coat. I felt like a great sponge. And suddenly I remembered my hat.

"I feel sure," I said, stopping still in the road, "that the chauffeur will go inside the car out of the rain and sit on my hat."

The officer thought this very likely. I felt extremely bitter about it. The more I thought of it the more I was convinced that he was exactly the sort of chauffeur who would get into a car and sit on an only hat.

At last we came to the town—to what had been a town. It was a town no longer. Walls without roofs, roofs almost without walls. Here and there only a chimney standing of what had been a home; a street so torn up by shells that walking was almost impossible —full of shell-holes that had become graves. There were now no lights, not even soldiers. In the silence our footsteps re-echoed against those desolate and broken walls.

A day or two ago I happened on a description of this town, written by a man who had seen it at the time I was there.

"The main street," he writes, "is like a great museum of prehistoric fauna. The house roofs, denuded of tiles and the joists left naked, have tilted forward on to the sidewalks, so that they hang in mid-air like giant vertebræ. . . . One house only of the whole village of ―― had been spared."

We stumbled down the street toward the trenches and at last stopped before a house. Through boards nailed across what had once been windows a few rays of light escaped. There was no roof; a side wall and an entire corner were gone. It was the residence of the ladies of the decoration.

Inside there was for a moment an illusion of entirety. The narrow corridor that ran through the centre of the house was weatherproof. But through some unseen gap rushed the wind of the night. At the right, warm with lamplight, was the reception room, dining room and bedroom—one small chamber about twelve by fifteen!

What a strange room it was, furnished with odds and ends from the shattered houses about! A bed in the corner; a mattress on the floor; a piano in front of the shell-holed windows, a piano so badly cracked by shrapnel that panels of the woodwork were missing and keys gone; two or three odd chairs and what had once been a bookcase, and in the centre a pine table laid for a meal.

Mrs. K――, whose uncle was a cabinet minister, was hurrying in with a frying-pan in her hand.

"The mutton!" she said triumphantly, and placed it on the table, frying-pan and all. The other lady of the decoration followed with the potatoes, also in the pan in which they had been cooked.

We drew up our chairs, for the mutton must not be allowed to get cold.

"It's quite a party, isn't it?" said one of the hostesses, and showed us proudly the dish of fruit on the centre of the table, flanked by bonbons and nuts which had just been sent from England.

True, the fruit was a little old and the nuts were few; but they gave the table a most festive look.

Some one had taken off my shoes and they were drying by the fire, stuffed with paper to keep them in shape. My soaking outer garments had been carried to the lean-to kitchen to hang by the stove, and dry under the care of a soldier servant who helped with the cooking. I looked at him curiously. His predecessor had been killed in the room where he stood.

The German batteries were firing, and every now and then from the trenches at the foot of the street came the sharp ping of rifles. No one paid any attention. We were warm and sheltered from the wind. What if the town was being shelled and the Germans were only six hundred feet away? We were getting dry, and there was mutton for dinner.

It was a very cheerful party—the two young ladies, and a third who had joined them temporarily, a doctor who was taking influenza and added little to the conversation, the chauffeur attached to the house, who was a count in ordinary times, a Belgian major who had come up from the trenches to have a real meal, and the English officer who had taken me out.

Outside the door stood the major's Congo servant, a black boy who never leaves him, following with dog-like fidelity into the trenches and sleeping outside his door when the major is in billet. He had picked him up in the Congo years before during his active service there.

The meal went on. The frying-pan was passed. The food was good and the talk was better. It was indiscriminately rapid French and English. When it was English I replied. When it was French I ate.

The hostess presented me with a shrapnel case which had arrived that day on the doorstep.

"If you are collecting trophies," said the major, "I shall get you a German sentry this evening. How would you like that?"

There was a reckless twinkle in the major's eye. It developed that he had captured several sentries and liked playing the game.

But I did not know the man. So I said: "Certainly, it would be most interesting."

Whereupon he rose. It took all the combined effort of the dinner party to induce him to sit down and continue his meal. He was vastly disappointed. He was a big man with a humorous mouth. The idea of bringing me a German sentry to take home as a trophy appealed to him.

The meal went on. No one seemed to consider the circumstances extraordinary. Now and then I remembered the story of the street fighting a few nights before. I had an idea that these people would keep on eating and talking English politics quite calmly in the event of a German charge. I wondered if I could live up to my reputation for courage in such a crisis.

CHAPTER XXIV

FLIGHT

THE first part of the meal over, the hostess picked up a nut and threw it deftly at a door leading into the lean-to-kitchen.

"Our table bell," she explained to me. And, true enough, a moment later the orderly appeared and carried out the plates.

Then we had dessert, which was fruit and candy, and coffee.

And all the time the guns were firing, and every opening of the door into the corridor brought a gale of wind into the room.

Suddenly it struck me that hardly a foot of the plaster interior of that room was whole. The ceiling was riddled. So were the walls.

"Shrapnel," said the major, following my gaze. "It gets worse every day."

"I think the ceiling is going to fall," said one of the hostesses.

True enough, there was a great bulge in the centre. But it held for that night. It may be holding now.

Everybody took a hand at clearing the table. The lamp was burning low, and they filled it without putting it out. One of the things that I have always been taught is never to fill a lighted lamp. I explained this to them carefully. But they were quite calm. It seems at the front one does a great many extraordinary things. It is part and parcel of that utter indifference to danger that comes with war.

Now appeared the chauffeur, who brought the information that the car had been dragged out of the mud and towed as far as the house.

"Towed?" I said blankly.

"Towed, madame. There is no more petrol."

The major suggested that we kill him at once. But he was a perfectly good chauffeur and young. Also it developed that he had not sat on my hat. So we let him live.

"Never mind," said Miss C——; "we can give you the chauffeur's bed and he can go somewhere else."

But after a time I decided that I would rather walk back than stay overnight in that house. For the major explained that at eleven o'clock the batteries behind the town would bombard the German trenches and the road behind them, along which they had information that an ammunition train would pass.

"Another night in the cellar!" said some one. "That means no one will need any beds, for there will be a return fire, of course."

"Is there no petrol to be had?" I inquired anxiously.

"None whatever."

None, of course. There had been shops in the town, and presumably petrol and other things. But now there was nothing but ruined walls and piles of brick and mortar. However, there was a cellar.

My feet were swollen and painful, for the walk had been one long agony. I was chilled, too, from my wetting, in spite of the fire. I sat by the tiny stove and tried to forget the prospect of a night in the cellar, tried to ignore the pieces of shell and shrapnel cases lined up on the mantelpiece, shells and shrapnel that had entered the house and destroyed it.

The men smoked and talked. An officer came up from the trenches to smoke his after-dinner pipe, a bearded individual, who apologised for his muddy condition. He and the major played a duet. They made a great fuss about their preparation for it. The stool must be so, the top of the cracked piano raised. They turned and bowed to us profoundly. Then sat down and played—CHOP STICKS!

But that was only the beginning. For both of them were accomplished musicians. The major played divinely. He played a Rhapsodie Hongroise, the Moonlight Sonata, one of the movements of the Sonata Appassionata. He played without notes, a bull-dog pipe gripped firmly in his teeth, blue clouds encircling his fair hair. Gone was the reckless soldier who would have taken his life in his hands for the whim of bringing in a German sentry. Instead there was a Belgian whose ruined country lay behind him, whose people lay dead in thousands of hideous graves, whose heart was torn and aching with the things that it knew and buried. We sat silent. His pipe died in his mouth; his eyes, fixed on the shell-riddled wall, grew sombre. When the music ceased his hands still lay lingeringly on the keys. And, beyond the foot of the street, the ominous guns of the army that had ruined his country crashed steadily.

We were rather subdued when the music died away. But he evidently regretted having put a weight on the spirits of the party. He rose and brought me a charming little water-colour sketch he had made of the bit of No Man's Land in front of his trench, with the German line beyond it.

"By the way," he said in his exact English, "I went to art school in Dresden with an American named Reinhart. Afterward he became a great painter—Charles Stanley Reinhart. Is he by any chance a relative?"

"Charles Stanley Reinhart is dead," I said. "He was a Pittsburgher, too, but the two families are connected only by marriage."

"Dead! So he is dead too! Everybody is dead. He—he was a very nice boy."

Suddenly he stood up and stretched his long arms.

"It was a long time ago," he said. "Now I go for the sentry."

They caught him at the door, however, and brought him back.

"But it is so simple," he protested. "No one is hurt. And the American lady——"

The American lady protested.

"I don't want a German sentry," I said. "I shouldn't know what to do with a German sentry if I had one."

So he sat down and explained his method to me. I wish I could tell his method here. It sounded so easy. Evidently it was a safety-valve, during that long wait of the deadlock, for his impetuous temperament. One could picture him sitting in his trench day after day among the soldiers who adored him, making little water-colour sketches and smoking his bulldog pipe, and then suddenly, as now, rising and stretching his long arms and saying:

"Well, boys, I guess I'll go out and bring one in."

And doing it.

I was taken for a tour of the house—up a broken

staircase that hung suspended, apparently from nothing, to what had been the upper story.

It was quite open to the sky and the rain was coming in. On the side toward the German line there was no wall. There were no partitions, no windows, only a few broken sticks of what had been furniture. And in one corner, partly filled with rain water, a child's cradle that had miraculously escaped destruction.

Downstairs to the left of the corridor was equal destruction. There was one room here that, except for a great shell-hole and for a ceiling that was sagging and almost ready to fall, was intact. Here on a stand were surgical supplies, and there was a cot in the corner. A soldier had just left the cot. He had come up late in the afternoon with a nosebleed, and had now recovered.

"It has been a light day," said my guide. "Sometimes we hardly know which way to turn—when there is much going on, you know. Probably to-night we shall be extremely busy."

We went back into the living room and I consulted my watch. It was half past ten o'clock. At eleven the bombardment was to begin!

The conversation in the room had turned to spies. Always, everywhere, I found this talk of spies. It appeared that at night a handful of the former inhabitants of the town crept back from the fields to sleep in the cellars of what had been their homes, and some of them were under suspicion.

"Every morning," said Miss C——, "before the German bombardment begins, three small shells are sent over in quick succession. Then there is about fifteen minutes' wait before the real shelling. I am convinced that it is a signal to some one to get out."

The officers pooh-poohed the idea. But Miss C——
stuck to her point.

"They are getting information somehow," she said.
"You may laugh if you like. I am sure I am right."

Later on an officer explained to me something about
the secret service of the war.

"It is a war of spies," he said. "That is one reason
for the deadlock. Every movement is reported to the
other side and checkmated almost before it begins.
In the eastern field of war the system is still inadequate; that accounts for the great movements that
have taken place there."

Perhaps he is right. It sounds reasonable. I do
not know with what authority he spoke. But certainly
everywhere I found this talk of spies. One of the
officers that night told of a recent experience of
his.

"I was in a church tower at ——," he said. "There
were three of us. We had been looking over toward
the German lines. Suddenly I looked down into the
street below. Some one with an electric flash was
signalling across. It was quite distinct. All of us
saw it. There was an answer from the German
trenches immediately. While one of us kept watch
on the tower the others rushed down into the street.
There was no one there. But it is certain that that
sort of thing goes on all the time."

A quarter to eleven!

Suddenly the whole thing seemed impossible—that
the noise at the foot of the street was really guns;
that I should be there; that these two young women
should live there day and night in the midst of such
horrors. For the whole town is a graveyard. Bodies
in numbers have been buried in shell-holes and hastily

covered, or float in the stagnant water of the canal. Every heavy rain uncovers shallow graves in the fields, allowing a dead arm, part of a rotting trunk, to show.

And now, after this lapse of time, it still seems incredible. Are they still there? Report has it that the Germans captured this town and held it for a time, only to lose it later. What happened to the little "sick and sorry" house during those fearful days? Did the German officers sit about that pine table and throw a nut to summon an orderly? Did they fill the lamp while it was lighted, and play on the cracked piano, and pick up shrapnel cases as they landed on the doorstep and set them on the mantel?

Ten minutes to eleven!

The chauffeur came to the door and stuck his head in.

"I have found petrol in a can in an empty shed," he explained. "It is now possible to go."

We went. We lost no time on the order of our going. The rain was over, but the fog had descended again. We lighted our lamps, and were curtly ordered by a sentry to put them out. In the moment that they remained alight, carefully turned away from the trenches, it was possible to see the hopeless condition of the street.

At last we reached a compromise. One lamp we might have, but covered with heavy paper. It was very little. The car bumped ominously, sagged into shell-holes.

I turned and looked back at the house. Faint rays of light shone through its boarded windows. A wounded soldier had been brought up the street and stood, leaning heavily on his companion, at the doorstep. The door opened, and he was taken in.

Good-bye, little "sick and sorry" house, with your laughter and tears, your friendly hands, your open door!   Good-bye!

Five minutes later, as we reached the top of the street, the bombardment began.

CHAPTER XXV

VOLUNTEERS AND PATRIOTS

I HOLD a strong brief for the English: For the English at home, restrained, earnest, determined and unassuming; for the English in the field, equally all of these things.

The British Army has borne attacks at La Bassée and Ypres, positions so strategically difficult to hold that the Germans have concentrated their assaults at these points. It has borne the horrors of the retreat from Mons, when what the Kaiser called "General French's contemptible little army" was forced back by oncoming hosts of many times its number. It has fought, as the English will always fight, with unequalled heroism but without heroics.

To-day, after many months of war, the British Army in the field is as smart, in a military sense, as tidy—if it will forgive me the word—as well ordered, as efficiently cared for, as the German Army was in the beginning. Partly this is due to its splendid equipment. Mostly it is due to that fetish of the British soldier wherever he may be—personal neatness.

Behind the lines he is jaunty, cheerful, smart beyond belief. He hates the trenches—not because they are dangerous or monotonous but because it is difficult to take a bath in them. He is four days in the trenches and four days out. On his days out he drills and marches, to get back into condition after the forced inaction of the trenches. And he gets his hair trimmed.

There is something about the appearance of the British soldier in the field that got me by the throat. Perhaps because they are, in a sense, my own people, speaking my tongue, looking at things from a viewpoint that I could understand. That partly. But it was more than that.

These men and boys are volunteers, the very flower of England. They march along the roads, heads well up, eyes ahead, thousands of them. What a tragedy for the country that gives them up! Who will take their places?—these splendid Scots with their picturesque kilts, their bare, muscular knees, their great shoulders; the cheery Irish, swaggering a bit and with a twinkle in their blue eyes; these tall young English boys, showing race in every line; these dashing Canadians, so impressive that their every appearance on a London street was certain to set the crowds to cheering.

I saw them in London, and later on I saw them at the front. Still later I saw them again, prostrate on the ground, in hospital trains, on hospital ships. I saw mounds, too, marked with wooden crosses.

Volunteers and patriots! A race incapable of a mean thing, incapable of a cruelty. A race of sportsmen, playing this horrible game of war fairly, almost too honestly. A race, not of diplomats, but of gentlemen.

"You will always be fools," said a captured German naval officer to his English captors, "and we shall never be gentlemen!"

But they are not fools. It is that attitude toward the English that may defeat Germany in the end.

Every man in the British Army to-day has counted the cost. He is there because he elected to be there. He is going to stay by until the thing is done, or he is. He says very little about it. He is uncomfortable if any one else says anything about it. He is rather matter of fact, indeed, and nonchalant as long as things are being done fairly. But there is nothing calm about his attitude when his opponent hits below the belt. It was a sense of fair play, as well as humanity, that made England rise to the call of Belgium. It is England's sense of fair play that makes her soldiers and sailors go white with fury at the drowning of women and children and noncombatants; at the unprincipled employment of such trickery in war as the use of asphyxiating gases, or at the insulting and ill-treating of those of their army who have been captured by the Germans. It is at the English, not at the French or the Belgians, that Germany is striking in this war. Her whole attitude shows it. British statesmen knew this from the beginning, but the people were slow to believe it. But escaped prisoners have told that they were discriminated against. I have talked with a British officer who made a sensational escape from a German prison camp. German soldiers have called across to the French trenches that it was the English they were after.

In his official order to his troops to advance, the German Emperor voiced the general sentiment.

"It is my Royal and Imperial Command that you concentrate your energies, for the immediate present, upon one single purpose, and that is that you address all your skill and all the valour of my soldiers to exterminate first the treacherous

English and walk over General French's contemptible little army.

"Headquarters,

"Aix-la-Chapelle, August 19th, 1914."

In the name of the dignity of great nations, compare that order with Lord Kitchener's instructions to his troops, given at the same time.

"You are ordered abroad as a soldier of the King to help our French comrades against the invasion of a common enemy. You have to perform a task which will need your courage, your energy, your patience. Remember that the honour of the British Army depends on your individual conduct. It will be your duty not only to set an example of discipline and perfect steadiness under fire, but also to maintain the most friendly relations with those whom you are helping in this struggle.

"The operations in which you are engaged will, for the most part, take place in a friendly country, and you can do your own country no better service than in showing yourselves in France and Belgium in the true character of a British soldier.

"Be invariably courteous, considerate, and kind. Never do anything likely to injure or destroy property, and always look upon looting as a disgraceful act. You are sure to meet with a welcome and to be trusted; your conduct will justify that welcome and that trust. Your duty cannot be done unless your health is sound. So keep constantly on your guard against any excesses. In this new experience you may find temptations both in wine and women. You must entirely resist both temptations, and, while treating all women with perfect courtesy, you should avoid any intimacy.

"Do your duty bravely,

"Fear God,

"Honour the King.

"(Signed) KITCHENER, Field Marshal."

CHAPTER XXVI

A LUNCHEON AT BRITISH HEADQUARTERS

THE same high-crowned roads, with pitfalls of mud at each side; the same lines of trees; the same coating of ooze, over which the car slid dangerously. But a new element—khaki.

Khaki everywhere—uniforms, tents, transports, all of the same hue. Skins, too, where one happens on the Indian troops. It is difficult to tell where their faces end and their yellow turbans begin.

Except for the slightly rolling landscape and the khaki one might have been behind the Belgian or French Army. There were as usual aëroplanes overhead, clouds of shrapnel smoke, and not far away the thunder of cannonading. After a time even that ceased, for I was on my way to British General Headquarters, well back from the front.

I carried letters from England to Field Marshal Sir John French, to Colonel Brinsley Fitzgerald, aidde-camp to the "Chief," as he is called, and to General Huguet, the *liaison* between the French and English Armies. His official title is something entirely different, but the French word is apt. He is the connecting link between the English and French Armies.

I sent these letters to headquarters, and waited in the small hotel for developments. The British antipathy to correspondents was well known. True, there were indications that a certain relaxation was about to take place. Frederick Palmer in London had been notified that before long he would be sent across, and I had heard that some of the London newspapers, the *Times* and a few others, were to be allowed a day at the lines.

But at the time my machine drew into that little French town and deposited me in front of a wretched inn, no correspondent had been to the British lines. It was *terra incognita*. Even London knew very little. It was rumoured that such part of the Canadian contingent as had left England up to that time had been sent to the eastern field, to Egypt or the Dardanelles. With the exception of Sir John French's reports and the "Somewhere in France" notes of "Eyewitness," a British officer at the front, England was taking her army on faith.

And now I was there, and there frankly as a writer. Also I was a woman. I knew how the chivalrous English mind recoiled at the idea of a woman near the front. Their nurses were kept many miles in the rear. They had raised loud protests when three English women were permitted to stay at the front with the Belgian Army.

My knees were a bit weak as I went up the steps and into the hotel. They would hardly arrest me. My letters were from very important persons indeed. But they could send me away with expedition and dispatch. I had run the Channel blockade to get there, and I did not wish to be sent away with expedition and dispatch.

The hotel was cold and bare. Curious-eyed officers came in, stared at me and went out. A French gentleman in a military cape walked round the bare room, spoke to the canaries in a great cage in the corner, and came back to where I sat with my fur coat, lap-robe fashion, over my knees.

"*Pardon!*" he said. "Are you the Duchess of Sutherland?"

I regretted that I was not the Duchess of Sutherland.

"You came just now in a large car?"

"I did."

"You intend to stay here for some time?"

"I have not decided."

"Where did you come from?"

"I think," I said after a rather stunned pause, "that I shall not tell you."

"Madame is very cautious!"

I felt convinced that he spoke with the authority of the army, or of the town *gendarmerie,* behind him. But I was irritated. Besides, I had been cautioned so much about telling where I had been, except in general terms, that I was even afraid to talk in my sleep.

"I think," I said, "that it does not really matter where I came from, where I am going, or what I am doing here."

I expected to see him throw back his cape and exhibit a sheriff's badge, or whatever its French equivalent. But he only smiled.

"In that case," he said cheerfully, "I shall wish you a good-morning."

"Good-bye," I said coldly. And he took himself off.

I have never solved the mystery of that encounter. Was he merely curious? Or scraping acquaintance with the only woman he had seen in months? Or was he as imposing a person as he looked, and did he go away for a warrant or whatever was necessary, and return to find me safe in the lap of the British Army?

The canary birds sang, and a porter with a leather apron, having overcome a national inability to light a fire in the middle of the day, came to take me to my room. There was an odour of stewing onions in the air, and soapsuds, and a dog sniffed at me and barked because I addressed him in English.

And then General Huguet came, friendly and smiling, and speaking English. And all was well.

Afterward I learned how that same diplomacy which made me comfortable and at home with him at once has made smooth the relations between the English and French Armies. It was Chesterfield, wasn't it, who spoke of *"Suaviter in modo, fortiter in re"*? That is General Huguet. A tall man, dark, keen and of most soldierly bearing; beside the genial downrightness of the British officers he was urbane, suave, but full of decision. His post requires diplomacy but not concession.

Sir John French, he regretted to say, was at the front and would not return until late in the evening. But Colonel Fitzgerald hoped that I would come to luncheon at headquarters, so that we might talk over what was best to be done. He would, if the arrangement suited me, return at one o'clock for me.

It was half past twelve. I made such concessions to the occasion as my travelling bag permitted, and, prompt to the minute, General Huguet's car drew up at the inn door. It was a wonderful car. I used it all that afternoon and the next day, and I can testify both to its comfort and to its speed. I had travelled fast in cars belonging to the Belgian and French staffs, but never have I gone as I did in that marvel of a car. Somewhere among my papers I have a sketch that I made of the interior of the limousine body, with the

two soldier-chauffeurs outside in front, the two carbines strapped to the speedometer between the *vis-à-vis*
seats inside the car, and the speedometer registering
ninety kilometres and going up.

We went at once to British Headquarters, with its
sentries and its flag; a large house, which had belonged
to a notary, its grim and forbidding exterior gave little
promise of the comfort within. A passage led to a
square centre hall from which opened various rooms—
a library, with a wood fire, the latest possible London
and Paris papers, a flat-topped desk and a large map; a
very large drawing-room, which is Sir John French's
private office, with white walls panelled with rose brocade, a marble mantel, and a great centre table, covered, like the library desk, with papers; a dining room,
wainscoted and comfortable. There were other rooms,
which I did not see. In the square hall an orderly sat
all day, waiting for orders of various sorts.

Colonel Fitzgerald greeted me amiably. He regretted that Sir John French was absent, and was
curious as to how I had penetrated to the fastnesses
of British Headquarters without trouble. Now and
then, glancing at him unexpectedly during the excellent luncheon that followed, I found his eyes fixed
on me thoughtfully, intently. It was not at all an
unfriendly gaze. Rather it was the look of a man
who is painstakingly readjusting his mental processes
to meet a new situation.

He made a delightful host. I sat at his right. At
the other end of the table was General Huguet, and
across from me a young English nobleman, attached to
the field marshal's staff, came in, a few minutes late,
and took his place. The Prince of Wales, who lives
there, had gone to the trenches the day before.

Two soldier-servants served the meal. There was red wine, but none of the officers touched it. The conversation was general and animated. We spoke of public opinion in America, of the resources of Germany and her starvation cry, of the probable length of the war. On this opinions varied. One of the officers prophesied a quick ending when the Allies were finally ready to take the offensive. The others were not so optimistic. But neither here, nor in any of the conversations I have heard at the headquarters of the Allies, was there a doubt expressed as to ultimate victory. They had a quiet confidence that was contagious. There was no bluster, no assertion; victory was simply accepted as a fact; the only two opinions might be as to when it would occur, and whether the end would be sudden or a slow withdrawal of the German forces.

The French Algerian troops and the Indian forces of Great Britain came up for discussion, their bravery, their dislike for trench fighting and intense longing to charge, the inroads the bad weather had made on them during the winter.

One of the officers considered the American press rather pro-German. The recent American note to Sir Edward Grey and his reply, with the press comments on both, led to this statement. The possibility of Germany's intentionally antagonising America was discussed, but not at length.

From the press to the censorship was but a step. I objected to the English method as having lost us our perspective on the war.

"You allow anything to go through the censor's office that is not considered dangerous or too explicit," I said. "False reports go through on an equality with true ones. How can America know what to believe?"

It was suggested by some one that the only way to make the censorship more elastic, while retaining its usefulness in protecting military secrets and movements, was to establish such a censorship at the front, where it is easier to know what news would be harmful to give out and what may be printed with safety.

I mentioned what a high official of the admiralty had said to me about the censorship—that it was "an infernal nuisance, but necessary."

"But it is not true that messages are misleadingly changed in transmission," said one of the officers at the table.

I had seen the head of the press-censorship bureau, and was able to repeat what he had said—that where the cutting out of certain phrases endangered the sense of a message, the words "and" or "the" were occasionally added, that the sense might be kept clear, but that no other additions or changes of meaning were ever made.

Luncheon was over. We went into the library, and there, consulting the map, Colonel Fitzgerald and General Huguet discussed where I might go that afternoon. The mist of the morning had turned to rain, and the roads at the front would be very bad. Besides, it was felt that the "Chief" should give me permission to go to the front, and he had not yet returned.

"How about seeing the Indians?" asked Colonel Fitzgerald, turning from the map.

"I should like it very much."

The young officer was turned to, and agreed, like a British patriot and gentleman, to show me the Indian villages. General Huguet offered his car. The officer got his sheepskin-lined coat, for the weather was cold.

"Thirty shillings," he said, "and nothing goes through it!"

I examined that coat. It was smart, substantial, lined throughout with pure white fur, and it had cost seven dollars and a half.

There is a very popular English word just making its place in America. The word is "swank." It is both noun and verb. One swanks when one swaggers. One puts on swank when one puts on side. And because I hold a brief for the English, and because I was fortunate enough to meet all sorts of English people, I want to say that there is very little swank among them. The example of simplicity and genuineness has been set by the King and Queen. I met many different circles of people. From the highest to the lowest, there was a total absence of that arrogance which the American mind has so long associated with the English. For fear of being thought to swagger, an Englishman will understate his case. And so with the various English officers I met at the front. There was no swank. They were downright, unassuming, extremely efficient-looking men, quick to speak of German courage, ready to give the benefit of the doubt where unproved outrages were in question, but rousing, as I have said, to pale fury where their troops were being unfairly attacked.

While the car was being brought to the door General Huguet pointed out to me on the map where I was going. As we stood there his pencil drew a light semicircle round the town of Ypres.

"A great battle," he said, and described it. Colonel Fitzgerald took up the narrative. So it happened that, in the three different staff headquarters, Belgian, French and English, executive officers of the three

armies in the western field described to me that great
battle—the frightful slaughter of the English, their
re-enforcement at a critical time by General Foch's
French Army of the North, and the final holding of
the line.

The official figures of casualties were given me
again: English forty-five thousand out of a hundred
and twenty thousand engaged; the French seventy
thousand, and the German over two hundred thousand.

Turning to the table, Colonel Fitzgerald picked up a
sheet of paper covered with figures.

"It is interesting," he said, "to compare the disease
and battle mortality percentages of this war with the
percentages in other wars; to see, considering the
frightful weather and the trenches, how little disease
there has been among our troops. Compare the figures
with the Boer War, for instance. And even then our
percentage has been somewhat brought up by the Indian troops."

"Have many of them been ill?"

"They have felt the weather," he replied; "not the
cold so much as the steady rain. And those regiments
of English that have been serving in India have felt
the change. They particularly have suffered from
frostbitten feet."

I knew that. More than once I had seen men being
taken back from the British lines, their faces twisted
with pain, their feet great masses of cotton and bandages which they guarded tenderly, lest a chance blow
add to their agony. Even the English system of allowing the men to rub themselves with lard and oil
from the waist down before going into flooded
trenches has not prevented the tortures of frostbite.

It was time to go and the motor was waiting. We set off in a driving sleet that covered the windows of the car and made motoring even more than ordinarily precarious. But the roads here were better than those nearer the coast; wider, too, and not so crowded. To Ham, where the Indian regiment I was to visit had been retired for rest, was almost twenty miles. "Ham!" I said. "What a place to send Mohammedans to!"

In his long dispatch of February seventeenth Sir John French said of the Indian troops:

"The Indian troops have fought with the utmost steadfastness and gallantry whenever they have been called upon."

This is the answer to many varying statements as to the efficacy of the assistance furnished by her Indian subjects to the British Empire at this time. For Sir John French is a soldier, not a diplomat. No question of the union of the Empire influences his reports. The Indians have been valuable, or he would not say so. He is chary of praise, is the Field Marshal of the British Army.

But there is another answer—that everywhere along the British front one sees the Ghurkas, slant-eyed and Mongolian, with their broad-brimmed, khaki-coloured hats, filling posts of responsibility. They are little men, smaller than the Sikhs, rather reminiscent of the Japanese in build and alertness.

When I was at the English front some of the Sikhs had been retired to rest. But even in the small villages on billet, relaxed and resting, they were a fine and soldierly looking body of men, showing race and their ancient civilisation.

It has been claimed that England called on her Indian troops, not because she expected much assistance from them but to show the essential unity of the British Empire. The plain truth is, however, that she needed the troops, needed men at once, needed experienced soldiers to eke out her small and purely defensive army of regulars. Volunteers had to be equipped and drilled—a matter of months.

To say that she called to her aid barbarians is absurd. The Ghurkas are fierce fighters, but carefully disciplined. Compare the lances of the Indian cavalry regiments and the *kukri*, the Ghurka knife, with the petrol squirts, hand grenades, aëroplane darts and asphyxiating bombs of Germany, and call one barbarian to the advantage of the other! The truth is, of course, that war itself is barbarous.

CHAPTER XXVII

A STRANGE PARTY

THE road to Ham turned off the main highway south of Aire. It was a narrow clay road in unspeakable condition. The car wallowed along. Once we took a wrong turning and were obliged to go back and start again.

It was still raining. Indian horsemen beat their way stolidly along the road. We passed through hamlets where cavalry horses in ruined stables were scantily protected, where the familiar omnibuses of London were parked in what appeared to be hundreds. The cocoa and other advertisements had been taken off and they had been hastily painted a yellowish grey. Here and there we met one on the road, filled and overflowing with troops, and looking curiously like the "rubber-neck wagons" of New York.

Aside from the transports and a few small Indian ammunition carts, with open bodies made of slats, and drawn by two mules, with an impassive turbaned driver calling strange words to his team, there was no sign of war. No bombarding disturbed the heavy atmosphere; no aëroplanes were overhead. There was no barbed wire, no trenches. Only muddy sugarbeet fields on each side of the narrow road, a few winter trees, and the beat of the rain on the windows.

At last, with an extra lurch, the car drew up in

the village of Ham. At a gate in a brick wall a Scotch soldier in kilts, carrying a rifle, came forward. Our errand was explained and he went off to find Makand Singh, a major in the Lahore Lancers and in charge of the post.

It was a curious picture that I surveyed through the opened door of the car. We were in the centre of the village, and at the intersection of a crossroads was a tall cross with a life-size Christ. Underneath the cross, in varying attitudes of dampness and curiosity, were a dozen Indians, Mohammedans by faith. Some of them held horses which, in spite of the rain, they had been exercising. One or two wore long capes to the knees, with pointed hoods which fitted up over their great turbans. Bearded men with straight, sensitive noses and oval faces, even the absurdity of the cape and pointed hood failed to lessen their dignity. They were tall, erect, soldierly looking, and they gazed at me with the bland gravity of the East.

Makand Singh came hastily forward, a splendid figure of a man, six foot two or thereabout, and appearing even taller by reason of his turban. He spoke excellent English.

"It is very muddy for a lady to alight," he said, and instructed one of the men to bring bags of sacking, which were laid in the road.

"You are seeing us under very unfavourable conditions," he said as he helped me to alight. "But there is a fire if you are cold."

I was cold. So Makand Singh led the way to his living quarters. To go to them it was necessary to pass through a long shed, which was now a stable for perhaps a dozen horses. At a word of command the Indian grooms threw themselves against the horses' heads and pushed them back. By stepping over the ground pegs to which they were tethered I got through the shed somehow and into a small yard.

Makand Singh turned to the right, and, throwing open the low door of a peasant's house, stood aside to allow me to enter. "It is not very comfortable," he explained, "but it is the best we have."

He was so tall that he was obliged to stoop as he entered the doorway. Within was an ordinary peasant's kitchen, but cleaner than the average. In spite of the weather the floor boards were freshly scrubbed. The hearth was swept, and by the stove lay a sleek tortoise-shell cat. There was a wooden dresser, a chimney shelf with rows of plates standing on it, and in a doorway just beyond an elderly peasant woman watching us curiously.

"Perhaps," said Makand Singh, "you will have coffee?"

I was glad to accept, and the young officer, who had followed, accepted also. We sat down while the kettle was placed on the stove and the fire replenished. I glanced at the Indian major's tall figure. Even sitting, he was majestic. When he took the cape off he was discovered clothed in the khaki uniform of his rank in the British Army. Except for the olive colour of his skin, his turban, and the fact that his beard—the soft beard of one who has never shaved—was drawn up into a black net so that it formed a perfect crescent around the angle of his jaw, he might have been a gallant and interested English officer.

For the situation assuredly interested him. His eyes were alert and keen. When he smiled he showed rows of beautiful teeth, small and white. And although his face in repose was grave, he smiled often.

He superintended the making of the coffee by the peasant woman and instructed her to prepare the table.

She obeyed pleasantly. Indeed, it was odd to see that between this elderly Frenchwoman and her strange guests—people of whose existence on the earth I dare say she had never heard until this war—there was the utmost good will. Perhaps the Indians are neater than other troops. Certainly personal cleanliness is a part of their religion. Anyhow, whatever the reason, I saw no evidence of sulkiness toward the Indians, although I have seen surly glances directed toward many of the billeted troops of other nationalities.

Conversation was rather difficult. We had no common ground to meet on, and the ordinary currency of polite society seemed inadequate, out of place.

"The weather must be terrible after India," I ventured.

"We do not mind the cold. We come from the north of India, where it is often cold. But the mud is bad. We cannot use our horses."

"You are a cavalry regiment?" I asked, out of my abysmal ignorance.

"We are Lancers. Yes. And horses are not useful in this sort of fighting."

From a room beyond there was a movement, followed by the entrance of a young Frenchman in a British uniform. Makand Singh presented him and he joined the circle that waited for coffee.

The newcomer presented an enigma—a Frenchman in a British uniform quartered with the Indian troops! It developed that he was a pupil from the Sorbonne, in Paris, and was an interpreter. Everywhere after-

ward I found these interpreters with the British Army
—Frenchmen who for various reasons are disqualified
from entering the French Army in active service and
who are anxious to do what they can. They wear
the British uniform, with the exception that instead
of the stiff crown of the British cap theirs is soft.
They are attached to every battalion, for Tommy At-
kins is in a strange land these days, a land that knows
no more English than he knows French.

True, he carries little books of French and English
which tell him how to say "Porter, get my luggage
and take it to a cab," or "Please bring me a laundry
list," or "Give my kind regards to your parents." Imagine him trying to find the French for "Look out,
they're coming!" to call to a French neighbour, in the
inevitable mix-up of the line during a *mêlée,* and finding only "These trousers do not fit well," or "I would
like an ice and then a small piece of cheese."

It was a curious group that sat in a semicircle around
that peasant woman's stove, waiting for the kettle to
boil—the tall Indian major with his aristocratic face
and long, quiet hands, the young English officer in his
Headquarters Staff uniform, the French interpreter,
and I. Just inside the door the major's Indian servant, tall, impassive and turbaned, stood with folded
arms, looking over our heads. And at the table the
placid-faced peasant woman cut slices of yellow bread,
made with eggs and milk, and poured our coffee.

It was very good coffee, served black. The woman
brought a small decanter and placed it near me.

"It is rum," said the major, "and very good in
coffee."

I declined the rum. The interpreter took a little.
The major shook his head.

"Although they say that a Sikh never refuses rum!"
he said, smiling.

Coffee over, we walked about the village. Hardly a
village—a cluster of houses along unpaved lanes
which were almost impassable. There were tumbling
stables full of horses, groups of Indians standing under dripping eaves for shelter, sentries, here and there
a peasant. The houses were replicas of the one where
Makand Singh had his quarters.

Although it was still raining, a dozen Indian Lancers were exercising their horses. They dismounted
and stood back to let us pass. Behind them, as they
stood, was the great Cross.

That was the final picture I had of the village of
Ham and the Second Lahore Lancers—the turbaned
Indians with their dripping horses, the grave bow of
Makand Singh as he closed the door of the car, and
behind him a Scotch corporal in kilt and cap, with a
cigarette tucked behind his ear.

We went on. I looked back. Makand Singh was
making his careful way through the mud; the horses
were being led to a stable. The Cross stood alone.

CHAPTER XXVIII

SIR JOHN FRENCH

THE next day I was taken along the English front, between the first and the second line of trenches, from Béthune, the southern extremity of the line, the English right flank, to the northern end of the line just below Ypres. In a direct line the British front at that time extended along some twenty-seven miles. But the line was irregular, and I believe was really well over thirty.

I have never been in an English trench. I have been close enough to the advance trenches to be shown where they lay, and to see the slight break they make in the flat country. I was never in a dangerous position at the English front, if one excepts the fact that all of that portion of the country between the two lines of trenches is exposed to shell fire.

No shells burst near me. Béthune was being intermittently shelled, but as far as I know not a shell fell in the town while I was there. I lunched on a hill surrounded by batteries, with the now celebrated towns of Messines and Wytschaete just across a valley, so that one could watch shells bursting over them. And still nothing threatened my peace of mind or my physical well-being. And yet it was one of the most interesting days of a not uneventful period.

In the morning I was taken, still in General Huguet's car, to British Headquarters again, to meet Sir John French.

I confess to a thrill of excitement when the door into his private office was opened and I was ushered in. The Field Marshal of the British Army was standing by his table. He came forward at once and shook hands. In his khaki uniform, with the scarlet straps of his rank on collar and sleeves, he presented a most soldierly and impressive appearance.

A man of middle height, squarely and compactly built, he moves easily. He is very erect, and his tanned face and grey hair are in strong contrast. A square and determined jaw, very keen blue eyes and a humorous mouth—that is my impression of Sir John French.

"We are sending you along the lines," he said when I was seated. "But not into danger. I hope you do not want to go into danger."

I wish I might tell of the conversation that followed. It is impossible. Not that it dealt with vital matters; but it was understood that Sir John was not being interviewed. He was taking a little time from a day that must have been crowded, to receive with beautiful courtesy a visitor from overseas. That was all.

There can be no objection, I think, to my mentioning one or two things he spoke of—of his admiration for General Foch, whom I had just seen, of the tribute he paid to the courage of the Indian troops, and of the marvellous spirit all the British troops had shown under the adverse weather conditions prevailing. All or most of these things he has said in his official dispatches.

Other things were touched on—the possible dura-

tion of the war, the new problems of what is virtually
a new warfare, the possibility of a pestilence when
warm weather came, owing to inadequately buried
bodies. The Canadian troops had not arrived at the
front at that time, although later in the day I saw
their transports on the way, or I am sure he would
have spoken of them. I should like to hear what he
has to say about them after their recent gallant fighting. I should like to see his fine blue eyes sparkle.

The car was at the door, and the same young officer
who had taken me about on the previous day entered
the room.

"I am putting you in his care," said Sir John, indicating the new arrival, "because he has a charmed
life. Nothing will happen if you are with him." He
eyed the tall young officer affectionately. "He has
been fighting since the beginning," he said, "handling
a machine gun in all sorts of terrible places. And nothing ever touches him."

A discussion followed as to where I was to be taken.
There was a culm heap near the Givenchy brickyards
which was rather favoured as a lookout spot. In spite
of my protests, that was ruled out as being under fire
at the time. Béthune was being shelled, but not se-
verely. I would be taken to Béthune and along the
road behind the trenches. But nothing was to happen
to me. Sir John French knitted his grey brows, and
suggested a visit to a wood where the soldiers had
built wooden walks and put up signs, naming them
Piccadilly, Regent Street, and so on.

"I should like to see something," I put in feebly.

I appreciated their kindly solicitude, but after all I
was there to see things; to take risks, if necessary, but
to see.

"Then," said Sir John with decision, "we will send you to a hill from which you can see."

The trip was arranged while I waited. Then he went with me to the door and there we shook hands. He hoped I would have a comfortable trip, and bowed me out most courteously. But in the doorway he thought of something.

"Have you a camera with you?"

I had, and said so; a very good camera.

"I hope you do not mind if I ask you not to use it."

I did not mind. I promised at once to take no pictures, and indeed at the end of the afternoon I found my unfortunate camera on the floor, much buffeted and kicked about and entirely ignored.

The interview with Sir John French had given me an entirely unexpected impression of the Field Marshal of the British Army. I had read his reports fully, and from those unemotional reports of battles, of movements and countermovements, I had formed a picture of a great soldier without imagination, to whom a battle was an issue, not a great human struggle— an austere man.

I had found a man with a fighting jaw and a sensitive mouth; and a man greatly beloved by the men closest to him. A human man; a soldier, not a writer.

And after seeing and talking with Sir John French I am convinced that it is not his policy that dictates the silence of the army at the front. He is proud of his men, proud of each heroic regiment, of every brave deed. He would like, I am sure, to shout to the world the names of the heroes of the British Army, to publish great rolls of honour. But silence, or comparative silence, has been the decree.

There must be long hours of suspense when the Field Marshal of the British Army paces the floor of that grey and rose brocade drawing-room; hours when the orders he has given are being translated into terms of action, of death, of wounds, but sometimes —thank God!—into terms of victory. Long hours, when the wires and the dispatch riders bring in news, valiant names, gains, losses; names that are not to be told; brave deeds that, lacking chroniclers, must go unrecorded.

Read this, from the report Sir John French sent out only a day or so before I saw him:

"The troops composing the Army of France have been subjected to as severe a trial as it is possible to impose upon any body of men. The desperate fighting described in my last dispatch had hardly been brought to a conclusion when they were called upon to face the rigours and hardships of a winter campaign. Frost and snow have alternated with periods of continuous rain.

"The men have been called upon to stand for many hours together almost up to their waists in bitterly cold water, separated by only one or two hundred yards from a most vigilant enemy.

"Although every measure which science and medical knowledge could suggest to mitigate these hardships was employed, the sufferings of the men have been very great.

"In spite of all this they present a most soldierlike, splendid, though somewhat war-worn appearance. Their spirit remains high and confident; their general health is excellent, and their condition most satisfactory.

"I regard it as most unfortunate that circumstances have prevented any account of many splendid instances of courage and endurance, in the face of almost unparalleled hardship and fatigue in war, coming regularly to the knowledge of the public."

So it is clearly not the fault of Sir John French that England does not know the names of her heroes, or that their families are denied the comfort of knowing that their sons fought bravely and died nobly. It is not the fault of the British people, waiting eagerly for news that does not come. Surely, in these inhuman times, some concession should be made to the humanities. War is not moving pawns in a game; it is a struggle of quivering flesh and agonised nerves, of men fighting and dying for ideals. Heroism is much more than duty. It is idealism. No leader is truly great who discounts this quality.

America has known more of the great human interest of this war than England. English people get the news from great American dailies. It is an unprecedented situation, and so far the English people have borne it almost in silence. But as the months go on and only bare official dispatches reach them, there is a growing tendency to protest. They want the truth, a picture of conditions. They want to know what their army is doing; what their sons are doing. And they have a right to know. They are making tremendous sacrifices, and they have a right to know to what end.

The greatest agent in the world for moulding public opinion is the press. The Germans know this, and have used their journals skilfully. To underestimate the power of the press, to fail to trust to its good will

and discretion, is to refuse to wield the mightiest instrument in the world for influencing national thought
and national action. At times of great crisis the press
has always shown itself sane, conservative, safe, eminently to be trusted.

The English know the power of the great modern
newspaper, not only to reflect but to form public opinion. They have watched the American press because
they know to what extent it influences American
policy.

There is talk of conscription in England to-day.
Why? Ask the British people. Ask the London
Times. Ask rural England where, away from the
tramp of soldiers in the streets, the roll of drums,
the visual evidence of a great struggle, patriotism is
asked to feed on the ashes of war.

Self-depreciation in a nation is as great an error as
over-complacency. Lack of full knowledge is the
cause of much of the present British discontent.

Let the British people be told what their army is
doing. Let Lord Kitchener announce its deeds, its
courage, its vast unselfishness. Let him put the torch
of publicity to the national pride and see it turn to a
white flame of patriotism. Then it will be possible to
tear the recruiting posters from the walls of London,
and the remotest roads of England will echo to the
tramp of marching men.

CHAPTER XXIX

ALONG THE GREAT BETHUNE ROAD

A GAIN and again through these chapters I have
felt apologetic for the luxurious manner in
which I frequently saw the war. And so now I hesi-
tate to mention the comfort of that trip along the
British lines; the substantial and essentially British
foresight and kindness that had stocked the car with
sandwiches wrapped in white paper; the good roads;
the sense of general well-being that spread like a contagion from a well-fed and well-cared-for army. There
is something about the British Army that inspires one
with confidence. It is a pity that those people who sit
at home in Great Britain and shrug their shoulders
over the daily papers cannot see their army at the
front.

It is not a roast-beef stolidity. It is rather the
steadiness of calm eyes and good nerves, of physically
fit bodies and clean minds. I felt it when I saw
Kitchener's army of clear-eyed boys drilling in Hyde
Park. I got it from the quiet young officer, still in his
twenties, who sat beside me in the car, and who, having been in the war from the beginning, handling a
machine gun all through the battle of Ypres, when his
regiment, the Grenadier Guards, suffered so horribly,
was willing to talk about everything but what he had
done.

We went first to Béthune. The roads as we approached the front were crowded, but there was no disorder. There were motor bicycles and side-cars carrying dispatch riders and scouts, travelling kitchens, great lorries, small light cars for supplies needed in a hurry—cars which make greater speed than the motor vans—omnibuses full of troops, and steam tractors or caterpillar engines for hauling heavy guns.

The day was sunny and cold. The rain of the day before had turned to snow in the night, and the fields were dazzling.

"In the east," said the officer with me, "where there is always snow in the winter, the Germans have sent out to their troops white helmet covers and white smocks to cover the uniforms. But snow is comparatively rare here, and it has not been considered necessary."

At a small bridge ten miles from Béthune he pointed out a house as marking the farthest advance of the German Army, reached about the eleventh of October. There was no evidence of the hard fighting that had gone on along this road. It was a peaceful scene, the black branches of the overarching trees lightly powdered with snow. But the snowy fields were full of unmarked mounds. Another year, and the mounds will have sunk to the level of the ground. Another year, and only history will tell the story of that October of 1914 along the great Béthune road.

An English aëroplane was overhead. There were armoured cars on the road, going toward the front; top-heavy machines that made surprisingly little noise, considering their weight. Some had a sort of conning tower at the top. They looked sombre, menacing. The driving of these cars over slippery roads must be difficult. Like the vans, they keep as near the centre of the road as possible, allowing lighter traffic to turn out to pass them. A van had broken down and was being repaired at one of the wayside repair shops maintained everywhere along the roads for this war of machinery. Men in khaki with leather aprons were working about it, while the driver stood by, smoking a pipe.

As we went on we encountered the Indian troops again. The weather was better, and they thronged the roads, driving their tiny carts, cleaning arms and accoutrements in sunny doorways, proud and haughty in appearance even when attending to the most menial duties. From the little ammunition carts, like toy wagons, they gazed gravely at the car, and at the unheard-of spectacle of a woman inside. Side by side with the Indians were Scots in kilts, making up with cheerful impudence for the Indians' lack of curiosity.

There were more Ghurkas, carrying rifles and walking lightly beside forage carts driven by British Tommies. There were hundreds of these carts taking hay to the cavalry divisions. The Ghurkas looked more Japanese than ever in the clear light. Their broad-brimmed khaki hats have a strap that goes under the chin. The strap or their black slanting eyes or perhaps their rather flattened noses and pointed chins give them a look of cruelty that the other Indian troops do not have. They are hard and relentless fighters, I believe; and they look it.

The conversation in the car turned to the feeding of the army.

"The British Army is exceedingly well fed," said the young officer.

"In the trenches also?"

"Always. The men are four days in the trenches and four out. When the weather is too bad for anything but sniping, the inactivity of the trench life and the abundant ration gets them out of condition. On their four days in reserve it is necessary to drill them hard to keep them in condition."

This proved to be the explanation of the battalions we met everywhere, marching briskly along the roads. I do not recall the British ration now, but it includes, in addition to meat and vegetables, tea, cheese, jam and bacon—probably not all at once, but giving that variety of diet so lacking to the unfortunate Belgian Army. Food is one of the principal munitions of war. No man fights well with an empty stomach. Food sinks into the background only when it is assured and plentiful. Deprived of it, its need becomes insistent, an obsession that drives away every other thought.

So the wise British Army feeds its men well, and lets them think of other things, such as war and fighting and love of country and brave deeds.

But food has not always been plentiful in the British Army. There were times last fall when, what with German artillery bombardment and shifting lines, it was difficult to supply the men.

"My servant," said the officer, "found a hare somewhere, and in a deserted garden a handful of carrots. Word came to the trench where I was stationed that at dark that night he would bring out a stew. We were very hungry and we waited eagerly. But just as it was cooked and ready a German shell came down the chimney of the house where he was working and blew up stove and stew and everything. It was one of the greatest disappointments I ever remember."

We were in Béthune at last—a crowded town, larger than any I had seen since I left Dunkirk. So congested were its narrow streets with soldiers, mounted and on foot, and with all the ghastly machinery of war, that a traffic squad had taken charge and was directing things. On some streets it was possible to go only in one direction. I looked about for the signs of destruction that had grown so familiar to me, but I saw none. Evidently the bombardment of Béthune had not yet done much damage.

A squad of artillerymen marched by in perfect step; their faces were keen, bronzed. They were fine-looking, well-set-up men, as smart as English artillerymen always are. I watched them as long as I could see them.

We had lost our way, owing to the regulations of the traffic squad. It was necessary to stop and inquire. Then at last we crossed a small bridge over the canal, and were on our way along the front, behind the advanced trenches and just in front of the second line.

For a few miles the country was very level. The firing was on our right, the second line of trenches on our left. The congestion of Béthune had given way to the extreme peace in daylight of the region just behind the trenches. There were few wagons, few soldiers. Nothing could be seen except an occasional cloud where shrapnel had burst. The British Army was keeping me safe, as it had promised!

There were, however, barbed-wire entanglements everywhere, built, I thought, rather higher than the French. Roads to the right led to the advanced trenches, empty roads which at night are thronged with men going to the front or coming back.

Here and there one saw a sentry, and behind him a tent of curious mottled shades of red, brown and green.

"They look as though they were painted," I said, rather bewildered.

"They are," the officer replied promptly. "From an aëroplane these tents are absolutely impossible to locate. They merge into the colors of the fields."

Now and then at a crossroads it was necessary to inquire our way. I had no wish to run into danger, but I was conscious of a wild longing to have the car take the wrong turning and land abruptly at the advance trenches. Nothing of the sort happened, however.

We passed small buildings converted into field hospitals and flying the white flag with a red cross.

"There are no nurses in these hospitals," explained the officer. "Only one surgeon and a few helpers. The men are brought here from the trenches, and then taken back at night in ambulances to the railroad or to base hospitals."

"Are there no nurses at all along the British front?"

"None whatever. There are no women here in any capacity. That is why the men are so surprised to see you."

Here and there, behind the protection of groves and small thickets, were temporary camps, sometimes tents, sometimes tent-shaped shelters of wood. There were batteries on the right everywhere, great guns concealed in farmyards or, like the guns I had seen on the French front, in artificial hedges. Some of them were firing; but the firing of a battery amounts to nothing but a great noise in these days of long ranges. Somewhere across the valley the shells would burst, we knew that; that was all.

The conversation turned to the Prince of Wales, and to the responsibility it was to the various officers to have him in the trenches. Strenuous efforts had been made to persuade him to be satisfied with the work at headquarters, where he is attached to Sir John French's staff. But evidently the young heir to the throne of England is a man in spite of his youth. He wanted to go out and fight, and he had at last secured permission.

"He has had rather remarkable training," said the young officer, who was also his friend. "First he was in Calais with the transport service. Then he came to headquarters, and has seen how things are done there. And now he is at the front."

Quite unexpectedly round a turn in the road we came on a great line of Canadian transports—American-built lorries with khaki canvas tops. Canadians were driving them, Canadians were guarding them. It gave me a homesick thrill at once to see these other Americans, of types so familiar to me, there in Northern France.

Their faces were eager as they pushed ahead. Some of the tent-shaped wooden buildings were to be temporary barracks for them. In one place the transports had stopped and the men were cooking a meal beside the road. Some one had brought a newspaper and a crowd of men had gathered round it. I wondered if it was an American paper. I would like to have stood on the running board of the machine, as we went past, and called out that I, too, was an American, and God bless them!

But I fancy the young officer with me would have been greatly disconcerted at such an action. The English are not given to such demonstrations. But the Canadians would have understood, I know.

Since that time the reports have brought great news of these Canadian troops, of their courage, of the loss of almost all their officers in the fighting at Neuve Chapelle. But that sunny morning, when I saw them in the north of France, they were untouched by battle or sudden death. Their faces were eager, intent, earnest. They had come a long distance and now they had arrived. And what next?

Into this scene of war unexpectedly obtruded itself a bit of peace. A great cart came down a side road, drawn by two white oxen with heavy wooden yokes. Piled high in the cart were sugar beets. Some thrifty peasant was salvaging what was left of his crop. The sight of the oxen reminded me that I had seen very few horses.

"They are farther back," said the officer. "Of course, as you know, for the last two or three months it has been impossible to use the cavalry at all."

Then he told me a curious thing. He said that during the long winter wait the cavalry horses got much out of condition. The side roads were thick with mud and the main roads were being reserved for transports. Adequate exercises for the cavalry seemed impossible. One detachment discovered what it considered a bright solution, and sent to England for beagle hounds. Morning after morning the men rode after the hounds over the flat fields of France. It was a welcome distraction and it kept the horses in working trim.

But the French objected. They said their country

was at war, was being devastated by an alien army. They considered riding to hounds, no matter for what purpose, an indecorous, almost an inhuman, thing to do under the circumstances. So the hounds were sent back to England, and the cavalry horses are now exercised in dejected strings along side roads.

As we went north the firing increased in intensity. More English batteries were at work; the German response was insistent.

We were approaching Ypres, this time from the English side, and the great artillery duel of late February was in progress.

The country was slightly rolling. Its unevenness permitted more activity along our road. Batteries were drawn up at rest in the fields here and there. In one place a dozen food kitchens in the road were cooking the midday meal, the khaki-clad cooks frequently smoking as they worked.

Ahead of this loomed two hills. They rose abruptly, treeless and precipitous. On the one nearest to the German lines was a ruined tower.

"The tower," said the officer, "would have been a charming place for luncheon. But the hill has been shelled steadily for several days. I have no idea why the Germans are shelling it. There is nobody there."

CHAPTER XXX

THE MILITARY SECRET

THE second hill was our destination. At the foot of it the car stopped and we got out. A steep path with here and there a wooden step led to the summit. At the foot of the path was a sentry and behind him one of the multicoloured tents.

"Are you a good climber?" asked the officer.

I said I was and we set out. The path extended only a part of the way, to a place perhaps two hundred feet beyond the road, where what we would call a cyclone cellar in America had been dug out of the hillside. Like the others of the sort I had seen, it was muddy and uninviting, practically a cave with a roof of turf.

The path ceased, and it was necessary to go diagonally up the steep hillside through the snow. From numberless guns at the base of the hill came steady reports, and as we ascended it was explained to me that I was about to visit the headquarters of Major General H——, commanding an army division.

"The last person I brought here," said the young officer, smiling, "was the Prince of Wales."

We reached the top at last. There was a tiny farmhouse, a low stable with a thatched roof, and, towering over all, the arms of a great windmill. Chickens cackled round my feet, a pig grunted in a corner, and apparently from directly underneath came the ear-splitting reports of a battery as it fired.

"Perhaps I would better go ahead and tell them you are coming," said the officer. "These people have probably not seen a woman in months, and the shock would be too severe. We must break it gently."

So he went ahead, and I stood on the crest of that wind-swept hill and looked across the valley to Messines, to Wytschaete and Ypres.

The battlefield lay spread out like a map. As I looked, clouds of smoke over Messines told of the bursting of shells.

Major General H—— came hurrying out. His quarters occupy the only high ground, with the exception of the near-by hill with its ruined tower, in the neighbourhood of Ypres. Here, a week or so before, had come the King of Belgium, to look with tragic eyes at all that remained to him of his country. Here had come visiting Russian princes from the eastern field, the King of England, the Prince of Wales. No obscurities—except myself—had ever penetrated so far into the fastness of the British lines.

Later on in the day I wrote my name in a visitors' book the officers have established there, wrote under sprawling royal signatures, under the boyish hand of the Prince of Wales, the irregular chirography of Albert of Belgium, the blunt and soldierly name of General Joffre.

There are six officers stationed in the farmhouse, composing General H——'s staff. And, as things turned out, we did not require the white-paper sandwiches, for we were at once invited to luncheon.

"Not a very elaborate luncheon," said General H——, "but it will give us a great deal of pleasure to share it."

While the extra places were being laid we went to the brow of the hill. Across the valley at the foot of a wooded ridge were the British trenches. The ground rose in front of them, thickly covered with trees, to the German position on the ridge.

"It looks from here like a very uncomfortable position," I said. "The German position is better, isn't it?"

"It is," said General H—— grimly. "But we shall take that hill before long."

I am not sure, and my many maps do not say, but there is little doubt in my mind that the hill in question is the now celebrated Hill 60, of which so much has been published.

As we looked across shells were bursting round the church tower of Messines, and the batteries beneath were sending out ear-splitting crashes of noise. Ypres, less than three miles away, but partly hidden in mist, was echoing the bombardment. And to complete the pandemonium of sound, as we turned, a *mitrailleuse* in the windmill opened fire behind us.

"Practice!" said General H—— as I started. "It is noisy here, I'm afraid."

We went through the muddy farmyard back to the house. The staff was waiting and we sat down at once to luncheon at a tiny pine table drawn up before a window. It was not a good luncheon. The French wine was like vinegar, the food the ordinary food of the peasant whose house it was. But it was a cheerful meal in spite of the food, and in spite of a boil on General H——'s neck. The marvel of a woman being there seemed to grow, not diminish, as the meal went on.

"Next week," said General H——, "we are to have two parties of correspondents here. The penny papers come first, and later on the ha'pennies!"

That brought the conversation, as usual, to the feeling about the war in America. Like all the other officers I had met, these men were anxious to have things correctly reported in America, being satisfied that the true story of the war would undoubtedly influence any wavering of public opinion in favour of the Allies.

One of the officers was a Canadian, and for his benefit somebody told the following story, possibly by now familiar to America.

Some of the Canadian troops took with them to England a bit of the dash and impatience of discipline of the great Northwest. The story in question is of a group of soldiers at night passing a sentry, who challenges them:

"Halt! Who goes there?"

"Black Watch."

"Advance, Black Watch, and all's well."

The next group is similarly challenged:

"Halt! Who goes there?"

"Cameronians."

"Advance, Cameronians."

The third group comes on.

"Halt! Who goes there?"

"What the devil is that to you?"

"Advance, Canadians!"

In the burst of mirth that followed the Canadian officer joined. Then he told an anecdote also:

"British recruits, practising passing a whispered order from one end of a trench to the other, received this message to pass along: 'Enemy advancing on right flank. Send re-enforcements.' When the message reached the other end of the trench," he said, "it was: 'Enemy advancing with ham shank. Send three and fourpence!'"

It was a gay little meal, the only breaks in the conversation when the great guns drowned out our voices. I wonder how many of those round that table are living to-day. Not all, it is almost certain. The German Army almost broke through the English line at that very point in the late spring. The brave Canadians have lost almost all their officers in the field and a sickening percentage of their men. That little valley must have run deep with blood since I saw it that day in the sunlight.

Luncheon was over. I wrote my name in the visitors' book, to the tune of such a bombardment as almost forbade speech, and accompanied by General H—— we made our way down the steep hillside to the car.

"Some time to-night I shall be in England," I said as I settled myself for the return trip.

The smile died on the general's face. It was as if, in speaking of home, I had touched the hidden chord of gravity and responsibility that underlay the cheerfulness of that cheery visit.

"England!" he said. That was all.

I looked back as the car started on. A battery was moving up along the road behind the hill. The sentry stood by his low painted tent. The general was watching the car, his hand shading his eyes against the glare of the winter sun. Behind him rose his lonely hill, white with snow, with the little path leading, by devious ways, up its steep and shining side.

It was not considered advisable to return by the
road behind the trenches. The late afternoon artillery duel was going on. So we turned off a few
miles south of the hill and left war behind us.

Not altogether, of course. There were still transports and troops. And at an intersection of three
roads we were abruptly halted. A line of military
cars was standing there, all peremptorily held up by
a handful of soldiers.

The young officer got out and inquired. There was
little time to spare, for I was to get to Calais that
evening, and to run the Channel blockade some time
in the night.

The officer came back soon, smiling.

"A military secret!" he said. "We shall have to
wait a little. The road is closed."

So I sat in the car and the military secret went by.
I cannot tell about it except that it was thrillingly
interesting. My hands itched to get out my camera
and photograph it, just as they itch now to write about
it. But the mystery of what I saw on the highroad
back of the British lines is not mine to tell. It must
die with me!

My visit to the British lines was over.

As I look back I find that the one thing that stands
out with distinctness above everything else is the
quality of the men that constitute the British Army in
the field. I had seen thousands in that one day. But
I had seen them also north of Ypres, at Dunkirk, at
Boulogne and Calais, on the Channel boats. I have
said before that they show race. But it is much more
than a matter of physique. It is a thing of steady
eyes, of high-held heads, of a clean thrust of jaw.

The English are not demonstrative. London, compared with Paris, is normal. British officers at the front and at headquarters treat the war as a part of the day's work, a thing not to talk about but to do. But my frequent meetings with British soldiers, naval men, members of the flying contingent and the army medical service, revealed under the surface of each man's quiet manner a grimness, a red heat of patriotism, a determination to fight fair but to fight to the death.

They concede to the Germans, with the British sense of fairness, courage, science, infinite resource and patriotism. Two things they deny them, civilisation and humanity—civilisation in its spiritual, not its material, side; humanity of the sort that is the Englishman's creed and his religion—the safeguarding of noncombatants, the keeping of the national word and the national honour.

My visit to the English lines was over. I had seen no valiant charges, no hand-to-hand fighting. But in a way I had had a larger picture. I had seen the efficiency of the methods behind the lines, the abundance of supplies, the spirit that glowed in the eyes of every fighting man. I had seen the colonial children of England in the field, volunteers who had risen to the call of the mother country. I had seen and talked with the commander-in-chief of the British forces, and had come away convinced that the mother country had placed her honour in fine and capable hands. And I had seen, between the first and second lines of trenches, an army of volunteers and patriots —and gentlemen.

CHAPTER XXXI

QUEEN MARY OF ENGLAND

THE great European war affects profoundly all the women of each nation involved. It affects doubly the royal women. The Queen of England, the Czarina of Russia, the Queen of the Belgians, the Empress of Germany, each carries in these momentous days a frightful burden. The young Prince of Wales is at the front; the King of the Belgians has been twice wounded; the Empress of Germany has her sons as well as her husband in the field.

In addition to these cares these women of exalted rank have the responsibility that comes always to the very great. To see a world crisis approaching, to know every detail by which it has been furthered or retarded, to realise at last its inevitability—to see, in a word, every movement of the great drama and to be unable to check its *dénouement*—that has been a part of their burden. And when the *dénouement* came, to sink their private anxieties in the public welfare, to assume, not a double immunity but a double responsibility to their people, has been the other part.

It has required heroism of a high order. It is, to a certain extent, a new heroism, almost a demonstration of the new faith whose foundation is responsibility—responsibility of a nation to its sons, of rulers to their people, of a man to his neighbour.

It has been my privilege to meet and speak with two of these royal women, with the Queen of England and with the Queen of the Belgians. In each instance I carried away with me an ineradicable impression of this quality—of a grave and wearing responsibility borne quietly and simply, of a quiet courage that buries its own griefs and asks only to help.

From the beginning of the war I had felt a keen interest in the Queen of England. Here was a great queen who had chosen to be, first of all, a wife and mother; a queen with courage and a conscience. And into her reign had come the tragedy of a war that affected every nation of the world, many of them directly, all of them indirectly. The war had come unsought, unexpected, unprepared for. Peaceful England had become a camp. The very palace in which the royal children were housed was open to an attack from a brutal enemy, which added to the new warfare of this century the ethics of barbarism.

What did she think of it all? What did she feel when that terrible Roll of Honour came in, week by week, that Roll of Honour with its photographs of splendid types of young manhood that no Anglo-Saxon can look at without a clutch at his throat? What did she think when, one by one, the friends of her girlhood put on the black of bereavement and went uncomplainingly about the good works in which hers was the guiding hand? What thoughts were hers during those anxious days before the Prince of Wales went to the front, when, like any other mother, she took every possible moment to be with him, walking about arm-in-arm with her boy, talking of everything but the moment of parting?

And when at last I was permitted to see the Queen of England, I understood a part at least of what she was suffering. I had been to the front. I had seen the English army in the field. I had been quite close to the very trenches where the boyish Prince of Wales was facing the enemies of his country and doing it with high courage. And I had heard the rumble of the great German guns, as Queen Mary of England must hear them in her sleep.

Even with no son in the field the Queen of England would be working for the soldiers. It is a part of the tradition of her house. But a good mother is a mother to all the world. When Queen Mary is supervising· the great work of the Needlework Guild one feels sure that into each word of direction has gone a little additional tenderness, because of this boy of hers at the front.

It is because of Her Majesty's interest in the material well-being of the soldiers at the front, and because of her most genuine gratitude for America's part in this well-being, that I took such pleasure in meeting the Queen of England.

It was characteristic of Her Majesty that she put an American woman—a very nervous American woman—at her ease at once, that she showed that American woman the various departments of her Needlework Guild under way, and that she conveyed, in every word she said, a deep feeling of friendship for America and her assistance to Belgium in this crisis.

Although our ambassadors are still accredited to the Court of St. James's, the old palace has ceased to be the royal residence. The King still holds there his levees, to which only gentlemen are admitted. But the formal Drawing Rooms are held at Buckingham Palace. To those who have seen St. James's during a levee, or to those London tourists who have watched the Scots Guards, or the Coldstream or the Grenadiers, preceded by a splendid band, swinging into the old Friary Court to perform the impressive ceremony of changing guard, the change in these days of war is most amazing. Friary Court is guarded by London policemen, and filled with great vans piled high with garments and supplies for the front—that front where the Coldstream and the Grenadiers and the others, shorn of their magnificence, are waiting grimly in muddy trenches or leading charges to victory—or the Roll of Honour. Under the winter sky of London the crenelated towers and brick walls of the old palace give little indication of the former grandeur of this most historic of England's palaces, built on the site of an old leper hospital and still retaining the name of the saint to whom that hospital was dedicated.

There had been a shower just before I arrived; and, although it was February, there was already a hint of spring in the air. The sun came out, drying the roads in the park close by, and shining brightly on the lovely English grass, green even then with the green of June at home. Riders, caught in the shower and standing by the sheltered sides of trees for protection, took again to the bridle paths. The hollows of Friary Court were pools where birds were splashing. As I got out of my car a Boy Scout emerged from the palace and carried a large parcel to a waiting van.

"Do you want the Q. M. N. G.?" said a tall policeman.

This, being interpreted, I was given to understand was Queen Mary's Needlework Guild.

Later on, when I was taken to Buckingham Palace to write my name in the Queen's book, which is etiquette after a presentation, there was all the formality the visit to St. James's had lacked—the drive into the inclosure, where the guard was changing, the stately footmen, the great book with its pages containing the dignitaries and great people of all the earth.

But the Boy Scout and the policeman had restored my failing courage that day at St. James's Palace. Except for a tendency to breathe at twice my normal rate as the Queen entered the room I felt almost calm.

As she advanced toward us, stopping to speak cordially to the various ladies who are carrying on the work of the Guild for her, I had an opportunity to see this royal woman who has suffered so grossly from the camera.

It will be a surprise to many Americans to learn that the Queen of England is very lovely to look at. So much emphasis has always been placed on her virtues, and so little has been written of her charm, that this tribute is only fair to Her Majesty. She is tall, perhaps five feet eight inches, with deep-blue eyes and beautiful colouring. She has a rather wide, humorous mouth. There is not a trace of austerity in her face or in any single feature. The whole impression was of sincerity and kindliness, with more than a trace of humour.

I could quite believe, after I saw Her Majesty, the delightful story that I had heard from a member of her own circle, that now and then, when during some court solemnity an absurdity occurred, it was positively dangerous to catch the Queen's eye!

Queen Mary came up the long room.   As she paused and held out her hand, each lady took it and curtsied at the same time.   The Queen talked, smiling as she spoke.   There was no formality.   Near at hand the lady-in-waiting who was in attendance stood, sometimes listening, sometimes joining in the conversation.   The talk was all of supplies, for these days in England one thinks in terms of war.   Certain things had come in; other things had gone or were going. For the Queen of England is to-day at the head of a great business, one that in a few months has already collected and distributed over a million garments, all new, all practical, all of excellent quality.

The Queen came toward me and paused.   There was an agonised moment while the lady-in-waiting presented me.   Her Majesty held out her hand.   I took it and bowed.   The next instant she was speaking.

She spoke at once of America, of what had already been done by Americans for the Belgians both in England and in their desolated country.   And she hastened to add her gratitude for the support they have given her Guild.

"The response has been more than generous," said Her Majesty.   "We are very grateful.   We are glad to find that the sympathy of America is with us."

She expressed a desire also to have America know fully just what was being done with the supplies that are being constantly sent over, both from Canada and from the United States.

"Canada has been wonderful," she said.   "They are doing everything."

The ready response of Canada to the demand for both troops and supplies appeared to have touched Her Majesty.   She spoke at length about the troops, the distance they had come, the fine appearance the men made, and their popularity with the crowds when they paraded on the streets of London. I had already noticed this. A Canadian regiment was sure to elicit cheers at any time, although London, generally speaking, has ceased any but silent demonstration over the soldiers.

"Have you seen any of the English hospitals on the Continent?" the Queen asked.

"I have seen a number, Your Majesty."

"Do they seem well supplied?"

I replied that they appeared to be thoroughly equipped, but that the amount of supplies required was terrifying and that at one time some of the hospitals had experienced difficulty in securing what they needed.

"One hospital in Calais," I said, "received twelve thousand pairs of bed socks in one week last autumn, and could not get a bandage."

"Those things happened early in the war. We are doing much better now. England had not expected war. We were totally unprepared."

And in the great analysis that is to come, that speech of the Queen of England is the answer to many questions. England had not expected war. Every roll of the drum as the men of the new army march along the streets, every readjustment necessary to a peaceful people suddenly thrust into war, every month added to the length of time it has taken to put England in force into the field, shifts the responsibility to where it belongs. Back of all fine questions of diplomatic negotiation stands this one undeniable fact. To deny it is absurd; to accept it is final.

"What is your impression of the French and Belgian hospitals?" Her Majesty inquired.

I replied that none were so good as the English, that France had always depended on her nuns in such emergencies, and, there being no nuns in France now, her hospital situation was still not good.

"The priests of Belgium are doing wonderful work," I said. "They have suffered terribly during the war."

"It is very terrible," said Her Majesty. "Both priests and nuns have suffered, as England has reason to know."

The Queen spoke of the ladies connected with the Guild.

"They are really much overworked," she said. "They are giving all their time day after day. They are splendid. And many of them, of course, are in great anxiety."

Already, by her tact and her simplicity of manner, she had put me at my ease. The greatest people, I have found, have this quality of simplicity. When she spoke of the anxieties of her ladies, I wished that I could have conveyed to her, from so many Americans, their sympathy in her own anxieties, so keen at that time, so unselfishly borne. But the lady-in-waiting was speaking:

"Please tell the Queen about your meeting with King Albert."

So I told about it. It had been unconventional, and the recital amused Her Majesty. It was then that I realised how humorous her mouth was, how very blue and alert her eyes. I told it all to her, the things that insisted on slipping off my lap, and the King's picking them up; the old envelope he gave me on which to make notes of the interview; how I had asked him whether he would let me know when the interview was over, or whether I ought to get up and go! And finally, when we were standing talking before my departure, how I had suddenly remembered that I was not to stand nearer to His Majesty than six feet, and had hastily backed away and explained, to his great amusement.

Queen Mary laughed. Then her face clouded.

"It is all so very tragic," she said. "Have you seen the Queen?"

I replied that the Queen of the Belgians had received me a few days after my conversation with the King.

"She is very sad," said Her Majesty. "It is a terrible thing for her, especially as she is a Bavarian by birth."

From that to the ever-imminent subject of the war itself was but a step. An English officer had recently made a sensational escape from a German prison camp, and having at last got back to England, had been sent for by the King. With the strange inconsistencies that seem to characterise the behaviour of the Germans, the man to whom he had surrendered after a gallant defence had treated him rather well. But from that time on his story was one of brutalities and starvation.

The officer in question had told me his story, and I ventured to refer to it. Her Majesty knew it quite well, and there was no mistaking the grief in her voice as she commented on it, especially on that part of it which showed discrimination against the British prisoners. Major V—— had especially emphasised the lack of food for the private soldiers and the fearful trials of being taken back along the lines of communication, some fifty-two men being locked in one of the small Continental box cars which are built to carry only six horses. Many of them were wounded. They were obliged to stand, the floor of the car being inches deep with filth. For thirty hours they had no water and no air, and for three days and three nights no food.

"I am to publish Major V——'s statement in America, Your Majesty," I said.

"I think America should know it," said the Queen. "It is most unjust. German prisoners in England are well cared for. They are well fed, and games and other amusements are provided for them. They even play football!"

I stepped back as Her Majesty prepared to continue her visit round the long room. But she indicated that I was to accompany her. It was then that one realised that the Queen of England is the intensely practical daughter of a practical mother. Nothing that is done in this Guild, the successor of a similar guild founded by the late Duchess of Teck, Her Majesty's mother, escapes her notice. No detail is too small if it makes for efficiency. She selected at random garments from the tables, and examined them for warmth, for quality, for utility.

Generally she approved. Before a great heap of heavy socks she paused.

"The soldiers like the knitted ones, we are told," she said. "These are not all knitted but they are very warm."

A baby sweater of a hideous yellow roused in her something like wrath.

"All that labour!" she said, "and such a colour for a little baby!" And again, when she happened on a pair of felt slippers, quite the largest slippers I have ever seen, she fell silent in sheer amazement. They amused her even while they shocked her. And again, as she smiled, I regretted that the photographs of the Queen of England may not show her smiling.

A small canvas case, skilfully rolled and fastened, caught Her Majesty's attention. She opened it herself and revealed with evident pride its numerous contents. Many thousands of such cases had already been sent to the army.

This one was a model of packing. It contained in its small compass an extraordinary number of things —changes of under flannels, extra socks, an abdominal belt, and, in an inclosure, towel, soap, toothbrush, nailbrush and tooth powder. I am not certain, but I believe there was also a pack of cards.

"I am afraid I should never be able to get it all back again!" said Her Majesty. So one of the ladies took it in charge, and the Queen went on.

My audience was over. As Her Majesty passed me she held out her hand. I took it and curtsied.

"Were you not frightened the night you were in the Belgian trenches?" she inquired.

"Not half so frightened as I was this afternoon, Your Majesty," I replied.

She passed on, smiling.

And now, when enough time has elapsed to give perspective to my first impression of Queen Mary of England, I find that it loses nothing by this supreme test. I find that I remember her, not as a great Queen but as a gracious and kindly woman, greatly beloved by those of her immediate circle, totally without arrogance, and of a simplicity of speech and manner that must put to shame at times those lesser lights that group themselves about a throne.

I find another impression also—that the Queen of

England is intensely and alertly mental—alive to her finger tips, we should say in America. She has always been active. Her days are crowded. A different type of royal woman would be content to be the honoured head of the Queen's Guild. But she is in close touch with it at all times. It is she who dictates its policy, and so competently that the ladies who are associated with the work that is being done speak of her with admiration not unmixed with awe.

From a close and devoted friend of Queen Mary I obtained other characteristics to add to my picture: That the Queen is acutely sensitive to pain or distress in others—it hurts her; that she is punctual—and this not because of any particular sense of time but because she does not like to keep other people waiting. It is all a part of an overwhelming sense of that responsibility to others that has its origin in true kindliness.

The work of the Queen's Guild is surprising in its scope. In a way it is a vast clearing house. Supplies come in from every part of the world, from India, Ceylon, Java, Alaska, South America, from the most remote places. I saw the record book. I saw that a woman from my home city had sent cigarettes to the soldiers through the Guild, that Africa had sent flannels! Coming from a land where the sending, as regards Africa, is all the other way, I found this exciting. Indeed, the whole record seems to show how very small the earth is, and how the tragedy of a great war has overcome the barriers of distance and time and language.

From this clearing house in England's historic old palace, built so long ago by Bluff King Hal, these offerings of the world are sent wherever there is need, to Servia, to Egypt, to South and East Africa, to the

Belgians. The work was instituted by the Queen the moment war broke out, and three things are being very carefully insured: That a real want exists, that the clothing reaches its proper destination, and that there shall be no overlapping.

The result has been most gratifying to the Queen, but it was difficult to get so huge a business—for, as I have already said, it is a business now—under way at the beginning. Demand was insistent. There was no time to organise a system in advance. It had to be worked out in actual practice.

One of the Queen's ladies-in-waiting wrote in February, apropos of the human element in the work:

"There was a great deal of human element in the start with its various mistakes. The Queen wished, on the breaking out of war, to start the Guild in such a way as to prevent the waste and overlapping which occurred in the Boer War. . . . The fact that the ladies connected with the work have toiled daily and unceasingly for seven months is the most wonderful part of it all."

Before Christmas nine hundred and seventy thousand belts and socks were collected and sent as a special gift to the soldiers at the front, from the Queen and the women of the empire. That in itself is an amazing record of efficiency.

It is rather comforting to know that there were mistakes in the beginning. It is so human. It is comforting to think of this exceedingly human Queen being a party to them, and being divided between annoyance and mirth as they developed. It is very comforting also to think that, in the end, they were rectified.

We had a similar situation during our Civil War.

There were mistakes then also, and they too were rectified. What the heroic women of the North and South did during that great conflict the women of Great Britain are doing to-day. They are showing the same high and courageous spirit, the same subordination of their personal griefs to the national cause, the same cheerful relinquishment of luxuries. It is a United Britain that confronts the enemy in France. It is a united womanhood, united in spirit, in labour, in faith and high moral courage, that looks east across the Channel to that land beyond the horizon, "somewhere in France," where the Empire is fighting for life.

A united womanhood, and at its head a steadfast and courageous Queen and mother, Mary of England.

CHAPTER XXXII

THE QUEEN OF THE BELGIANS

ON the third of August, 1914, the German Army crossed the frontier into Belgium. And on the following day, the fourth, King Albert made his now famous speech to the joint meeting of the Belgian Chamber and Senate. Come what might, the Belgian people would maintain the freedom that was their birthright.

"I have faith in our destinies," King Albert concluded. "A country which defends itself wins respect and cannot perish."

With these simple and dignified words Belgium took up the struggle. She was beaten before she began, and she knew it. No matter what the ultimate outcome of the war, she must lose. The havoc would be hers. The old battleground of Europe knew what war meant; no country in the world knew better. And, knowing, Belgium took up the burden.

To-day, Belgium is prostrate. That she lives, that she will rise again, no Belgian doubts. It may be after months—even after years; but never for a moment can there be any doubt of the national integrity. The Germans are in Belgium, but not of it. Belgium is still Belgium—not a part of the German Empire. Until the Germans are driven out she is waiting.

As I write this, one corner of her territory remains

to her, a wedge-shaped piece, ten miles or so in width at the coast, narrowing to nothing at a point less than thirty miles inland. And in that tragic fragment there remains hardly an undestroyed town. Her revenues are gone, being collected as an indemnity, for God knows what, by the Germans. King Albert himself has been injured. The Queen of the Belgians has pawned her jewels. The royal children are refugees in England. Two-thirds of the army is gone. And, of even that tiny remaining corner, much is covered by the salt floods of the sea.

The King of the Belgians is often heard of. We hear of him at the head of his army, consulting his staff, reviewing his weary and decimated troops. We know his calibre now, both as man and soldier. He stands out as one of the truly heroic figures of the war.

But what of the Bavarian-born Queen of the Belgians? What of this royal woman who has lost the land of her nativity through the same war that has cost her the country of her adoption; who must see her husband go each day to the battle line; who must herself live under the shadow of hostile aëroplanes, within earshot of the enemy's guns? What was she thinking of during those fateful hours when, all night long, King Albert and his Ministers debated the course of Belgium—a shameful immunity, or a war? What does she think now, when, before the windows of her villa at La Panne, the ragged and weary remnant of the brave Belgian Army lines up for review? What does she hope for and pray for—this Queen without a country?

What she thinks we cannot know. What she hopes for we may guess—the end of war; the return of her faithful people to their homes; the reunion of families;

that the guns will cease firing, so the long lines of ambulances will no longer fill the roads; that the wounded will recover; and that those that grieve may be comforted.

She has pawned her jewels. When I saw her she wore a thin gold chain round her neck, and on it a tiny gold heart. I believe she has sacrificed everything else. Royal jewels have been pawned before this—to support extravagant mistresses or to bolster a crumbling throne; but Elisabeth of Belgium has pawned her jewels to buy supplies for wounded soldiers. Battle-scarred old Belgium has not always had a clean slate; but certainly this act of a generous and devoted queen should mark off many scores.

The Queen is living at La Panne, a tiny fishing village and resort on the coast—an ugly village, robbed of quaintness by its rows of villas owned by summer visitors. The villas are red and yellow brick, built château fashion and set at random on the sand. Efforts at lawns have proved abortive. The encroaching dunes gradually cover the grass. Here and there are streets; and there is one main thoroughfare, along which is a tramway that formerly connected the town with other villages.

On one side the sea; on the other the dunes, with little shade and no beauty—such is the location of the new capital of Belgium. And here, in one of the six small villas that house the court, the King and Queen of Belgium, with the Crown Prince, are living. They live very quietly, walking together along the sands at those times when King Albert is not with his troops, faring simply, waiting always—as all Belgium is waiting to-day. Waiting for the end of this terrible time.

I asked a member of the royal household what they did during those long winter evenings, when the only sounds in the little village were the wash of the sea and the continual rumble of the artillery at Nieuport.

"What can we do?" he replied. "My wife and children are in Brussels. It is not possible to read, and it is not wise to think too much. We wait."

But waiting does not imply inaction. The members of His Majesty's household are all officers in the army. I saw only one gentleman in civilian dress, and he was the King's secretary, M. Ingenbleek. The King heads this activity, and the Queen of the Belgians is never idle. The Ocean Ambulance, the great Belgian base hospital, is under her active supervision, and its location near the royal villa makes it possible for her to visit it daily. She knows the wounded soldiers, who adore her. Indeed, she is frankly beloved by the army. Her appearance is always the signal for a demonstration; and again and again I saw copies of her photograph nailed up in sentry huts, in soldiers' billets, in battered buildings that were temporary headquarters for divisions of the army.

In return for this devotion the young Queen regards the welfare of the troops as her especial charge. She visits them when they are wounded, and many tales are told of her keen memory for their troubles. One, a wounded Frenchman, had lost his pipe when he was injured. As he recovered he mourned his pipe. Other pipes were offered, but they were not the same. There had been something about the curve of the stem of the old one, or the shape of the bowl—whatever it was, he missed it. And it had been his sole possession.

At last the Queen of the Belgians had him describe the old pipe exactly. I believe he made a drawing—

and she secured a duplicate of it for him. He told me the story himself.

The Queen had wished to go to the trenches to see the wretchedness of conditions at the front, and to discover what she could do to ameliorate them. One excursion she had been permitted at the time I saw her, to the great anxiety of those who knew of the trip. She was quite fearless, and went into one of the trenches at the railroad embankment of Pervyse. I saw that trench afterward. It was proudly decorated with a sign that said: *Repose de la Reine.* And above the board was the plaster head of a saint, from one of the churches. Both sign and head, needless to say, were carefully protected from German bullets.

Everywhere I went I found evidences of devotion to this girlish and tender-hearted Queen. I was told of her farewell to the leading officials of the army and of the court, when, having remained to the last possible moment, King Albert insisted on her departure from Brussels. I was told of her incognito excursions across the dangerous Channel to see her children in England. I was told of her single-hearted devotion to the King; her belief in him; her confidence that he can do no wrong.

So, when a great and bearded individual, much given to bowing, presented himself at the door of my room in the hotel at Dunkirk, and extended to me a notification that the Queen of the Belgians would receive me the next day at the royal villa at La Panne, I was keenly expectant.

I went over my wardrobe. It was exceedingly limited and more than a little worn. Furs would cover some of the deficiencies, but there was a difficulty about shoe buttons. Dunkirk apparently laces its shoes.

After a period of desperation, two top buttons were removed and sewed on lower down, where they would do the most good. That and much brushing was all that was possible, my total war equipment comprising one small suitcase, two large notebooks and a fountain pen.

I had been invited to lunch at a town on my way to La Panne, but the luncheon was deferred. When I passed through my would-be entertainer was eating bully beef out of a tin, with a cracker or two; and shells were falling inhospitably. Suddenly I was not hungry. I did not care for food. I did not care to stop to talk about food. It was a very small town, and there were bricks and glass and plaster in the streets. There were almost no people, and those who were there were hastily preparing for flight.

It was a wonderful Sunday afternoon, brilliantly sunny. A German aëroplane hung overhead and called the bull's-eyes. From the plain near they were firing at it, but the shells burst below. One could see how far they fell short by the clouds of smoke that hung suspended beneath it, floating like shadowy balloons.

I felt that the aëroplane had its eyes on my car. They drop darts—do the aëroplanes—two hundred and more at a time; small pencil-shaped arrows of steel, six inches long, extremely sharp and weighted at the point end. I did not want to die by a dart. I did not want to die by a shell. As a matter of fact, I did not want to die at all.

So the car went on; and, luncheonless, I met the Queen of the Belgians.

The royal villa at La Panne faces the sea. It is at the end of the village and the encroaching dunes have ruined what was meant to be a small lawn. The long grass that grows out of the sand is the only vegetation about it; and outside, half-buried in the dune, is a marble seat. A sentry box or two, and sentries with carbines pacing along the sand; the constant swish of the sea wind through the dead winter grass; the half-buried garden seat—that is what the Queen of the Belgians sees as she looks from the window of her villa.

The villa itself is small and ugly. The furnishing is the furnishing of a summer seaside cottage. The windows fit badly and rattle in the gale. In the long drawing room—really a living room—in which I waited for the Queen, a heavy red curtain had been hung across the lower part of the long French windows that face the sea, to keep out the draft. With that and an open coal fire the room was fairly comfortable.

As I waited I looked about. Rather a long room this, which has seen so many momentous discussions, so much tragedy and real grief. A chaotic room too; for, in addition to its typical villa furnishing of chintz-covered chairs and a sofa or two, an ordinary pine table by a side window was littered with papers.

On a centre table were books—H. G. Wells' "The War in the Air"; two American books writen by correspondents who had witnessed the invasion of Belgium; and several newspapers. A hideous marble bust on a pedestal occupied a corner, and along a wall was a very small cottage piano. On the white marble mantel were a clock and two candlesticks. Except for a great basket of heather on a stand—a gift to Her Majesty— the room was evidently just as its previous owners had left it. A screen just inside the door, a rather worn rug on the floor, and a small brocade settee by the fireplace completed the furnishing.

The door opened and the Queen entered without ceremony. I had not seen her before. In her simple blue dress, with its white lawn collar and cuffs, she looked even more girlish than I had anticipated. Like Queen Mary of England, she had suffered from the camera. She is indeed strikingly beautiful, with lovely colouring and hair, and with very direct wide eyes, set far apart. She is small and slender, and moves quickly. She speaks beautiful English, in that softly inflected voice of the Continent which is the envy of all American women.

I bowed as she entered; and she shook hands with me at once and asked me to sit down. She sat on the sofa by the fireplace. Like the Queen of England, like King Albert, her first words were of gratitude to America.

It is not my intention to record here anything but the substance of my conversation with Queen Elisabeth of Belgium. Much that was said was the free and unrestricted speech of two women, talking over together a situation which was tragic to them both; for Queen Elisabeth allowed me to forget, as I think she had ceased to remember, her own exalted rank, in her anxiety for her people.

A devoted churchwoman, she grieved over the treatment accorded by the invading German Army to the priests and nuns of Belgium. She referred to her own Bavarian birth, and to the confidence both King Albert and she had always felt in the friendliness of Germany.

"I am a Bavarian," she said. "I have always, from my childhood, heard this talk that Germany must grow, must get to the sea. I thought it was just talk—a pleasantry!"

She had seen many of the diaries of German soldiers, had read them in the very room where we were sitting. She went quite white over the recollection and closed her eyes.

"It is the women and children!" she said. "It is terrible! There must be killing. That is war. But not this other thing."

And later on she said, in reference to German criticism of King Albert's course during the early days of the war:

"Any one who knows the King knows that he cannot do a wrong thing. It is impossible for him. He cannot go any way but straight."

And Queen Elisabeth was right. Any one who knows King Albert of Belgium knows that "he cannot go any way but straight."

The conversation shifted to the wounded soldiers and to the Queen's anxiety for them. I spoke of her hospital as being a remarkable one—practically under fire, but moving as smoothly as a great American institution, thousands of miles from danger. She had looked very sad, but at the mention of the Ocean Ambulance her face brightened. She spoke of its equipment; of the difficulty in securing supplies; of the new surgery, which has saved so many limbs from amputation. They were installing new and larger sterilisers, she said.

"Things are in as good condition as can be expected now," she said. "The next problem will come when we get back into our own country. What are the people to do? So many of the towns are gone; so many farms are razed!"

The Queen spoke of Brand Whitlock and praised highly his work in Brussels. From that to the relief

work was only a step. I spoke of the interest America
was taking in the relief work, and of the desire of so
many American women to help.

"We are grateful for anything," she said. "The
army seems to be as comfortable as is possible under
the circumstances; but the people, of course, need
everything."

Inevitably the conversation turned again to the treatment of the Belgian people by the Germans; to the
unnecessary and brutal murders of noncombatants; to
the frightful rapine and pillage of the early months of
the war. Her Majesty could not understand the scep-
ticism of America on this point. I suggested that it
was difficult to say what any army would do when it
found itself in a prostrate and conquered land.

"The Belgian Army would never have behaved so,"
said Her Majesty. "Nor the English; nor the French.
Never!"

And the Queen of the Belgians is a German! True,
she has suffered much. Perhaps she is embittered; but
there was no bitterness in her voice that afternoon in
the little villa at La Panne—only sadness and great
sorrow and, with it, deep conviction. What Queen
Elisabeth of Belgium says, she believes; and who
should know better? There, to that house on the sea
front, in the fragment of Belgium that remains, go all
the hideous details that are war. She knows them all.
King Albert is not a figure-head; he is the actual fighting head of his army. The murder of Belgium has
been done before his very eyes.

In those long evenings when he has returned from
headquarters; when he and Queen Elisabeth sit by the
fire in the room that overlooks the sea; when every
blast that shakes the windows reminds them both of

that little army, two-thirds gone, shivering in the trenches only a mile or two away, or of their people beyond the dead line, suffering both deprivation and terror—what pictures do they see in the glowing coals?

It is not hard to know. Queen Elisabeth sees her children, and the puzzled, boyish faces of those who are going down to the darkness of death that another nation may find a place in the sun.

What King Albert sees may not all be written; but this is certain: Both these royal exiles—this Soldier-King who has won and deserved the admiration of the world; this Queen who refuses to leave her husband and her wounded, though day after day hostile aëroplanes are overhead and the roar of German guns is in her ears—these royal exiles live in hope and in deep conviction. They will return to Belgium. Their country will be theirs again. Their houses will be restored; their fields will be sown and yield harvest—not for Germany, but for Belgium. Belgium, as Belgium, will live again!

CHAPTER XXXIII

THE RED BADGE OF MERCY

IMMEDIATELY on the declaration of war by the Powers the vast machinery of mercy was put in the field. The mobilisation of the Red Cross army began—that great army which is of no nation, but of all nations, of no creed but of all faiths, of one flag for all the world and that flag the banner of the Crusaders.

The Red Cross is the wounded soldier's last defence. Worn as a brassard on the left arm of its volunteers, it conveys a higher message than the Victoria Cross of England, the Iron Cross of Germany, or the Cross of the Legion of Honour of France. It is greater than cannon, greater than hate, greater than blood-lust, greater than vengeance. It triumphs over wrath as good triumphs over evil. Direct descendant of the cross of the Christian faith, it carries on to every battlefield the words of the Man of Peace: "Blessed are the merciful, for they shall obtain mercy."

The care of the wounded in war has been the problem of the ages. Richard the Lion-Hearted took a hospital ship to the coast of Palestine. The German people of the Middle Ages had their wounded in battle treated by their wives, who followed the army for that purpose. It remained for Frederick the First of Prussia to establish a military service in connection with a standing army.

With the invention of firearms battlefield surgery faced new problems, notably hemorrhage, and took a step forward to meet these altered conditions. It was a French surgeon who solved the problem of hemorrhage by tying the torn blood vessels above the injury. To England goes the credit for the prevention of sepsis, as far as it may be prevented on a battlefield.

As far as it may be prevented on a battlefield! For that is the question that confronts the machinery of mercy to-day. Transportation to the hospitals has been solved, to a large extent, by motor ambulances, by hospital trains, by converted channel steamers connecting the Continent with England. Hospitals in the western field of war are now plentiful and some are well equipped. The days of bedding wounded men down on straw are largely in the past, but how to prevent the ravages of dirt, the so-called "dirt diseases" of gaseous gangrene, blood poisoning, tetanus, is the problem.

I did not see the first exchange of hopelessly wounded prisoners that took place at Flushing, while I was on the Continent. It must have been a tragic sight. They lined up in two parties at the railroad station, German surgeons and nurses with British prisoners, British surgeons and nurses with German prisoners.

Then they were counted off, I am told. Ten Germans came forward, ten British, in wheeled chairs, on crutches, the sightless ones led. The exchange was made. Then ten more, and so on. What a sight! What a horror! No man there would ever be whole again. There were men without legs, without arms, blind men, men twisted by fearful body wounds. Two hundred and sixteen British officers and men, and as many Germans, were exchanged that day.

"They were, however, in the best of spirits," said the London Times of the next day!

At Folkestone a crowd was waiting on the quay, and one may be sure that heads were uncovered as the men limped, or were led or wheeled, down the gangplank. Kindly English women gave them nosegays of snowdrops and violets.

And then they went on—to what? For a few weeks, or months, they will be the objects of much kindly sympathy. In the little towns where they live visitors will be taken to see them. The neighbourhood will exert itself in kindness. But after a time interest will die away, and besides, there will be many to divide sympathy. The blind man, or the man without a leg or an arm, will cease to be the neighbourhood's responsibility and will become its burden.

What then? For that is the problem that is facing each nation at war—to make a whole life out of a fragment, to teach that the spirit may be greater than the body, to turn to usefulness these sad and hopeless by-products of battlefields.

The ravages of war—to the lay mind—consist mainly of wounds. As a matter of fact, they divide themselves into several classes, all different, all requiring different care, handling and treatment, and all, in their several ways, dependent for help on the machinery of mercy. In addition to injuries on the battlefield there are illnesses contracted on the field, septic conditions following even slight abrasions or minor wounds, and nervous conditions—sometimes approximating a temporary insanity—due to prolonged strain, to incessant firing close at hand, to depression following continual lack of success, to the sordid and hideous conditions of unburied dead, rotting in full view for weeks and even months.

During the winter frozen feet, sometimes requiring amputation, and even in mild cases entailing great suffering, took thousands of men out of the trenches. The trouble resulted from standing for hours and even days in various depths of cold water, and was sometimes given the name "waterbite." Soldiers were instructed to rub their boots inside and out with whale oil, and to grease their feet and legs. Unluckily, only fortunately situated men could be so supplied, and the suffering was terrible. Surgeons who have observed many cases of both frost and water bite say that, curiously enough, the left foot is more frequently and seriously affected than the right. The reason given is that right-handed men automatically use the right foot more than the left, make more movements with it. The order to remove boots twice a day, for a few moments while in the trenches, had a beneficial effect among certain battalions.

The British soldier who wraps tightly a khaki puttee round his leg and thus hampers circulation has been a particular sufferer from frostbite in spite of the precaution he takes to grease his feet and legs before going into the trenches.

The presence of septic conditions has been appalling.

This is a dirty war. Men are taken back to the hospitals in incredible states of filth. Their stiffened clothing must frequently be cut off to reveal, beneath, vermin-covered bodies. When the problem of transportation is a serious one, as after a great battle, men must lie in sheds or railway stations, waiting their turn. Wounds turn green and hideous. Their first-aid dressing, originally surgically clean, becomes infected. Lucky the man who has had a small vial of iodine to pour over the gaping surface of his wound. For the time, at least, he is well off.

The very soil of Flanders seems polluted. British surgeons are sighing for the clean dust of the Boer war of South Africa, although they cursed it at the time. That it is not the army occupation which is causing the grave infections of Flanders and France is shown by the fact that the trouble dates from the beginning of the war. It is not that living in a trench undermines the vitality of the men and lays them open to infection. On the contrary, with the exception of frost bite, there is a curious absence of such troubles as would ordinarily result from exposure, cold and constant wetting.

The open-air life has apparently built up the men. Again and again the extraordinary power of resistance shown has astonished the surgeons. It is as if, in forcing men to face overwhelming hardships, a watchful Providence had granted them overwhelming vitality.

Perhaps the infection of the soil, the typhoid-carrying waters that seep through and into the trenches, the tetanus and gangrene that may infect the simplest wounds, are due to the long intensive cultivation of that fertile country, to the fertilisation by organic matter of its fields. Doubtless the vermin that cover many of the troops form the connecting link between the soil and the infected men. In many places gasoline is being delivered to the troopers to kill these pests, and it is a German army joke that before a charge on a Russian trench it is necessary to send ahead men to scatter insect powder! So serious is the problem in the east indeed that an official order from Berlin now requires all cars returning from Russia to be placarded *"Aus Russland!* Before using again thoroughly sterilise and unlouse!" And no upholstered cars are allowed to be used.

Generally speaking, a soldier is injured either in his trench or in front of it in the waste land between the confronting armies. In the latter case, if the lines are close together the situation is still further complicated. It may be and often is impossible to reach him at all. He must lie there for hours or even for days of suffering, until merciful death overtakes him. When he can be rescued he is, and many of the bravest deeds of this war have been acts of such salvage. In addition to the work of the ambulance corps and of volunteer soldiers who often venture out into a rain of death to bring in fallen officers and comrades in the western field, some five hundred ambulance dogs are being used by the Allies to locate the wounded.

When a man is injured in the trenches his companions take care of him until night, when it is possible to move him. His first-aid packet is opened, a sterilised bandage produced, and the dressing applied to the wound. Frequently he has a small bottle of iodine and the wound is first painted with that. In cases where iodine is used at once, chances of infection are greatly lessened. But often he must lie in the trench until night, when the ambulances come up. His comrades make him as comfortable as they can. He lies on their overcoats, his head frequently on his own pack.

Fighting goes on about him, above him. Other comrades fall in the trench and are carried and laid near him. In the intervals of fighting, men bring the

injured men water. For that is the first cry—a great
and insistent need—water. When they cannot get
water from the canteens they drink what is in the
bottom of the trench.

At last night falls. The evening artillery duel, except when a charge is anticipated, is greatly lessened
at night, and infantry fire is only that of "snipers."
But over the trench and over the line of communication behind the trench hang always the enemy's "starlights."

The ambulances come up. They cannot come as far
as the trenches, but stretchers are brought and the
wounded men are lifted out as tenderly as possible.

Many soldiers have tried to tell of the horrors of a
night journey in an ambulance or transport; careful
driving is out of the question. Near the front the
ambulance can have no lights, and the roads everywhere have been torn up by shells.

Men die in transit, and, dying, hark back to early
days. They call for their mothers, for their wives.
They dictate messages that no one can take down.
Unloaded at railway stations, the dead are separated
from the living and piled in tiers on trucks. The
wounded lie about on stretchers on the station floor.
Sometimes they are operated on there, by the light of
a candle, it may be, or of a smoking lamp. When it
is a well-equipped station there is the mercy of chloroform, the blessed release of morphia, but more times
than I care to think of at night, there has been no
chloroform and no morphia.

France has sixty hospital trains, England twelve,
Belgium not so many.

I have seen trains drawing in with their burden of
wounded men. They travel slowly, come to a gradual

stop, without jolting or jarring; but instead of the
rush of passengers to alight, which usually follows the
arrival of a train, there is silence, infinite quiet.
Then, somewhere, a door is unhurriedly opened. Maybe a priest alights and looks about him. Perhaps it is
a nurse who steps down and takes a comprehensive
survey of conditions. There is no talking, no uproar.
A few men may come up to assist in lifting out the
stretchers, an ambulance driver who salutes and in-
dicates with a gesture where his car is stationed. There
are no onlookers. This is business, the grim business
of war. The line of stretchers on the station platform
grows. The men lie on them, impassive. They have
waited so long. They have lain on the battlefield, in
the trench, behind the line at the dressing shed, waiting, always waiting. What is a little time more or
less, now?

The patience of the injured! I have been in many
hospitals. I have seen pneumonia and typhoid patients
lying in the fearful apathy of disease. They are very
sad to see, very tragic, but their patience is the lethargy
of half consciousness. Their fixed eyes see visions.
The patience of the wounded is the resignation of alert
faculties.

Once I saw a boy dying. He was a dark-haired,
brown-eyed lad of eighteen. He had had a leg shattered the day before, and he had lain for hours unat-
tended on the battlefield. The leg had been amputated,
and he was dying of loss of blood.

He lay alone, in a small room of what had once
been a girls' school. He had asked to be propped up
with pillows, so that he could breathe. His face was
grey, and only his eyes were alive. They burned like
coals. He was alone. The hospital was crowded, and

there were others who could be saved. So he lay there, propped high, alone, and as conscious as I am now, and waited. The nurse came back at last, and his eyes greeted her.

There seemed to be nothing that I could do. Before his conscious eyes I was an intruder, gazing at him in his extremity. I went away. And now and then, when I hear this talk of national honour, and am carried away with a hot flame of resentment so that I, too, would cry for war, I seem to see that dying boy's eyes, looking through the mists that are vengeance and hatred and affronted pride, to war as it is—the end of hope, the gate of despair and agony and death.

After my return I received these letters. The woman who wrote them will, I know, forgive me for publishing extracts from them. She is a Belgian, married to an American. More clearly than any words of mine, they show where falls the burden of war:

"I have just learned that my youngest brother has been killed in action in Flanders. King Albert decorated him for conspicuous bravery on April 22d, and my poor boy went to his reward on April 26th. In my leaden heart, through my whirling brain, your words keep repeating themselves: 'For King and Country!' Yes, he died for them, and died a hero! I know only that his regiment, the Grenadiers, was decimated. My poor little boy! God pity us all, and save martyred Belgium!"

In a second letter:

"I enclose my dear little boy's obituary notice. He died at the head of his company and five hundred and seventy-four of his Grenadiers went down with him. Their regiment effectively checked the German advance, and in recognition General Joffre pinned the

Cross of the Legion of Honour to his regimental colours. But we are left to mourn—though I do not begrudge my share of sorrow. The pain is awful, and I pray that by the grace of God you may never know what it means."

For King and Country!

The only leaven in this black picture of war as I have seen it, as it has touched me, has been the scarlet of the Red Cross. To a faith that the terrible scenes at the front had almost destroyed, came every now and then again the flash of the emblem of mercy. Hope, then, was not dead. There were hands to soothe and labour, as well as hands to kill. There was still brotherly love in the world. There was a courage that was not of hate. There was a patience that was not a lying in wait. There was a flag that was not of one nation, but of all the world; a flag that needed no recruiting station, for the ranks it led were always full to overflowing; a flag that stood between the wounded soldier and death; that knew no defeat but surrender to the will of the God of Battles.

And that flag I followed. To the front, to the field hospitals behind the trenches, to railway stations, to hospital trains and ships, to great base hospitals. I watched its ambulances on shelled roads. I followed its brassards as their wearers, walking gently, carried stretchers with their groaning burdens. And, whatever may have failed in this war—treaties, ammunition, elaborate strategies, even some of the humanities —the Red Cross as a symbol of service has never failed.

I was a critical observer. I am a graduate of a hospital training-school, and more or less for years I have been in touch with hospitals. I myself was enrolled under the Red Cross banner. I was prepared for efficiency. What I was not prepared for was the absolute self-sacrifice, the indifference to cost in effort, in very life itself, of a great army of men and women. I saw English aristocrats scrubbing floors; I found American surgeons working day and night under the very roar and rattle of guns. I found cultured women of every nation performing the most menial tasks. I found an army where all are equal—priests, surgeons, scholars, chauffeurs, poets, women of the stage, young girls who until now have been shielded from the very name of death—all enrolled under the red badge of mercy.

CHAPTER XXXIV

IN TERMS OF LIFE AND DEATH

ONE of the first hospitals I saw was in Calais. We entered a muddy courtyard through a gate, and the building loomed before us. It had been a girls' convent school, and was now a military hospital for both the French and British armies, one half the building being used by each. It was the first war hospital I had seen, and I was taken through the building by Major S ——, of the Royal Army Medical Corps. It was morning, and the corridors and stairs still bore the mud of the night, when the ambulances drive into the courtyard and the stretchers are carried up the stairs. It had been rather a quiet night, said Major S ——. The operations were already over, and now the work of cleaning up was going on.

He opened a door, and we entered a long ward.

I live in a great manufacturing city. Day by day its mills take their toll in crushed bodies. The sight of broken humanity is not new to me. In a general way, it is the price we pay for prosperity. Individually, men so injured are the losers in life's great struggle for food and shelter.

I had never before seen men dying of an ideal.

There is a terrible sameness in war hospitals. There are rows of beds, and in them rows of unshaven, white-faced men. Some of them turn and look at visitors.

Others lie very still, with their eyes fixed on the ceiling, or eternity, or God knows what. Now and then one is sleeping.

"He has slept since he came in," the nurse will say; "utter exhaustion."

Often they die. If there is a screen, the death takes place decently and in order, away from the eyes of the ward. But when there is no screen, it makes little difference. What is one death to men who have seen so many?

Once men thought in terms of a day's work, a night's sleep, of labour and play and love. But all over Europe to-day, in hospital and out, men are learning to think in terms of life and death. What will be the result? A general brutalising? The loss of much that is fine? Perhaps. There are some who think that it will scourge men's souls clean of pettiness, teach them proportion, give them a larger outlook. But is it petty to labour and love? Is the duty of the nation greater than the duty of the home? Is the nation greater than the individual? Is the whole greater than the sum of its parts?

Ward after ward. Rows of quiet men. The occasional thump of a convalescent's crutch. The swish of a nurse's starched dress. The strangled grunt of a man as the dressing is removed from his wound. The hiss of coal in the fireplace at the end of the ward. Perhaps a priest beside a bed, or a nun. Over all, the heavy odour of drugs and disinfectants. Brisk nurses go about, cheery surgeons, but there is no real cheer. The ward is waiting.

I saw a man who had been shot in the lungs. His lungs were filled with jagged pieces of steel. He was inhaling oxygen from a tank. There was an inhaler strapped over his mouth and nostrils, and the oxygen passed through a bottle of water, to moisten it before it entered his tortured lungs.

The water in the bottle seethed and bubbled, and the man lay and waited.

He was waiting for the next breath. Above the mask his eyes were fixed, intent. Would it come? Ah, that was not so bad. Almost a full breath that time. But he must have another, and another.

They are all waiting; for death, maybe; for home; for health again, or such travesty of health as may come, for the hospital is not an end but a means. It is an interval. It is the connecting link between the trenches and home, between war and peace, between life and death.

That one hospital had been a school. The children's lavatory is now the operating room. There are rows of basins along one side, set a trifle low for childish hands. When I saw them they were faintly rimmed with red. There was a locker room too. Once these lockers had held caps, no doubt, and overshoes, balls and other treasures. Now they contained torn and stained uniforms, weapons, knapsacks.

Does it matter how many wards there were, or how many surgeons? Do figures mean anything to us any more? When we read in the spring of 1915 that the British Army, a small army compared with the others, had lost already in dead, wounded and missing more than a quarter of a million men we could not visualise it. Multiply one ward by infinity, one hospital by thousands, and then try to realise the terrible by-products of war!

In that Calais hospital I saw for the first time the apparatus for removing bits of shell and shrapnel di-

rectly under the X-ray. Four years ago such a pro-
cedure would have been considered not only marvelous
but dangerous.

At that time, in Vienna and Berlin, I saw men with
hands hopelessly burned and distorted as the result
of merely taking photographic plates with the X-ray.
Then came in lead-glass screens—screens of glass
made with a lead percentage.

Now, as if science had prepared for this great emergency, operators use gloves saturated with a lead solution, and right-angled instruments, and operate directly
in the ray. For cases where immediate extraction is
inadvisable or unnecessary there is a stereoscopic arrangement of plates on the principle of our familiar
stereoscope, which shows an image with perspective
and locates the foreign body exactly.

One plate I saw had a story attached to it.

I was stopping in a private house where a tall Belgian surgeon lived. In the morning, after breakfast,
I saw him carefully preparing a tray and carrying it
upstairs. There was a sick boy, still in his teens, up
there. As I passed the door I had seen him lying there,
gaunt and pale, but plainly convalescent.

Happening to go up shortly after, I saw the tall
surgeon by the side of the bed, the tray on his knees.
And later I heard the story:

The boy was his son. During the winter he had been
injured and taken prisoner. The father, in Calais, got
word that his boy was badly injured and lying in a
German hospital in Belgium. He was an only son.

I do not know how the frenzied father got into
Belgium. Perhaps he crept through the German lines.
He may have gone to sea and landed on the sand dunes
near Zeebrugge. It does not matter how, for he

found his boy. He went to the German authorities and got permission to move him to a private house. The boy was badly hurt. He had a bullet in the wall of the carotid artery, for one thing, and a fractured thigh. The father saw that his recovery, if it occurred at all, would be a matter of skillful surgery and unremitting care, but the father had a post at Calais and was badly needed.

He took a wagon to the hospital and got his boy. Then he drove, disguised I believe as a farmer, over the frontier into Holland. The boy was covered in the bottom of the wagon. In Holland they got a boat and went to Calais. All this, with that sharp-pointed German bullet in the carotid artery! And at Calais they took the plate I have mentioned and got out the bullet.

The last time I saw that brave father he was sitting beside his son, and the boy's hand was between both of his.

Nearly all the hospitals I saw had been schools. In one that I recall, the gentle-faced nuns, who by edict no longer exist in France, were still living in a wing of the school building. They had abandoned their quaint and beautiful habit for the ugly dress of the French provinces—odd little bonnets that sat gro-tesquely on the tops of their heads, stuffy black dresses, black cotton gloves. They would like to be useful, but they belonged to the old régime.

Under their bonnets their faces were placid, but their eyes were sad. Their schoolrooms are hospital wards, the tiny chapel is piled high with supplies; in the re-fectory, where decorous rows of small girls were wont to file in to the convent meals, unthinkable horrors of operations go on all day and far into the night. The

Hall of the Holy Rosary is a convalescent room, where soldiers smoke and play at cards. The Room of the Holy Angels contains a steriliser. Through the corridors that once re-echoed to the soft padding of their felt shoes brisk English nurses pass with a rustle of skirts.

Even the cross by which they lived has turned red, the colour of blood.

CHAPTER XXXV

THE LOSING GAME

I SAW a typhoid hospital in charge of two women doctors. It was undermanned. There were not enough nurses, not enough orderlies.

One of the women physicians had served through the Balkan war.

"There was typhoid there," she said, "but nothing to compare with this in malignancy. Nearly all the cases have come from one part of Belgium."

Some of the men were wounded, in addition to the fever. She told me that it was impossible to keep things in proper order with the help they had.

"And food!" she said. "We cannot have eggs. They are prohibitive at twenty-five centimes—five cents—each; nor many broths. Meat is dear and scarce, and there are no chickens. We give them stewed macaroni and farinaceous things. It's a terrible problem."

The charts bore out what she had said about the type of the disease. They showed incredible temperatures, with the sudden drop that is perforation or hemorrhage.

The odour was heavy. Men lay there, far from home, babbling in delirium or, with fixed eyes, picking at the bed clothes. One was going to die that day. Others would last hardly longer.

"They are all Belgians here," she said. "The British and French troops have been inoculated against typhoid."

So here again the Belgians were playing a losing game. Perhaps they are being inoculated now. I do not know. To inoculate an army means much money, and where is the Belgian Government to get it? It seems the tragic irony of fate that that heroic little army should have been stationed in the infested territory. Are there any blows left to rain on Belgium?

In a letter from the Belgian lines the writer says:

"This is just a race for life. The point is, which will get there first, disease and sickness caused by drinking water unspeakably contaminated, or sterilising plants to avoid such a disaster."

Another letter from a different writer, also in Belgium at the front, says:

"A friend of mine has just been invalided home with enteritis. He had been drinking from a well with a dead Frenchman in it!"

The Belgian Soldiers' Fund in the spring of 1915 sent out an appeal, which said:

"The full heat of summer will soon be upon the army, and the dust of the battlefield will cause the men to suffer from an intolerable thirst."

This is a part of the appeal:

"It is said that out of the 27,000 men who gave their lives in the South African war 7000 only were killed, whilst 20,000 died of enteritis, contracted by drinking impure water.

"In order to save their army from the fatal effects of contaminated water, the Belgian Army medical authorities have, after careful tests, selected the following means of sterilisation—boiling, ozone and violet rays—as the most reliable methods for obtaining large supplies of pure water rapidly.

"Funds are urgently needed to help the work of providing and distributing a pure water supply in the following ways:

"1.   By small portable sterilising plants for every company to produce and distribute from twenty to a hundred gallons of pure cold water per hour.

"2.   By sterilisers easy of adjustment for all field hospitals, convalescent homes, medical depots, and so forth.

"3.   By large sterilising plants, capable of producing from 150 gallons upward per hour, to provide a pure water supply for all the devastated towns through which the army must pass.

"4.   By the sterilisation of contaminated pools and all surface water, under the direction of leading scientific experts who have generously offered their services.

"5.   By pocket filters for all who may have to work out of reach of the sterilising plants, and so forth.

"6.   By two hundred field kitchens on the battlefield to serve out soup, coffee or other drinks to the men fighting in the trenches or on the march."

Everywhere, at the front, I found the gravest apprehension as to water supply in case the confronting armies remained in approximately the same position. Sir John French spoke of it, and the British are providing a system of sterilised water for their men. Merely providing so many human beings with water is a tremendous problem.   Along part of the line, quite aside from typhoid contamination, the water is now impregnated with salt water from the sea.   If even wells contain dead bodies, how about the open watercourses? Wounded men must have water. It is their first and most insistent cry.

People will read this who have never known the thirst of the battlefield or the parched throat that follows loss of blood; people who, by the turning of a tap, may have all the water they want. Perhaps among them there are some who will face this problem of water as America has faced Belgium's problem of food. For the Belgian Army has no money at all for sterilisers, for pocket filters; has not the means to inoculate the army against typhoid; has little of anything. The revenues that would normally support the army are being collected—in addition to a war indemnity—by Germany.

Any hope that conditions would be improved by a general spring movement into uncontaminated territory has been dispelled. The war has become a gigantic siege, varied only by sorties and assaults. As long ago as November, 1914, the situation as to drinking water was intolerable. I quote again from the diary taken from the body of a German officer after the battle of the Yser—a diary published in full in an earlier chapter.

"The water is bad, quite green, indeed; but all the same we drink it—we can get nothing else. Man is brought down to the level of the brute beast."

There is little or no typhoid among the British troops. They, too, no doubt, have realised the value of conservation, and to inoculation have added careful supervision of wells and of watercourses. But when I was at the front the Belgian Army of fifty thousand trained soldiers and two hundred thousand recruits was dependent on springs oozing from fields that were vast graveyards; on sluggish canals in which lay the bodies of men and horses; and on a few tank wagons that carried fresh water daily to the front.

A quarter of a million dollars would be needed to install a water supply for the Belgian Army and for the civilians—residents and refugees—gathered behind the lines. To ask the American people to shoulder this additional burden is out of the question. But perhaps, somewhere among the people who will read this, there is one great-hearted and wealthy American who would sleep better of nights for having lifted to the lips of a wounded soldier the cup of pure water that he craves; for having furnished to ten thousand wounds a sterile and soothing wet compress.

Dunkirk was full of hospitals when I was there. Probably the subsequent shelling of the town destroyed some of them. I do not know. A letter from Calais, dated May 21st, 1915, says:

"I went through Dunkirk again. Last time I was there it was a flourishing and busy market day. This time the only two living souls I saw were the soldiers who let us in at one gate and out at the other. In the interval, as you know, the town had been shelled by fifteen-inch guns from a distance of twenty-three miles. Many buildings in the main streets had been reduced to ruins, and nearly all the windows in the town had been smashed."

There is, or was, a converted Channel steamer at Dunkirk that is now a hospital. Men in all stages of mutilation are there. The salt winds of the Channel blow in through the open ports. The boat rises and falls to the swell of the sea. The deck cabins are occupied by wounded officers, and below, in the long saloon, are rows of cots.

I went there on a bright day in February. There

was a young officer on the deck. He had lost a leg at the hip, and he was standing supported by a crutch and looking out to sea. He did not even turn his head when we approached.

General M ———, the head of the Belgian Army medical service, who had escorted me, touched him on the arm, and he looked round without interest.

"For conspicuous bravery!" said the General, and showed me the medal he wore on his breast.

However, the young officer's face did not lighten, and very soon he turned again to the sea. The time will come, of course, when the tragedy of his mutilation will be less fresh and poignant, when the Order of Leopold on his breast will help to compensate for many things; but that sunny morning, on the deck of the hospital ship, it held small comfort for him.

We went below. At our appearance at the top of the stairs those who were convalescent below rose and stood at attention. They stood in a line at the foot of their beds, boys and grizzled veterans, clad in motley garments, supported by crutches, by sticks, by a hand on the supporting back of a chair. Men without a country, where were they to go when the hospital ship had finished with them? Those who were able would go back to the army, of course. But what of that large percentage who will never be whole again? The machinery of mercy can go so far, and no farther. France cannot support them. Occupied with her own burden, she has persistently discouraged Belgian refugees. They will go to England probably—a kindly land but of an alien tongue. And there again they will wait.

The waiting of the hospital will become the waiting of the refugee. The Channel coast towns of England are full of human derelicts who stand or sit for hours, looking wistfully back toward what was once home.

The story of the hospitals is not always gloomy. Where the surroundings are favourable, defeat is sometimes turned to victory. Tetanus is being fought and conquered by means of a serum. The open treatment of fractures—that is, by cutting down and exposing the jagged edges of splintered bones, and then uniting them—has saved many a limb. Conservation is the watchword of the new surgery, to save whenever possible. The ruthless cutting and hacking of previous wars is a thing of the past.

I remember a boy in a French hospital whose leg bones had been fairly shattered. Eight pieces, the surgeon said there had been. Two linear incisions, connected by a centre one, like a letter H, had been made. The boy showed me the leg himself, and a mighty proud and happy youngster he was. There was no vestige of deformity, no shortening. The incisions had healed by first intention, and the thin, white lines of the H were all that told the story.

As if to offset the cheer of that recovery, a man in the next bed was dying of an abdominal injury. I saw the wound. May the mother who bore him, the wife he loved, never dream of that wound!

I have told of the use of railway stations as temporary resting places for injured soldiers. One is typical of them all. As my visit was made during a lull in the fighting, conditions were more than usually favourable. There was no congestion.

On a bright afternoon early in March I went to the railway station three miles behind the trenches at E ——. Only a mile away a town was being shelled. One could look across the fields at the changing roof line, at a church steeple that had so far escaped. But no shells were falling in E ——.

The station was a small village one. In the room corresponding to our baggage-room straw had been spread over the floor, and men just out of the trenches lay there in every attitude of exhaustion. In a tiny room just beyond two or three women were making soup. As fast as one kettle was ready it was served to the hungry men. There were several kettles—all the small stove would hold. Soup was there in every state, from the finished product to the raw meat and vegetables on a table.

Beyond was a waiting-room, with benches. Here were slightly injured men, bandaged but able to walk about. A few slept on the benches, heads lolled back against the whitewashed wall. The others were paying no attention to the incessant, nearby firing, but were watching a boy who was drawing.

He had a supply of coloured crayons, and the walls as high as he could reach were almost covered. There were priests, soldier types, caricatures of the German Emperor, the arms of France and Belgium—I do not remember what all. And it was exceedingly well done. The boy was an artist to his finger tips.

At a clever caricature of the German Emperor the soldiers laughed and clapped their hands. While they were laughing I looked through an open door.

Three men lay on cots in an inner room—rather, two men and a boy. I went in.

One of the men was shot through the spine and paralysed. The second one had a bullet in his neck, and his face already bore the dark flush and anxious look of general infection. The boy smiled.

They had been there since the day before, waiting

for a locomotive to come and move the hospital train that waited outside. In that railway station the boy had had his leg taken off at the knee.

They lay there, quite alone. The few women were feeding starving men. Now and then one would look in to see if there was any change. There was nothing to be done. They lay there, and the shells burst incessantly a mile away, and the men in the next room laughed and applauded at some happy stroke of the young artist.

"I am so sorry," I said to the boy. The others had not roused at my entrance, but he had looked at me with quick, intelligent eyes.

"It is nothing!" was his reply.

Outside, in the village, soldiers thronged the streets. The sun was shining with the first promise of spring. In an area way regimental butchering was going on, and a great sow, escaping, ran frenzied down the street, followed by a throng of laughing, shouting men. And still the shells fell, across a few fields, and inside the station the three men lay and waited.

That evening at dusk the bombardment ceased, and I went through the shelled town. It was difficult to get about. Walls had fallen across the way, interiors that had been homes gaped open to the streets. Shattered beds and furnishings lay about—kitchen utensils, broken dishes. On some of the walls holy pictures still hung, grouped about a crucifix. There are many to tell how the crucifix has escaped in the wholesale destruction of towns.

A shoemaker had come back into the village for the night, and had opened his shop. For a time he seemed to be the only inhabitant of what I had known, a short time before, as a prosperous and thriving market town. Then through an aperture that had been a window I saw three women sitting round a candle. And in the next street I found a man on his knees on the pavement, working with bricks and a trowel.

He explained that he had closed up a small cellarway. His family had no place else to go and were coming in from the fields, where they had sought safety, to sleep in the cellar for the night. He was leaving a small aperture, to be closed with bags of sand, so that if the house was destroyed over them in the night they could crawl out and escape.

He knelt on the bricks in front of the house, a patient, resigned figure, playing no politics, interested not at all in war and diplomacy, in a way to the sea or to a place in the sun—one of the millions who must adapt themselves to new and fearsome situations and do their best.

That night, sitting at dinner in a hotel, I saw two pretty nurses come in. They had been relieved for a few hours from their hospital and were on holiday.

One of them had a clear, although musical voice. What she said came to me with great distinctness, and what she was wishing for was a glass of American soda water!

Now, long months before I had had any idea of going to the war I had read an American correspondent's story of the evacuation of Antwerp, and of a tall young American girl, a nurse, whom the others called Morning Glory. He never knew the rest of her name. Anyhow, Morning Glory leaped into my mind and stayed there, through soup, through rabbit, which was called on the menu something entirely different, through hard cakes and a withered orange.

So when a young lieutenant asked permission to

bring them over to meet me, I was eager. It was Morning Glory! Her name is really Glory, and she is a Southern girl. Somewhere among my papers I have a snapshot of her helping to take a wounded soldier out of an ambulance, and if the correspondent wants it I shall send it to him. Also her name, which he never knew. And I will verify his opinion that it is better to be a Morning Glory in Flanders than to be a good many other things that I can think of.

CHAPTER XXXVI

HOW AMERICANS CAN HELP

WITH the possible exception of Germany, which seems to have anticipated everything, no one of the nations engaged appears to have expected the fearful carnage of this war. The destructive effect of the modern, high-explosive shell has been well known, but it is the trench form of warfare which, by keeping troops in stationary positions, under grilling artillery fire, has given such shells their opportunity. Shrapnel has not been so deadly to the men in the trenches.

The result of the vast casualty lists has been some hundreds of isolated hospitals scattered through France, not affiliated with any of the Red Cross societies, unorganised, poverty-stricken, frequently having only the services of a surgeon who can come but once a week. They have no dressings, no nurses save peasants, no bedding, no coal to cook even the scanty food that the villagers can spare.

No coal, for France is facing a coal famine to-day. Her coal mines are in the territory held by the Germans. Even if she had the mines, where would she get men to labour in them, or trains to transport the coal?

There are more than three hundred such hospitals scattered through isolated French villages, hospitals where everything is needed. For whatever else held fast during the first year of the war, the nursing system of France absolutely failed. Some six hundred miles of hospital wards there are to-day in France, with cots so close together that one can hardly step between. It is true that with the passing of time, the first chaos is giving way to order. But France, unlike England, has the enemy within her boundaries, on her soil. Her every resource is taxed. And the need is still great.

The story of the town of D——, in Brittany, is very typical of what the war has brought into many isolated communities.

D—— is a little town of two thousand inhabitants, with a thirteenth-century church, with mediæval houses with quaint stone porticoes and outside staircases. There is one street, shaped like a sickle, with a handle that is the station road.

War was declared and the men of D——went away. The women and children brought in the harvest, and waited for news. What little came was discouraging.

One day in August one of the rare trains stopped at the station, and an inspector got off and walked up the sickle-handle to the schoolhouse. He looked about and made the comment that it would hold eighty beds. Whereupon he went away, and D—— waited for news and gathered the harvest.

On the fifth of September, 1914, the terrific battle of the Marne commenced. The French strategic retreat was at an end, and with her allies France resumed the offensive. What happened in the little village of D——?

And remember that D—— is only one of hundreds of tiny interior towns. D—— has never heard of the

Red Cross, but D—— venerated, in its thirteenth-century church, the Cross of Christ.

This is what happened:

One day in the first week of September a train drew up at the box-like station, a heterogeneous train—coaches, luggage vans, cattle and horse cars. The doors opened, and the work of emptying the cars began. The women and children, aghast and bewildered, ran down the sickle-handle road and watched. Four hundred wounded men were taken out of the cars, laid prone on the station platform, and the train went on.

There were no surgeons in D——, but there was a chemist who knew something of medicine and who, for one reason or another, had not been called to the ranks. There were no horses to draw carts. There was nothing.

The chemist was a man of action. Very soon the sickle and the old church saw a curious sight. They saw women and children, a procession, pushing wounded men to the school in the hand carts that country people use for milk cans and produce. They saw brawny peasant women carrying chairs in which sat injured men with lolling heads and sunken eyes.

Bales of straw were brought into the school. Tender, if unaccustomed, hands washed fearful wounds, but there were no dressings, no bandages.

Any one who knows the French peasant and his poverty will realise the plight of the little town. The peasant has no reserves of supplies. Life is reduced to its simplest elements. There is nothing that is not in use.

D—— solved part of its problem by giving up its

own wooden beds to the soldiers. It tore up its small stock of linen, its towels, its dusters; but the problem of food remained.

There was a tiny stove, on which the three or four teachers of the school had been accustomed to cook their midday meal. There was no coal, only wood, and green wood at that. All day, and all day now, D——— cooks the *pot-à-feu* for the wounded on that tiny stove. *Pot-à-feu* is good diet for convalescents, but the "light diets" must have eggs, broth, whatever can be found.

So the peasant woman of D——— comes to the hospital, bringing a few eggs, the midday meal of her family, who will do without.

I have spoken mainly in the past tense, but conditions in D——— are not greatly changed to-day. An old marquise, impoverished by the war, darns the pathetic socks of the wounded men and mends their uniforms. At the last report I received, the corridors and schoolrooms were still filled—every inch of space—with a motley collection of beds, on which men lay in their uniforms, for lack of other clothing. They were covered with old patchwork quilts, with anything that can be used. There were, of course, no sheets. All the sheets were used long ago for dressings. A friend of mine there recently saw a soldier with one leg, in the kitchen, rolling wretched scraps and dusters for bandages. There was no way to sterilise them, of course. Once a week a surgeon comes. When he goes away he takes his instruments with him.

This is not an isolated case, nor an exaggerated one. There are things I do not care to publish. Three hundred and more such hospitals are known. The French Government pays, or will pay, twenty-five

cents a day to keep these men.   Black bread and *pot-à-
jeu* is all that can be managed on that amount.

Convalescents sit up in bed and painfully unravel
their tattered socks for wool.   They tie the bits together, often two or three inches in length, and knit
new feet in old socks, or—when they secure enough—
new socks.   For the Germans hold the wool cities of
France.   Ordinarily worsted costs eighteen and nineteen francs in Dinard and Saint Malo, or from three
dollars and sixty cents to three dollars and eighty
cents a pound.   Much of the government reserves of
woollen underwear for the soldiers was in the captured
towns, and German prisoners have been found wearing woollens with the French Government stamp.

Every sort of building is being used for these isolated hospitals—garages, town halls, private dwellings,
schools.   At first they had no chloroform, no instruments.   There are cases on record where automobile
tools were used in emergency, kitchen knives, saws,
anything.   In one case, last spring, two hundred convalescents, leaving one of these hospitals on a cold day
in March, were called back, on the arrival of a hundred freshly wounded men, that every superfluous
bandage on their wounds might be removed, to be used
again.

Naturally, depending entirely on the unskilled
nursing of the village women, much that we regard as
fundamental in hospital practice is ignored.   Wounded
men, typhoid and scarlet fever cases are found in the
same wards.   In one isolated town a single clinical
thermometer is obliged to serve for sixty typhoid and
scarlet fever patients.*

Sometimes the men in these isolated and ill-equipped

*Written in June, 1915.

refuges realise the horror and hopelessness of their situation. The nights are particularly bad. Any one who knows hospitals well, knows the night terrors of the wards; knows, too, the contagion of excitement that proceeds from a hysterial or delirious patient.

In some of these lonely hospitals hell breaks loose at night. The peasant women must sleep. Even the tireless nuns cannot labour forever without rest. The men have come from battlefields of infinite horror. A frenzied dream, a delirious soldier calling them to the charge, and panic rages.

To offset these horrors of the night the peasants have, here and there, resorted to music. It is naïve, pathetic. Where there is a piano it is moved into the school, or garage, or whatever the building may be, and at twilight a nun or a volunteer musician plays quietly, to soothe the men to sleep. In one or two towns a village band, or perhaps a lone cornetist, plays in the street outside.

So the days go on, and the nights. Supplies are begged for and do not always come. Dressings are washed, to be used again and again.

An attempt is now being made to better these conditions. A Frenchwoman helping in one of these hospitals, and driven almost to madness by the outcries of men and boys undergoing operations without anæsthetics, found her appeals for help unanswered. She decided to go to England to ask her friends there for chloroform, and to take it back on the next boat. She was successful. She carried back with her, on numerous journeys, dressings, chloroform, cotton, even a few instruments. She is still doing this work. Others interested in isolated hospitals, hearing of her success, appealed to her; and now regular, if small, shipments of chloroform and dressings are going across the Channel.

Americans willing to take their own cars, and willing to work, will find plenty to do in distributing such supplies over there. A request has come to me to find such Americans. Surgeons who can spare a scalpel, an artery clip or two, ligatures—catgut or silk—and forceps, may be certain of having them used at once. Bandages rolled by kindly American hands will not lie unclaimed on the quay at Havre or Calais.

So many things about these little hospitals of France are touching, without having any particular connection. There was a surgeon in one of these isolated villages, with an X-ray machine but no gloves or lead screen to protect himself. He worked on, using the deadly rays to locate pieces of shell, bullets and shrapnel, and knowing all the time what would happen. He has lost both hands.

Since my return to America the problems of those who care for the sick and wounded have been further complicated, among the Allies, by the inhuman use of asphyxiating gases.

Sir John French says of these gases:

"The effect of this poison is not merely disabling, or even painlessly fatal, as suggested in the German press. Those of its victims who do not succumb on the field and who can be brought into hospitals suffer acutely and, in a large proportion of cases, die a painful and lingering death. Those who survive are in little better case, as the injury to their lungs appears to be of a permanent character and reduces them to a condition that points to their being invalids for life."

I have received from the front one of the respirators

given out to the troops to be used when the gas clouds appear.

"It is prepared with hypophosphite of soda," wrote the surgeon who sent it, "and all they have to do before putting it on is to dip it in the water in the trenches. They are all supplied in addition with goggles, which are worn on their caps."

This is from the same letter:

"That night a German soldier was brought in wounded, and jolly glad he was to be taken. He told us he had been turned down three times for phthisis—tuberculosis—and then in the end was called up and put into the trenches after eight weeks' training. All of which is very significant. Another wounded German told the men at the ambulance that they must move on as soon as they could, as very soon the Germans would be in Calais.

"All the German soldiers write home now on the official cards, which have Calais printed on the top of them!"

Not all. I have before me a card from a German officer in the trenches in France. It is a good-natured bit of raillery, with something of grimness underneath.

"Dear Madame:

" 'I nibble them'—Joffre. See your article in the *Saturday Evening Post* of May 29th, 1915. Really, Joffre has had time! It is September now, and we are not nibbled yet. Still we stand deep in France. Au revoir à Paris, Madame."

He signs it "Yours truly," and then his name.
Not Calais, then, but Paris!

CHAPTER XXXVII

AN ARMY OF CHILDREN

IT is undeniably true that the humanities are failing us as the war goes on. Not, thank God, the broad humanity of the Red Cross, but that individual compassion of a man for his wounded brother, of which the very fabric of mercy is woven. There is too much death, too much suffering. Men grow calloused. As yet the loss is not irretrievable, but the war is still only a matter of months. What if it is to be of years?

France and Belgium were suffering from a wave of atheism before the war. But there comes a time in the existence of nations, as in the lives of individuals, when human endeavour seems useless, when the world and the things thereof have failed. At such time nations and individuals alike turn at last to a Higher Power. France is on her knees to-day. Her churches are crowded. Not perhaps since the days of chivalry, when men were shriven in the churches before going out to battle, has France so generally knelt and bowed her head—but it is to the God of Battles that she prays.

On her battlefields the priests have most signally distinguished themselves. Some have exchanged the soutane for the uniform, and have fought bravely and well. Others, like the priests who stood firm in the midst of Jordan, have carried their message of hope to the dying into the trenches.

No article on the work of the Red Cross can be complete without a reference to the work of these priests, not perhaps affiliated with the society, but doing yeoman work of service among the wounded. They are everywhere, in the trenches or at the outposts, in the hospitals and hospital trains, in hundreds of small villages, where the entire community plus its burden of wounded turns to the *curé* for everything, from advice to the sacrament.

In prostrate Belgium the demands on the priests have been extremely heavy. Subjected to insult, injury and even death during the German invasion, where in one diocese alone thirteen were put to death—their churches destroyed, or used as barracks by the enemy —that which was their world has turned to chaos about them. Those who remained with their conquered people have done their best to keep their small communities together and to look after their material needs—which has, indeed, been the lot of the priests of battle-scarred Flanders for many generations.

Others have attached themselves to the hospital service. All the Belgian trains of wounded are cared for solely by these priests, who perform every necessary service for their men, and who, as I have said before, administer the sacrament and make coffee to cheer the flagging spirits of the wounded, with equal courage and resource.

Surgeons, nurses, priests, nuns, volunteer workers who substitute for lack of training both courage and zeal, these are a part of the machinery of mercy. There is another element—the boy scouts.

During the early days of the war the boy scouts

of England, then on school holiday, did marvellous
work.   Boys of fourteen made repeated trips across
the Channel, bringing back from France children, invalids, timorous women.   They volunteered in the
hospitals, ran errands, carried messages, were as useful
as only willing boys can be.   They did scout service,
too, guarding the railway lines and assisting in watching the Channel coast; but with the end of the holiday most of the English boy scouts were obliged to go
back to school.   Their activities were not over, but
they were largely curtailed.

There were five thousand boy scouts in Belgium at
the beginning of the war.   I saw them everywhere—
behind the battle lines, on the driving seats of ambulances, at the doors of hospitals.   They were very
calm.   Because I know a good deal about small boys I
smothered a riotous impulse to hug them, and spoke to
them as grown-up to grown-up.   Thus approached,
they met my advances with dignity, but without excitement.

And after a time I learned something about them
from the Chief Scout of Belgium; perhaps it will show
the boy scouts of America what they will mean to the
country in time of war.   Perhaps it will make them
realise that being a scout is not, after all, only camping in the woods, long hikes, games in the open.   The
long hikes fit a boy for dispatch carrying, the camping
teaches him to care for himself when, if necessity
arises, he is thrown on the country, like his older
brother, the fighting man.

A small cog, perhaps, in the machinery of mercy,
but a necessary one.   A vital cog in the vast machinery
of war—that is the boy scout to-day.

The day after the declaration of war the Belgian

scouts were mobilised, by order of the minister of war—five thousand boys, then, ranging in age from twelve to eighteen, an army of children. What a sight they must have been! How many grown-ups can think of it with dry eyes? What a terrible emergency was this, which must call the children into battle!

They were placed at the service of the military authorities, to do any and every kind of work. Some, with ordinary bicycles or motorcyles, were made dispatch riders. The senior scouts were enlisted in the regular army, armed, and they joined the soldiers in barracks. The younger boys, between thirteen and sixteen, were letter-carriers, messengers in the different ministries, or orderlies in the hospitals that were immediately organised. Those who could drive automobiles were given that to do.

Others of the older boys, having been well trained in scouting, were set to watch points of importance, or given carbines and attached to the civic guard. During the siege of Liège between forty and fifty boy scouts were constantly employed carrying food and ammunition to the beleaguered troops.

The Germans finally realised that every boy scout was a potential spy, working for his country. The uniform itself then became a menace, since boys wearing it were frequently shot. The boys abandoned it, the older ones assuming the Belgian uniform and the younger ones returning to civilian dress. But although, in the chaos that followed the invasion and particularly the fall of Liège, they were virtually disbanded, they continued their work as spies, as dispatch riders, as stretcher-bearers.

There are still nine boy scouts with the famous

Ninth Regiment, which has been decorated by the king.

One boy scout captured, single-handed, two German officers. Somewhere or other he had got a revolver, and with it was patrolling a road. The officers were lost and searching for their regiments. As they stepped out of a wood the boy confronted them, with his revolver levelled. This happened near Liège.

Trust a boy to use his wits in emergency! Here is another lad, aged fifteen, who found himself in Liège after its surrender, and who wanted to get back to the Belgian Army. He offered his services as stretcher-bearer in the German Army, and was given a German Red Cross pass. Armed with this pass he left Liège, passed successfully many sentries, and at last got to Antwerp by a circuitous route. On the way he found a dead German and, being only a small boy after all, he took off the dead man's stained uniform and bore it in his arms into Antwerp!

There is no use explaining about that uniform. If you do not know boys you will never understand. If you do, it requires no explanation.

Here is a fourteen-year-old lad, intrusted with a message of the utmost importance for military headquarters in Antwerp. He left Brussels in civilian clothing, but he had neglected to take off his boy scout shirt—boy-fashion! The Germans captured him and stripped him, and they burned the boy scout shirt. Then they locked him up, but they did not find his message.

All day he lay in duress, and part of the night. Perhaps he shed a few tears. He was very young, and things looked black for him. Boy scouts were being shot, remember! But it never occurred to him to destroy the message that meant his death if discovered.

He was clever with locks and such things, after the manner of boys, and for most of the night he worked with the window and shutter lock.   Perhaps he had a nail in his pocket, or some wire.   Most boys have.   And just before dawn he got window and shutter opened, and dropped, a long drop, to the ground.   He lay there for a while, getting his breath and listening.   Then, on his stomach, he slid away into the darkest hour that is just before the dawn.

Later on that day a footsore and weary but triumphant youngster presented himself at the headquarters of the Belgian Army in Antwerp and insisted on seeing the minister of war.   Being at last admitted, he turned up a very travel-stained and weary little boy's foot and proceeded to strip a piece of adhesive plaster from the sole.

Underneath the plaster was the message!

War is a thing of fearful and curious anomalies.   It has shown that humane units may comprise a brutal whole; that civilisation is a shirt over a coat of mail. It has shown that hatred and love are kindred emotions, boon companions, friends.   It has shown that in every man there are two men, devil and saint; that there are two courages, that of the mind, which is bravest, that of the heart, which is greatest.

It has shown that government by men only is not an appeal to reason, but an appeal to arms; that on women, without a voice to protest, must fall the burden.   It is easier to die than to send a son to death.

It has shown that a single hatred may infect a world, but it has shown that mercy too may spread among nations. That love is greater than cannon, greater than hate, greater than vengeance; that it triumphs over wrath, as good triumphs over evil.

Direct descendant of the cross of the Christian faith, the Red Cross carries onto every battlefield the words of the Man of Mercy:

"Blessed are the merciful, for they shall obtain mercy."

On a day in March I went back to England. March in England is spring. Masses of snowdrops lined the paths in Hyde Park. The grass was green, the roads hard and dry under the eager feet of Kitchener's great army. They marched gayly by. The drums beat. The passers-by stopped. Here and there an open carriage or an automobile drew up, and pale men, some of them still in bandages, sat and watched. In their eyes was the same flaming eagerness, the same impatience to get back, to be loosed against the old lion's foes.

All through England, all through France, all through the tragic corner of Belgium that remains to her, were similar armies drilling and waiting, equally young, equally eager, equally resolute. And the thing that they were going to I knew. I had seen it in that mysterious region that had swallowed up those who had gone before; in the trenches, in the operating rooms of field hospitals, at outposts where the sentries walked hand in hand with death.

War is not two great armies meeting in the clash and frenzy of battle. War is a boy carried on a stretcher, looking up at God's blue sky with bewildered eyes that are soon to close; war is a woman carrying a child that has been injured by a shell; war is spirited horses tied in burning buildings and waiting for death;

war is the flower of a race, battered, hungry, bleeding, up to its knees in filthy water; war is an old woman burning a candle before the Mater Dolorosa for the son she has given.

For King and Country!

THE END